The Relevance of the Radical

The Relevance of the Radical:
Simone Weil 100 Years Later

Edited by

A. Rebecca Rozelle-Stone
and
Lucian Stone

continuum

Continuum International Publishing Group

The Tower Building   80 Maiden Lane
11 York Road   Suite 704
London SE1 7NX   New York, NY 10038

www.continuumbooks.com

British Library Cataloguing-in-Publication Data
A catalogue record for this book is available from the British Library.

ISBN: 978-0-567-51728-9 (hardcover)
        978-0-567-38172-9 (paperback)

Library of Congress Cataloging-in-Publication Data
A catalog record for this book is available from the Library of Congress.

Typeset by Newgen Imaging Systems Pvt Ltd, Chennai, India
Printed in the United States of America

Contents

Part Two: Radical World

Acknowledgments

We would like to express our gratitude to the many individuals who helped us prior to and during the preparation of this manuscript in various capacities. Eric O. Springsted and E. Jane Doering provided us with the initial encouragement to pursue this project, and throughout its preparation they gave us invaluable practical advice. We would be remiss if we did not also acknowledge our indebtedness to Cynthia Gayman and Anthony J. Steinbock, who introduced us to Weil's works and explored the contours of her thought with us in great detail.

This book would not be possible, of course, without the dedication of the contributors. We thank them for authoring such thoughtful and timely essays and for the continued dialogues at the American Weil Society's annual colloquies.

Bryan Lueck, our colleague in the Department of Philosophy at Southern Illinois University Edwardsville, graciously agreed to put his love for Portuguese to work translating Maria Clara Lucchetti Bingemer's chapter, "Affliction and the Option for the Poor." In order to produce a high-quality translation, he took it upon himself to learn about Weil's life and philosophy, and in so doing he was an important interlocutor for us as we made progress on the manuscript. In the end, we learned a great deal more about Weil through our conversations with him, and we are in his debt for taking on this task in addition to his own research activities.

We also want to thank Burke Gerstenschläger, our initial editor at Continuum, who was very enthusiastic about this project from our first conversation with him. Without his help, this book would have never gotten off the ground. In addition, we would like to thank Thomas Kraft and Mr. P. Muralidharan for their support and for seeing this project through to the end.

We would like to thank Sylvie Weil for granting us permission to use Simone Weil's Renault factory identification card photo for the cover art. We also extend our deep gratitude to the family of Leonardo Alishan (Neli, Michael, Ara and Eileen) for giving us permission to reprint his poem "Tired Thoughts" in this volume.

Our students at Southern Illinois University Edwardsville and Webster University continue to inspire us to study and discuss Weil's life and works. Perhaps they are especially deserving of the subject matter of this work, Weil's relevance to contemporary philosophical, religious and social-political issues. During the course of our lectures and resulting discussions, they are keen to remind us of the issues they face on a daily basis and as they look toward their futures, and demand that Weil speak to those lingering concerns.

Our family and friends have had to endure the void of our absence and silence as we juggled the workload of this volume and our busy schedules. We thank them for their infinite patience, especially Ava and Hal Rozelle and Jacqueline Stone, our loving parents.

We would also like to acknowledge Southern Illinois University Edwardsville. Lucian received the Vaughnie Lindsay New Investigator Award, freeing him from some of his teaching responsibilities in order to concentrate his energies on research and the editorial responsibilities of this volume.

A. Rebecca Rozelle-Stone and Lucian Stone
St. Louis, MO
15 March 2009

Notes on Contributors

Maria Clara Luchettibingemer is Associate Professor of Theology and Dean of the Center for Theology and Human Sciences at the Pontifical Catholic University of Rio de Janeiro. She has published, in English, with Ivone Gebara, *Mary Mother of God and Mother of the Poor* (New York: Orbis, 1993), as well as many articles and book chapters. Her most recent publications include *Simone Weil. A força e a fraqueza do amor* (Rocco, 2007; Italian edition: Zona, 2007); and *Jesus Cristo: servo de Deus e Messias glorioso* (Paulinas, 2008).

Jacques Cabaud is the first biographer of Simone Weil. His biography, *Simone Weil: A Fellowship in Love* (London: Harvill Press, 1964), has been translated and published in five languages. He also authored *Simone Weil à New York et à Londre* (Paris: Plon, 1967; translated and published in Japanese), in addition to numerous articles published in the journal *Cahiers Simone Weil*. His latest article concerning Weil's thought, "Simone Weil: An Ethic for Esthetics," was published in *Cahiers Simone Weil* (Mars 2008).

E. Jane Doering is Associate Professor in the College Seminar Program at the University of Notre Dame, where she coordinates the Woodrow Wilson Teachers As Scholars Program and the Program of Liberal Studies Junior Great Books Teaching Project. She is an active writer and presenter on Simone Weil's social and political thought in light of her mystical experiences. She is coeditor, with Eric O. Springsted, of *The Christian Platonism of Simone Weil* (University of Notre Dame Press, 2004). Her articles: "Simone Weil: Le pouvoir des mots," "Jean Jacques Rousseua et Simone Weil: Deux théoriciens d'une politique moderne," and "Déclaration des droits et des devoirs: Problèmes contemporains à la lumière de Simone Weil," have all appeared in *Cahiers Simone Weil*. Currently she is completing her manuscript, *The Specter of Self-perpetuating Force: Simone Weil on Violence, War, Beauty, and Grace*, also for the Notre Dame Press.

Krista E. Duttenhaver is Assistant Professor of Theology, Program of Liberal Studies, at the University of Notre Dame. Representative publications include: "'Stretched out with Christ': God and suffering in Martin Luther and Simone Weil," in *The Global Luther: A Theologian for Modern Times* (Augsburg/Fortress Press, 2008); and "Relative freedoms: the influence of Spinoza on the systems of Schleiermacher and Whitehead," in *Schleiermacher and Whitehead: Open Systems in Dialogue* (Walter de Gruyter, 2004).

Bartomeu Estelrich is currently Assistant Director of The Jesuit Institute at Boston College, where he also teaches courses in the Department of Philosophy. He earned a Ph.D. in Philosophy at Universidad Pontificia Comillas (Madrid, Spain). He is the the author of *Ciencia y Ecología de la Creación* (Universidad Técnica Particular de Loja Press, 2004). Other representative publications include: "'Christ lui-même est descendu et m'a prise.' An approximation of the irruption of Christ in Simone Weil's life as interpreted through the Christian tradition," *Cahiers Simone Weil* (2008); "Simone Weil's concept of grace," *Modern Theology* Vol. 25, No. 2 (April 2009); and "Philosophy as a spiritual exercise: Simone Weil and Pierre Hadot" (Pontifícia Universidade Católica do Rio de Janeiro, forthcoming).

Cynthia Gayman is Associate Professor of Philosophy and coordinator of the philosophy program in the Department of English and Philosophy, Murray State University. Recent publications include: "Words, power, pluralism: are you talking to me?" in *Journal of Speculative Philosophy*, Vol. 22, No. 2 (2008); "Whose rights and what's the difference: a critique of Beth Singer's essay 'Human rights: some current issues,'" in *Metaphilosophy*, July 2007; "Not so funny: a Deweyan response," in *Contemporary Pragmatism*, December 2005; and "Applied existentialism: on Kristina Arp's *The Bonds of Freedom: Simone de Beauvoir's Existentialist Ethics*," in *Journal of Speculative Philosophy* (2003). In addition to many invited lectures, she has presented her research on Simone Weil, "Subject to affliction: Simone Weil and the suffering self," at the Society for Phenomenology and Existential Philosophy (2004).

Coy D. Jones is Adjunct Professor of Philosophy at Holy Cross College at Notre Dame, Indiana. He is a doctoral candidate at the Divinity School, the University of Chicago, having previously earned an M.A.T.S. from Claremont School of Theology. He has presented his research at the American Academy of Religion's annual meeting.

Bryan Lueck is Assistant Professor of Philosophy at Southern Illinois University Edwardsville. He earned a Ph.D. from The Pennsylvania State University in 2007. His research interests include contemporary continental philosophy and ethics.

Marie Cabaud Meaney is an Arthur J. Ennis Fellow at Villanova University. She obtained a D.Phil. in French literature and an M.Phil. in European literature (German and English) at Oxford University; previously she had received an M.Phil. in philosophy from the International Academy of Philosophy in Liechtenstein and a D.E.U.G. from the Sorbonne, Paris IV. She is the author of *Simone Weil's Apologetic Use of Literature: Her Christological Interpretations of Classic Greek Texts* (Oxford University Press, 2008).

Vance G. Morgan is Professor of Philosophy at Providence College in Providence, Rhode Island. He has published more than a dozen articles, ranging in topic from Simone Weil and Iris Murdoch to the metaphysical foundations of naturalism, in scholarly journals such as *The Review of Metaphysics, Faith and Philosophy, The Southern Journal of Philosophy, American Catholic Philosophical Quarterly, Philosophy and Theology, Journal of Philosophical Research, Dialogue, Philosophy Now,* and *Providence: Studies in Western Civilization.* His book, *Foundations of Cartesian Ethics,* was published by Humanities Press in 1994; his most recent book, *Weaving the World: Simone Weil on Mathematics, Science, and Love,* was published by University of Notre Dame Press in the fall of 2005.

Christopher A. P. Nelson is an Instructor of Philosophy and Chair of the Department of History and Philosophy at South Texas College. He earned a Ph.D. from Southern Illinois University at Carbondale, writing a dissertation on the Christology of Søren Kierkegaard. He is the author of a number of articles dealing with the confluence of the ethical and the religious in the writings of Kierkegaard, most of which have appeared in Mercer University Press's *International Kierkegaard Commentary* series, such as: "Revelation and the revealed: the crux of the ethical-religious *Stadium*"; and "Wonder, philosophy, and Kierkegaard's discourse, 'On the occasion of a confession.'" His article, "Kierkegaard, mysticism, and jest: the story of Little Ludvig" appeared in the *Continental Philosophy Review.*

Sarah Pinnock is Associate Professor of Religion at Trinity University. She is the author of *Beyond Theodicy: Jewish and Christian Continental Responses to the Holocaust* (State University of New York Press, 2002), and editor of *The Theology of Dorothee Soelle* (Trinity Press, 2003). She is also the author of many book chapters and articles including: "Vulnerable Bodies: Feminist Reflections on the Holocaust and Nature," in *The Holocaust and Nature*, edited by Didier Pollefeyt (University of Washington Press, forthcoming); and "Atrocity and Ambiguity: Recent Developments in Christian Holocaust Responses," *Journal of the American Academy of Religion* Vol. 75/3 (September 2007). Sarah has presented papers at international conferences such as the American Academy of Religion annual meeting, the Scholars' Conference on the Holocaust and the Churches, and the Irish School of Ecumenics at Trinity College Dublin, and she was a Fulbright scholar at Latvia University in 2006–2007. Currently, she is the President of the Southwest Regional AAR, and serves on the national AAR steering committees for Religion, Holocaust and Genocide, and Death and Beyond.

Inese Radzins is Assistant Professor of Theology at the Pacific School of Religion. Representative publications include: "Simone Weil's political philosophy: toward a post-colonial critique of power," in *New Topics in Feminist Philosophy of Religion: Resistance, Religion and Ethical-Political Relations*, Pamela Sue Anderson, ed. (Kluwer, 2008); and "Simone Weil's need for roots," in *Empire and Christian Tradition: New Readings of Classical Theologians*, Kwok Pui Lan et al., eds (Fortress Press, 2007). She is a regular participant in the American Weil Society's Annual Colloquy, and has presented her research at the American Academy of Religion's annual meetings.

A. Rebecca Rozelle-Stone is currently Assistant Professor of Philosophy at Southern Illinois University Edwardsville. She earned her Ph.D. from Southern Illinois University Carbondale, where she wrote a dissertation entitled "Voiding distraction: Simone Weil and the religio-ethics of attention." Her published articles on Weil include: "Le Déracinement of attention: Simone Weil on the institutionalization of distractedness," *Philosophy Today* Vol. 53, No. 1 (Spring 2009); and "Forgiveness through attention: Simone Weil's critique of the imagination," *Sacred Web: A Journal of Tradition and Modernity* (Summer 2005). She is a regular presenter at the American Weil Society's Annual Colloquy and has also presented her research at the Society for Phenomenology and Existential Philosophy, and the Society for the Advancement of American Philosophy.

Mario von der Ruhr is Lecturer in Philosophy at Swansea University (UK). He is the author of *Simone Weil: An Apprenticeship in Attention*

(Continuum, 2006), having previously assisted D. Z. Phillips in editing Rush Rhees' *Discussions of Simone Weil* (State University of New York Press, 2000). His coedited works include *Religion and the End of Metaphysics* (Mohr Siebeck, 2008), *Religion and Wittgenstein's Legacy* (Ashgate, 2005), and *Biblical Concepts* (Palgrave, 2004). He is an associate editor of the journal *Philosophical Investigations*, and Chairman of the *Welsh Philosophical Society*.

Lawrence E. Schmidt is Professor in the Department and Centre for the Study of Religion at the University of Toronto. He has coauthored a book, with Scott Marratto, *The End of Ethics in a Technological Society* (McGill-Queens University Press, 2008). Representative articles he has published include: "Simone Weil on religion: a Voegelinian critique," "George Grant on Simone Weil: the saint and the thinker," "The measure of justice: the language of limit as key to Simone Weil's political philosophy" (with Scott Marratto), and "The Christian materialism of Simone Weil."

Eric O. Springsted is co-founder of the American Weil Society and has been its president since its inception in 1981. After teaching for over twenty years at Illinois College, Princeton Theological Seminary and General Theological Seminary, he is currently engaged in pastoral work. He has written over twenty articles on Weil, and his books on her include: *Christus Mediator: Platonic Mediation in the Thought of Simone Weil* (Scholars Press, 1983); *Simone Weil and the Suffering of Love* (Cowley, 1986); and *Spirit, Nature and Community: Issues in the Thought of Simone Weil* (with Diogenes Allen; State University of New York Press, 1994). His work on Weil has appeared in half a dozen languages.

Lucian Stone is currently Assistant Professor of Philosophy at Southern Illinois University Edwardsville. He is coeditor of (with Lewis Hahn and Randall Auxier) and contributor to *The Philosophy of Seyyed Hossein Nasr*, Library of Living Philosophers, Volume XXVIII (Open Court Press, 2001). His research interests include Islamic philosophy, Sufism, comparative mystical philosophies, philosophy and literature, and the philosophy of humor. He has presented his research on Simone Weil at the American Weil Society's Annual Colloquy, and at the Annual Society for Phenomenology and Existential Philosophy Conference.

List of Abbreviations

Original Works in French

AD	*Attente de Dieu.* Paris: La Colombe, 1950.
AD¹	*Attente de Dieu.* Paris: Fayard, 1966.
C II	*Cahiers II.* Paris: Plon, 1972.
C III	*Cahiers III* (nouvelle edition). Paris: Plon, 1974.
CO	*La Condition ouvrière.* Paris: Gallimard, 1951–.
CS	*La Connaissance surnaturelle.* Paris: Gallimard, 1950.
E	*L'Enracinement.* Paris: Gallimard, 1990.
EHP	*Écrits historiques et politiques.* Paris: Gallimard, 1957.
EL	*Écrits de Londres et dernières lettres.* Paris: Gallimard, 1957.
IPC	*Intuitions pré-chrétiennes.* Paris: La Colombe, 1951.
LDP	*Leçons de philosophie de Simone Weil (Roanne 1933–1934).* Paris: Plon, 1959.
LR	*Lettre à un religieux.* Paris: Gallimard, 1951.
OC	*Œuvres completes.* Paris: Gallimard, 1981–.
OC I	*Premiers écrits philosophiques*
OC II.1	*Écrits historiques et politques: L'Engagement syndical (1927– juillet 1934)*
OC II.2	*Écrits historiques et politques: L'Expérience ouvrière et l'adieu à la revolution (juillet 1934–juin 1937)*
OC II.3	*Écrits historiques et politques: Vers la guerre (1937–1940)*
OC VI.1	*Cahiers (1933–septembre 1941)*
OC VI.2	*Cahiers (septembre–février 1942)*
OC VI.3	*Cahiers (février 1942–juin 1942)*
Oe	*Oeuvres.* Ed. F. de Lussy. Paris: Gallimard, 1999.
OEL	*Oppression et Liberté.* Paris: Gallimard, 1955.
P	*Poèmes.* Paris: Gallimard, 1963.
PSO	*Pensées sans ordre concernant l'amour de Dieu.* Paris: Gallimard, 1962.
SG	*La Source grecque.* Paris: Gallimard, 1963.
SS	*Sur la science.* Paris: Gallimard, 1966.

English Translations of Weil's Writings

FLN   *First and Last Notebooks.* Trans. Richard Rees. London: Oxford University Press, 1970.

FW   *Formative Writings 1929–1941.* Trans. Dorothy Tuck McFarland and Wilhelmina van Ness. Amherst, MA: University of Massachusetts Press, 1987.

GG   *Gravity and Grace.* Trans. Emma Crawford and Mario von der Ruhr. London: Routledge, 2002.

GG¹   *Gravity and Grace.* Trans. Arthur Wills. Lincoln, NE: University of Lincoln Press, 1997.

GTG   *Gateway to God.* Ed. David Raper. New York: Crossroad, 1982.

IC   *Intimations of Christianity among the Ancient Greeks.* Trans. E. C. Geissbuhler. London: Routledge, 1988.

LOP   *Lectures on Philosophy.* Trans. Hugh Price. Cambridge: Cambridge University Press, 1978.

LP   *Letter to a Priest.* Trans. Arthur Wills. London: Routledge, 2002.

NB   *The Notebooks of Simone Weil.* 2 Vols. Trans. Arthur Wills. London: Routledge & Kegan Paul, 1956, 1976.

NR   *The Need for Roots.* Trans. Arthur Wills. London: Routledge, 2002.

OL   *Oppression and Liberty.* Trans. Arthur Wills and John Petrie. London: Routledge, 2001.

OL¹   *Oppression and Liberty.* Trans. Arthur Wills and John Petrie. Amherst: The University of Massachusetts Press, 1973.

SE   *Selected Essays.* Trans. Richard Rees. London: Oxford University Press, 1962.

SL   *Seventy Letters.* Trans. Richard Rees. New York: Oxford University Press, 1965.

SN   *On Science, Necessity, and the Love of God.* Trans. Richard Rees. London: Oxford University Press, 1968.

SWA   *Simone Weil: An Anthology.* Ed. Siân Miles. New York: Weidenfeld and Nicolson, 1986.

SWC   *Simone Weil on Colonialism.* Trans. Patricia Little. New York: Rowman and Littlefield, 2003.

SWR   *Simone Weil Reader.* Ed. George A. Panichas. Wakefield, RI and London: Moyer Bell, 1977.

SWW   *Simone Weil: Writings.* Ed. Eric O. Springsted. Maryknoll, NY: Orbis Books, 1998.

WG   *Waiting for God.* Trans. Emma Craufurd. New York: Harper
            and Row, 1973.

WG[1]   *Waiting for God.* Trans. Emma Craufurd. New York: Harper-
            Collins, 2001.

The Relevance of Simone Weil (1909–1943): 100 Years Later

Throughout her life, Simone Weil was to find fault with those very convictions, institutions, or people with whom she seemed to have the most affinity.

As a teenager, she was attracted to the "party of the workers." She soon found out, however, that Communism was not instigating a fight for the liberation from oppression, but for its increase. Then, she wrote articles in favor of "non-affiliated" trade unions only to discover that they, too, would result in the misuse of power by bureaucracy. As Weil warned us: Since in modern society "oppression is exercised in the name of the function," the expertise of a few leads to the virtual slavery of many.[1]

When civil war broke out in Spain, she joined the international militia on the Republican side, but was soon laid off by a wound which kept her from fighting for a cause she had by then ceased to believe in. In her eyes, the end does not justify the means, since it is the means that give the end its meaning.

At heart she was a pacifist, willing for Sudetenland to be surrendered to Hitler. But since this dictator had shown at Prague that he could trample on values even more precious than human life, she renounced her ineffective convictions and proposed a corps of front-line nurses tailored to fit her own passion for self-sacrifice.

In the more intimate domain of personal belief, she had been an agnostic. But the absence of God left unanswered the problem of human suffering. Christianity provided this answer, since it is the "religion of the slaves."[2] Since beauty was a transcendent value, God could be found at the juncture between beauty and suffering. However, it was not Simone Weil that found God, but God who came to her. She would not pray until three years later, and when reciting by chance the Our Father, a mystical intimacy ensued. Henceforth a Catholic at heart, she would nonetheless stay out of the Church, as it was too safe a haven when so many could not share it.

In late 1942, having shepherded her parents to safety in the United States, she joined the Free French in London, volunteering for a mission as a spy in France. However, she was pigeonholed into a think-tank, mapping constitutional blueprints for a France of the future. This is a future that she would not share. After having broken up with the Gaullists, whom she suspected of compromising the integrity of their cause, she died of self-imposed austerities in August 1943.

Thus, with her early death, her influence could only be exercised posthumously.

What she had to say in her unfinished manuscripts can best be read as a commitment to the search for transcendental truth. Her very incapacity to fit, for any length of time, into any group, in spite of her gift of sympathy, is based on her rejection of a consensual ideal.

If there is a lesson to be drawn from her life, it is to be found in the tension between truth such as it reveals itself to the individual and as it is proposed by society: for Truth, in the perspective of the Good, and in the light of Beauty, is personal and cannot be collective – ultimately, because Truth is a Person.

Having died young, she remains forever young. Thus, in her quest for the absolute, she is for us closer to the choices she made, than she would have been if she had reached the more detached speculative maturity thinkers often achieve in middle age. Her appeal in part relies upon the freshness and immediacy of the events of her life. Yet, in her correspondence and in her notebooks, she frequently adopts a reflective attitude. She writes, for instance, to Père Perrin that there is such a thing as an implicit love of God in those who do not believe in Him, but live as if they did.[3] In Simone Weil's case, this was certainly true. Thus, she thinks it must have been equally true for Homer or Sophocles, who evoke a justice transcending partisanship.

If we can hardly learn much that is really worthwhile from the society we live in, we can at least do so from the cultures of the past, the sieve of time having separated the dross from the gold. It is the conventional thinking of today, however, that has become the basis for the formulation of an ideal for the majority. "Beware the prestige of numbers," Weil seems to say at times.[4] The pragmatics of democracy have nothing to do with the uniqueness of the truth. Opinion is the seedbed of error; "opinion is the devil,"[5] just as the evil spirits were "legion" in the possessed exorcised by Christ. The fact that they were many is significant. In fact, opinion is wrong even when it is right, because it is not an apprehension of truth, but consensus. René Girard would say that it is "mimetic" in its appeal. It provides a ready-made pattern for thought as a substitute for that inner awareness which Simone Weil calls "attention."

We tend to forget that people, considered individually or collectively, remain fairly consistently conformed to what they have been. If they improve on one point, they worsen on the other. There is in the Gospels a passage which is not often quoted. It is the one where Christ castigates the Pharisees,[6] calling them "Serpents!" and "Race of vipers!" and warning that they are on the way to hell. As we say in French: "*l'élite trahit toujours!*" ("The elite always betrays!") Thus when the Pharisees and Sadducees rejected the Messiah, they betrayed the expectations of the whole nation:

> Woe to you, scribes and Pharisees, hypocrites! For you build the tombs of the prophets and adorn the monuments of the righteous, saying, "If we had lived in the days of our fathers, we would not have taken part with them in shedding the blood of the prophets." Thus you witness against yourselves that you are sons of those who murdered the prophets.[7]

In short, these men of culture and power were about to repeat the very misdeeds of those forerunners of whom they strongly disapproved. How was this possible? Had they not learned from the lessons of the past? Yes, they had learned insofar as "they [built] the tombs of the prophets," but not so that they drew the right conclusions. If it is criminal "[to shed] the blood of the prophets," it is even more so to shed the blood of He whom the prophets had been announcing. While these Pharisees were no less dead than those they buried with pomp, they abstained cheerfully from emulating those they claimed as their models.

Thus Simone Weil's revulsion for the aimless massacres of World War I had led her to place trust at first in those fellow pacifists who would soon reveal their shallowness of heart by their willingness to collaborate with the Nazis in occupied France. These opportunists had shown that their lip-service to humanitarianism served as a screen for their readiness to betray their own country. Once tried, they were found wanting.

Each generation passes judgment on the preceding one, revoking with humor its mistakes or with aversion its crimes, but repeating both nonetheless, in due time, under another guise. Meanwhile, celebration of past heroes disguises in reality a massive readiness not to follow in their footsteps.

Simone Weil's life had been a constant search for a milieu in which this reiteration of what has been aberrant does not take place. Her reluctance to join the Church came from a fear of its institutional aspect. Her reading of the legendary deaths of early martyrs was so critical as to depreciate the quality of their sacrifice: she thought they were cushioned by their belief in an afterlife and conditioned by the approval of fellow Christians. She was ready to commit herself to a worthy cause, as long as it could not be considered a haven. It could be said that she felt more at home in the Greece of Plato than in the France of the twentieth century.

The past is our teacher, not the present, which is ontologically as fleeting and unsubstantial as a fraction of time, just as it is lived by most as a compromise of conflicting interests. The future, alas, is too unreal to provide anything but the virtuality of hope.

In terms of this past, how should we, followers of the Weilienne ethos, judge our present era? So many practices have been declared morally irrelevant, that the real world has become a mirror-image of the wasteland of values Simone Weil described in the virtual world of cheap literature.[8]

Progress is not before us, but above us, according to Simone Weil, because that is from whence the past received what it has to offer . . .

Jacques Cabaud
January 2009

Notes

[1] OC II.1, 268.

[2] WG, 19–20.

[3] See, "Formes de l'amour implicite de Dieu," in AD, 99–166.

[4] Editors' note: See, for example, "Human Personality," in SWA, 60, where it reads: "for men burdened with a fatigue that makes any effort of attention painful it is a relief to contemplate the unproblematic clarity of figures." On collectivities Weil writes: "The collective is the object of all idolatry" (GG, 216).

[5] CS, 272.

[6] Editors' note: Weil tells us, "A Pharisee is someone who is virtuous out of obedience to the Great Beast" (GG, 222).

[7] Matthew 23:29–30.

[8] See "Morale et literature," in OC IV.1, 90–95.

Introduction

A Call to Radicalism

A. Rebecca Rozelle-Stone and Lucian Stone

We are in a period of transition; but a transition towards what?
—*Simone Weil*[1]

When Simone Weil (1909–1943) asked the question cited above in 1933 (over three-quarters of a century ago), she was observing the increasing literal and moral "bankruptcy" of capitalism, as well as the naïveté of self-proclaimed Marxists who were setting up not emancipatory political systems, but new institutions of oppression, whether fascistic or managerial-bureaucratic. In all cases, her concern was that the individual was being subsumed to the collective, and as a result, the consciousness of these very transformations was suffering an increasing threat of annihilation. It is no wonder then, that Weil answers her own question about the direction of the transition: "No one has the slightest idea."[2] The irony, as she notes, is that oppressive governments, social forces, powerful institutions, and all the blind mechanisms of society, cannot stop people from striving towards a clear comprehension of their goals. "Nothing in the world," Weil wrote, "can prevent us from thinking clearly," from "comprehending the force by which we are crushed."[3] In saying this, she understood that there is no contradiction between theory and action, but that in fact, to have meaningful, efficacious and just actions, one must clarify one's intentions and illuminate the obstacles that are to be overcome.

In light of this necessity, her vocation appears all the more fundamental. Her calling, she insisted, was an "intellectual" one. So she demanded that her thought be like "water," in its indifference to the objects (or ideas) that fall into it, equally open with regard to everything that presents itself: "[Water] does not weigh them; they weigh themselves, after a certain time of oscillation."[4] The search for truth, then, requires us to put aside preconceived categories and compartments of knowledge; economics, politics, art and religion will not each have their own separate, isolated truths. Rather, to understand wholly these aspects of human existence, we must come to see their underlying interconnections, the relationships between the supposedly disparate facts. Perhaps it was because Weil was committed to this method—the love of and search for universal truth—that she is now notoriously difficult to locate in one field or another: religious studies, Christian theology, political science, literature, or philosophy? Moreover, just as she asserted that there was and should be no divorce between thought and genuine action, Weil herself was not only a scholar, but also a labor activist, a participant in the Spanish Civil War, a teacher, a factory worker, a farm laborer, and for some, a saint. All of these marks she made on the world were infused with her critical consciousness, her awareness of her own role and culpability in systemic evils, and her carefully considered and radical positions on the issues of her day.

It is a grave mistake we continue to make in supposing that there should be classes of people who are the "thinkers" and classes who are the "actors," as if these—thinking and acting—are specialties unto themselves that are not perverted by the absence of the other. Weil realized, for example, that something as basic as clarifying thought "might be a way of saving human lives."[5] Although this imperative was basic, in insisting on its application, it was and is radical, so accustomed we are to moralizing lip service and policies that continually uphold an oppressive status quo.

Are we, situated 100 years after Simone Weil's birth, any more prepared to receive the invocation to this basic radicalism? In 1934, questioning whether her own fellow citizens were ready to begin grasping essential relationships and clarifying their muddled ideas, she concluded, "Our age seems almost entirely unfitted for such a task."[6] Although the observations and beliefs that "the glossy surface" of her civilization hid "a real intellectual decadence"[7] were proffered in the early 1930s, we have good reason to think that the twenty-first century has ushered in new extremes of intellectual impoverishment. While in recent decades philosophers, theologians, cultural critics and sociologists have been warning us of the effects of technologies generally considered benign— from mass media transmission of disinformation and "infotainment" propaganda to communications technologies rendering us increasingly detached and illiterate—we have neglected to see that our social ills frequently have common origins and causes. Too often, solutions cannot be realized because even the most well-intentioned philosophers and moral theorists are struggling within the same framework and set of assumptions that have caused the problems in the first place. Real solutions are then dismissed as being too "radical", and hence "irrelevant."

But we would do well to remember the etymology of the word "radical." The Latin *radicalis* denotes "of or having roots," and "going to the origin and the essential." While our colloquial usage of "radical" suggests that which is marginal, extreme or unconventional, its origin and our current usage of it appear consistent when we consider the uprooted and thoughtless nature of our society. Becoming rooted in reality and in what is essential, especially in a context of mechanical action and abstracted intellectualism, *is unconventional*. Might we not desperately need a radical new ethic, a new paradigm of "the good"? Might we not, as Weil has declared, require "a new type of sanctity," which would amount to "a large portion of truth and beauty hitherto concealed under a thick layer of dust," revealed . . . as radically basic?[8]

If we are tempted to complain that Simone Weil's invocation to radicalism holds us to standards that are impossibly high, we should also heed her words: "An educational method which is not inspired by the conception of *a certain form of human perfection* is not worth very much."[9] This form of "human perfection," we contend, strongly resembles the idea of the "new saint" whom Weil espoused. In such a person, there would exist "a focal point of greatness where the genius creating beauty, the genius revealing truth, heroism and holiness are indistinguishable."[10] Although the new saint and her qualities are not something that can be manufactured, such persons should be sought out and beheld as exemplars, and attention should be given to the many ways in which our current societal structures fall short of this conception of "human perfection." It is important to remember that in contradistinction to the leaders of secular or even mass religious hierarchies, the exemplar has no followers, but only "'emulators' in a relationship of emulation" who come to love, esteem, hate and scorn what the exemplar loves, esteems, and so on.[11] In light of this re-valuation, it is easy to see why the exemplar is "not a goal after which one strives," but is rather the goal-determiner for the emulator.[12]

T. S. Eliot, who considered Weil to be such a saint and a genius, recognized that many people would not agree with her views; some, in fact, may violently disagree with them. "But," he wrote, "agreement and rejection are secondary: what matters is to make contact with a great soul."[13] We think there is truth in this claim, and we would argue that the force of exemplarity of Simone Weil's "great soul" may serve to orient those who would attend to her in ways that take them straight to the root of our social, economic, educational, religious, personal, aesthetic and moral problems. Thus, we were inspired, 100 years after Weil's birth, to bring together serious considerations of her ideas and life, and the messages they carry for us today, in the infancy of the 21st century. While Weil's ideas are impossible to separate from her praxis, the first section of this book analyzes the "Radical Orientation" suggested in her writings, emphasizing the role of notions like "equilibrium," "the supernatural," and "the void" in grounding her life's work in general, including her perspectives on religion, idolatry, atheism, education, and mystery . The second section examines the "Radical World" that follows from the orientation described, and contributors in this half consider pertinent themes such as science and technology, violence, war, power, resistance, responsibility, feminism, liberation theology, Marxism and propagandistic language, as they are related to and illuminated by the writings and life of Weil.

We want to make clear, from the beginning, that while the following chapters are written by sixteen renowned or newly emerging scholars of Weil's thought, as is often the case with scholars of any philosopher or historical thinker, there are disagreements in interpretation. Readers will observe, especially, the differing perspectives on Weil's understanding of the supernatural and the natural, the degree of her heterodoxy with regard to Christianity, and what it means to say that Weil was "religious" in general. Additionally, there are divergent stances on her notion of power, and on her cosmology. This pluralism is as it should be; to portray Weil in a static way would be a misrepresentation and negation of the mysteries and subtleties of her ideas. Moreover, the fact that the contributors have backgrounds in philosophy, theology, religious studies and feminism is *a propos* in reflecting the universal nature of Weil's thought and its resistance to being compartmentalized within one field. We hope to arouse the interest of scholars and laypeople from other disciplines as well, and would be pleased if we provoked a sustained dialogue about some of the challenges (logical and practical) that arise from these meditations on Simone Weil.

Through the revolutionary insights of this remarkable woman, then, we are proposing a framework for understanding and creating a more just world, one that challenges our metaphysical, epistemological and ethical assumptions which have led to pervasive forms of uprootedness, or what Weil calls *déracinement*. We hope these diverse essays will enable readers not only to see the relevance of Weil's life and thought for pressing issues today, but also to see ourselves and our socio-political milieu in a radically different light. This new framework centers on a notion of absolute selflessness and humility, and is radical both in the sense of being "unconventional" and in the sense of the aforementioned Latin *radicalis*, "returning to essential roots." In this sense, we aim to demonstrate that the radical *is* absolutely relevant, and that Simone Weil is the paradigm for effective socio-political and personal redress.

Notes

1   OL, 1.
2   OL, 1.
3   OL, 23.
4   WG, 85.
5   SWA, 222.
6   SWA, 222.
7   SWA, 222.
8   WG, 99.
9   NR 216 (emphasis added).
10 NR 232.
11 Anthony Steinbock, "Interpersonal attention through exemplarity," *Journal of Consciousness Studies* Vol. 8, Nos. 5–7 (2001), 188.
12 Ibid., 190.
13 T. S. Eliot, "Preface," in Simone Weil, *The Need for Roots: Prelude to a Declaration of Duties towards Mankind*, trans. Arthur Wills (New York: Routledge, 2002), viii.

Part One

Radical Orientation

Chapter 1

Simone Weil on Modern Disequilibrium

Bartomeu Estelrich

You could not be born at a better period than the present, when we have lost everything.[1]

The twentieth century has seen the birth in Europe of several philosophical movements, which have tried, as a common trend, to respond "in various ways to a world increasingly dominated by technocracy, the positive sciences, and the threat of total control over human intelligence."[2] Among them, phenomenology, existentialism, structuralism, and critical theory have proved to be especially relevant for the construction of new methods of inquiry more keenly attuned to the particular circumstances of Western culture in the last century.[3] For example,

> Phenomenology and Existentialism [have] attempt[ed] to relocate the origins of meaning in our lived experience prior to the impersonal "objectivism" of a narrow scientific attitude. Structuralism [has] emphasize[d] the hidden or "unconscious" structures of language, which underpin our current established discourses—social, cultural, and economic. And Critical Theory [has] develope[d] the insights of Hegel and Marx into a radical interrogation of the ideologies at work in advanced industrial societies.[4]

Even though this classification may tend to oversimplify matters, and under its broad heading, makes it "very difficult to do justice to the complex . . . the multi-dimensional relations existing between the four movements,"[5] it is undeniable that those philosophical currents can be considered as some of the most influential, and therefore most "relevant," movements of twentieth-century European thought.

If that is so, two obvious sets of problems arise when we wonder about the "relevance" of Simone Weil's philosophy. The first set—which I will call the "contextual" set of problems—appears when we realize that Weilienne philosophy: a) had no part in any of the above-mentioned movements; b) barely mentions twentieth-century philosophers;[6] c) regarded itself as an heir of the Platonic and Christian traditions at a time when both traditions were under suspicion;[7] and d) is hardly mentioned in any manual on the history of philosophy. The second set of problems—which I will refer to as the "terminological" ones—arises, when we inquire about the very meaning of the concept of "relevance." First, these problems arise because that "relevance" entails the problem of determining the limits of what can be considered as such during a given period of time, and second, because it also entails the difficulty of pinpointing an authoritative subject capable of establishing those limits.

To address these contextual and terminological problems, I will divide my analysis into two parts. The first part will focus on analyzing the historical moment that Weilienne philosophy was conceived as well as the context to which it was primarily responding (modernity), and the second part will concentrate on the meaning of relevance in view of her philosophy in our present time. To address the former, I will assume that a philosophy can be considered as "relevant," on one level, if it deals with the questions/problems that were significant during its historical time, and if the answers/solutions that it provided were accurate. That is, I will explore some of the most "relevant" events of Weil's time, underlining the fact that those events were, at the same time, the detonators of her philosophy. Additionally, I will analyze the most important topics raised by modern philosophy and the answers that Simone Weil gave to them. To address the latter problems, I will contend that a philosophy is "relevant" (on another level) if the problems that gave rise to it are still currently in force, either in their original forms or in modern-day versions, and if the solutions provided in the past by this philosophy are still applicable to present problems. In particular, I will argue that the "irrelevant" principles underlined by Simone Weil in her time are in fact still relevant today, for us to understand and to transform our present reality.

Relevant Themes in Weil's Historical Moment

Four major phenomena shaped Western society in the twentieth century: a) two World Wars; b) the spread of capitalism, socialism and totalitarianism; c) the social impact of those systems on populations—poverty, the emergence of the new economic caste of the proletariat, and the accompanying affliction and oppression; and d) the increasing importance of technology in all aspects of human life. In her desire to unravel the causes of these phenomena, Weil did not resign herself to a peripheral analysis of these events. She probed and discovered that, for instance, beneath the wars of her time there was a hidden, atemporal element common to all of them. She named that element "force" and depicted it as an "evil principle,"[8] a "mechanism"[9] that "reigns everywhere"[10] and "make[s] a thing of anybody who comes under its sway."[11] For Weil, war was nothing but the art of the force: the art of crushing[12] and petrifying[13] persons, destroying anything that is essential to them.

Weil also analyzed the social structures of her time, and discovered that beneath their benign appearance they hid a strong, invisible power that tends to take control over individuals, to dominate them, and to convert them into submissive servants. Weil, following Plato's *Republic*,[14] likened the power of society to a "great beast,"[15] "essentially evil,"[16] that "crushes whomever it touches."[17] Because of its transcendent and quasi-divine characteristics,[18] society acts like "a trap"[19] that catches the attention of individuals, entices their souls, and offers them a false sense of collective security.[20] In doing so, society becomes the most dangerous "object of idolatry"[21] on earth and the main "obstacle between man and God."[22] In light of these recognitions, Weil examined the conditions of affliction and oppression in which the population of her time was living, and discovered that what caused them was a latent tendency, increasingly present in all aspects of modern life, toward immoderation: a tendency that gives more prominence to ambition than to measure, to excess than to proportion, to intemperance than to self-control.

However, Weil went a step further and discovered three main causes for these problems. First, the modern concept of science[23] which, by shedding its ancient connotation of "equilibrium," became an autonomous and technological power, developed "for its own sake," and with an inner tendency to stray "further and further away from any human meaning."[24] According to her, this tendency had "its roots in a [modern] mistake [of overestimating] the nature of the algebraic symbols."[25] Such a mistake is based upon the presumption that the more we abstractly represent our surrounding world, the better we understand it. Secondly, a new concept of money, which in leaving behind its original value as an intermediary, became an algebraic symbol independent of human life. According to Weil it is possible to perceive this new concept in the modern "phenomenon of money generating money and, even more oddly, [of] money itself becoming irrelevant and being replaced by credit, and by credit to the second or third degree."[26] Finally, she noted the increasing importance of machinery, which, by a process of depersonalization, starved "the worker intellectually and spiritually, and [. . .] destroy[ed] the proper relation of mind and body."[27] For Weil, the best example of this is the modern factory. "The 'fragmentation' of the work, isolating each worker in a tiny, seemingly unrelated part, creates the situation in which these broken-off pieces can be taken over by machines,"[28] or by the workers themselves, becoming more machine-like as they work.

Weil called these aspects "the three monstrosities of contemporary civilization."[29] In order to fully understand them, she delved even deeper into her analysis and discovered that they originated, firstly, from the loss, in modern times, of the notion of "measure:"

> The idea of measure has been lost in every sphere [of our civilization] [. . .]. Everything is corrupted by [the notion of quantity]. Including private life, because *temperance* (σωφροσύνη) has become unthinkable. Outside the sphere of external observances (bourgeois formality) the whole moral trend of the post-war years (and even before) has been an *apology* for *intemperance* (surrealism) and therefore, ultimately, for madness. . .[30]

And, secondly, these monstrosities resulted from the loss of the idea of "equilibrium:"

> Modern life is *given over to excess*. Everything is steeped in it—thought as well as action, private life as well as public. (Sports: championship— pleasure to the point of intoxication and nausea—fatigue to the point of passing out—etc., etc., etc.). Hence the decadence of art. There is no more equilibrium anywhere [. . .] Every equilibrium has been upset. For example: between labour and the fruits of labour. Even the peasants have been corrupted indirectly by speculation . . . There is no longer any visible relation between action and its results, so that even in action man has become passive.[31]

According to Weil, "intemperance," "excess," "immoderation," and loss of the sense of "limit," "measure" and "proportion" are the causes of modern disequilibrium, and hence the causes of affliction and oppression. To fight against such disequilibrium is the primary goal of her philosophy. For only a philosophy that "seek[s] for an equilibrium between man and himself, between man and things"[32] is capable of breaching the madness in which modern civilization finds itself immersed, to invert the "monstrous" logic that modern philosophy started, and to return the world to an orderly, "*cosmo-logic*" (κόσμοσ), state.[33]

Even though the tendency towards "immoderation" is as old as human history, and its consequences can be traced in any culture, Weil saw that the roots of *modern* immoderation started when, at the outset of modernity, philosophy cut itself off from its humble origins, and forgot its search for a harmonious principle. For that reason, if we want to understand the relevance of Weil's philosophy, and to reach the very core of her proposal, it is necessary to analyze its connection with, and response to, modern philosophy.

From a historical point of view, modern philosophy can be divided into three main periods. The first one started at the outset of the sixteenth century with the arrival of the Machiavellian, Lutheran and Copernican revolutions. These three revolutions, occurring almost simultaneously, abruptly woke Old Europe from its medieval dream. The Machiavellian revolution, to begin with, changed the very concept of politics as based in a moral vision by analyzing the proper functions of a "modern" prince from a "realistic" and "pragmatic" viewpoint. The Lutheran revolution, concurrently, fueled the emergence of the modern autonomous subject by reinforcing the supremacy of the individual in his/her relationship with God and with the Scriptures. The Copernican revolution, finally, paved the way for a new notion of science by formulating a mathematically based heliocentric cosmology.

The second period of modern philosophy started during the seventeenth century and lasted until the mid-nineteenth century. It can be described as a euphoric moment in which it was thought possible to dissipate the darkness of error and superstition left over from the medieval period by the sole "light" of reason. Its program can be defined by the belief in an almighty science capable of totally explaining reality; in the notion of an individual-egotistic subject, related to nothing, and only responsible for its own betterment; and in the idea of an unstoppable progress towards an ever-improving future.

However, this overall optimism came to an end when, by the late nineteenth and early twentieth century, Marx, Freud and Nietzsche cast suspicion on the philosophical premises of the previous period. This subversive triumvirate rebelled, using different approaches, and in their own unique ways, against the former (second) period of modernity by unveiling the causal forces that surreptitiously rule the world. Marx, by rejecting Hegel's idealism, discovered that society, under a superficial appearance of calm, was ruled by covert economic forces, capable of creating an impregnable barrier between those who have the power—the bourgeoisie—and those who simply obey—the working class, or proletariat. Freud, by analyzing hidden human desires, posited that the mind was governed by unconscious "pulsions." He suggested that human behavior was conducted by two conflicting central desires—the life drive (*libido*) and the death drive (*thanatos*)—and that human beings were therefore not fully in charge of their lives. Finally, Nietzsche challenged the foundations of Christianity and traditional morality by proposing a total break with the Platonic-Judeo-Christian tradition. His recourse of opposing the Apollonian instinct (the instinct to create order, moderation and symmetry) to the Dionysian one (the instinct towards chaos, excess, and dissolution of all boundaries), led him to exalt life, creativity, health, and the realities of the world we live in, rather than those situated in a world beyond. For that reason he regarded himself as the prophet of a new morality, which by "transvaluating" (*Umwertung*) all values, set the basis for the appearance of a new race of men, the *Übermensch*, emancipated from any idea of God, and fully adapted to the demands of a nihilistic culture.

According to Weil, these modern values can be seen in three aspects of the culture of her time. First, she observed the destruction of the mind-body equilibrium:

> The conditions of modern life destroy the mind-body equilibrium in everything, in thought and in action—in all actions: in work, in fighting . . . [*in the margin*: and in love, which is now a luxurious sensation and a game. . .] (and, inevitably, the emotional life itself is affected by it. . .) In its every aspect, the civilization we live in overwhelms the human *body*. Mind and body have become strangers to one another. Contact has been lost.[34]

Second, she witnessed the erosion of the spiritual and material bases of contemporary civilization:

> The contemporary *unconscious* domination is turning against itself and is in process of destroying not only the spiritual but the material bases of contemporary civilization—(destruction of products—anarchy of the productive system—war).[35]

And thirdly, she realized the dissolution of every value whose demise Nietzsche had prophesied:

In our day, everything [. . .] has lost its value. Production and technical progress . . . science . . . art . . . social action. . . Man has lost contact with himself and with the world.[36]

Weil, in order to redirect these tendencies, proposed a philosophy grounded in principles diametrically opposed to those proclaimed by modernity. In opposition to the deductive-geometric method of rationalism and the inductive-experimental one of the Enlightenment, Weil looked for a philosophical method that, instead of starting with the ideas that reason assumes as clear and distinct, or with the observational facts provided by experimentation, starts from those problems that reason rejects as insoluble. She embraced a method that instead of reaching conclusions by exploring our surrounding world and adhering to scientific procedures, tends to detach itself from the facts and use them as a springboard to jump toward the transcendent; she favored a method that, instead of being content with analytical explanations of the structures of this world, aspires to a direct contact with the reality that supports it.

The proper method of philosophy consists in clearly conceiving the insoluble problems in all their insolubility and then in simply contemplating them, fixedly and tirelessly, year after year, without any hope, patiently waiting. . .

There is no entry into the transcendent until the human faculties—intelligence, will, human love—have come up against a limit, and the human being waits at this threshold, which he can make no move to cross, without turning away and without knowing what he wants, in fixed, unwavering attention.[37]

Weil also broke with the Hegelian postulate that equates the rational with the real and vice versa. For her, the way to reach the real is not by a dialectical process but by a phenomenological one, the key element of which is attention. She defines attention as "a negative effort,"[38] which "consists of suspending our thought, leaving it detached, empty, and ready to be penetrated by the object."[39] During this process the subject should be "motionless, in expectation, unshaken and unmoved by any external shock,"[40] "not seeking anything, but ready to receive in its naked truth the object that is to penetrate it."[41] By doing so, the self ceases to be in charge of the subject, and the soul enters into a state of waiting (*attende*), silence (*silence*), and immobility (*immobilité*)[42] that allows him/her to go through the appearances of this world and reach the real one.

Weil also reacted against two modern interpretations of God. First, she moved away from the cold idea of an *ex-machina—Watchmaker God—* assumed during the early stages of modernity in movements like Deism— which, outside the empirical world, endowed with total power, and exceedingly perfect, sets in motion the great machine of the Universe without sentiment and love, grants it an end, and afterwards, disappears. Secondly, she also refused the skeptical interpretations of God—common during the last stages of modernity—which either by considering Him as the ultimate "opiate of the people" (Marx), or as a "psychological delusion" (Freud), or, by simply asserting His death (Nietzsche), eradicated Him from the modern discourse once and for all. For Weil, God is neither a psychological construct nor a constructor of artifacts. God is an Artist[43] that models the Universe with beauty and sentiment. He is the creator[44] that produces the world with care and toil. He is the origin[45] of all that exists, and the center of our harmonic Cosmos. For Weil, God is love:[46] a total and perfect love that keeps unity in the bosom of the Trinity,[47] that was revealed to the world in Christ's passion,[48] and is the ultimate reason for God to create.[49] However, the love that God feels for his creation neither controls nor baffles the conscience of the people. For Weil, God is also, and paradoxically, an impersonal[50] and absent God that does not interfere in the course of creation;[51] a God that willingly has withdrawn from the Universe;[52] a God that even though *the center* of creation, is not *at* its center;[53] a God, finally, that, for the sake of humanity, has "abdicated from his divine omnipotence"[54] and has "emptied himself of his divinity."[55]

Finally, Weil also reacted against the modern concept of an autonomous, self-determining subject. For her, a subject who is locked into his/her ego is unable to take a step further towards the unknown. The Weilienne subject, on the contrary, is a pilgrim of the absolute; a subject aware of the social problems of his/her age, open to the transcendent, and eager for mystery; a subject that is not attached to the certainties that his/her mind produces, but open to the uncertainties that his/her search for truth generates; a subject that is not defined by what he/she already "is," but by his/her consent "not to be;"[56] a subject that rejects being at the center, and is capable of sacrifice, renunciation and obedience; a subject, finally, that by inhabiting the limits of the transcendent, is able to warn us about the irrational consequences of a purely rational existence.

Taking into account all these responses, Weilienne philosophy cannot be considered, in a strict sense, modern. Even though Simone Weil was fully aware of the problems of her time, she refused the answers/ solutions that the mainstream of modern philosophy gave to them. For her, those problems should have been addressed from a different perspective. Such a perspective, instead of underlining the immanent, would have emphasized the transcendent; instead of adopting an objective-subjective standpoint, would have accentuated an impersonal one; instead of accepting the promise of an ever-improving progress, would have stressed the attitude of attention to the present. Moreover, instead of placing emphasis on the rights of the individual, this perspective would have demanded universal justice, and instead of explaining the present situation by recourse to "pulsions," instincts, or hidden economic structures, it would have looked for the seeds of goodness, truth and beauty sown in this world. For her, philosophy, more than being a rational interpretation of reality, is a way of life, a method of spiritual progress that pursues a purification and conversion of the soul, and a transformational process that allows beholding the reality as it is, with its inevitable contradictions.[57] For Weil, philosophy should rediscover its place and proper function in contemporary society. And that implies calling attention to what is perceived as minute, insignificant, or irrelevant. That is, philosophy implies becoming aware of the seeds of pure love and generosity that invigorate our communities, discerning the germs of social change concealed in the movements and civil organizations of our time, discovering the particles of good hidden in the multiple layers of our souls, looking for the secret presence of God in our lives, and detecting the glimmer of truth, beauty and justice scattered among our cultures. For only by stressing those values is it possible to invert the modern logic of immoderation, to re-establish the primeval harmony "between man and [. . .] nature,"[58] and to restore "*measure* and *equilibrium*"[59] in our societies.

The Relevance of Weil's Philosophy Today

Our present time is very similar to the one in which Simone Weil lived. We still are under the threat of war (now camouflaged under the idea of terrorism); poverty has not been eradicated, and in the current economic crisis it is expanding rapidly; affliction and oppression reign everywhere; technology is pervasive in all aspects of human life; and pollution has increased exponentially, endangering all forms of life on the planet. In addition, if we compare the effects of these situations in our culture to the ones described by Weil, we see that they are basically the same, with the only difference that they have notably increased: the gap between mind and body has widened greatly; the spiritual and material bases of our civilization have shrunken dangerously; our societies are more fragmented, accelerated, disorientated and disenchanted than before; many essential aspects of human life (for example communication, art, love, work and leisure) have lost their original meaning, purpose and value; and people are increasingly alienated from themselves and from the world. In fact, if we analyze all these problems in detail, we can see that they all share a common denominator. They all are expressions of our contemporary tendency toward disequilibrium and are due, as Weil has already diagnosed, to "intemperance," "excess," "immoderation," and the loss of our sense of "limit," "measure," and "proportion."

If this analysis is correct, the question about the relevance of Weil's philosophy in our time can be answered straightforwardly. Weil's philosophy is still relevant not only because our situation is essentially the same as in Weil's time, but also because she has accurately described the causes that have sparked those problems, and has offered a solution to them that is still applicable today. In my view, that solution can be synthesized with three aspects of her philosophy: first, with her emphasis on a new experience of time; secondly, with her proposal of a new concept of the self; and thirdly, with her insights into a new spirituality of work.

For Weil, the modern concept of time must be transformed. According to her, modernity, by idealizing the idea of progress, has overemphasized the perspectives of past and future. In doing so, modernity has hindered the capacity of the individual to live in the present, and enhanced his/her tendency to dwell in an imaginary world (whether in the past or in the future). For that reason, Weil suggests that the first step for a person to restore equilibrium in his/her life is by renouncing his/her tendency to live in an "imaginary future" or in an "idealized past":

> The past and the future hinder the wholesome effect of affliction by providing an unlimited field for imaginary elevation. That is why the renunciation of past and future is the first of all renunciations.[60]

In renouncing escape into the past and the future, a person becomes attentive to the present and detached from the surrounding world, allowing him/her to break the dynamic of "intemperance," "excess," and "immoderation" in which modern society finds itself immersed. He/she is permitted to restore a "true hierarchy among values:"

Detachment is a renouncement of all possible goals without exception, a renouncement that sets a void in place of the future . . . But the detachment that is in question here does not lack an object; detached thought has as its object the establishment of a true hierarchy among values . . .; it has as its object a way of living, a better life, not elsewhere but in this world and immediately.[61]

The second aspect that must be transformed in order to restore equilibrium is the self. The self has two main connotations in Weil's philosophy. The self is, on the one hand, the only thing that a person truly possesses—"We possess nothing in the world . . . except the power to say 'I.'"[62] On the other hand, the self is the source of sin—"the sin in me says 'I.'"[63] It is because of this second connotation that the self has the power to introduce disequilibrium into the world:

Our sin introduces a discordance in the perfect harmony; it is only possible to reconstitute this perfect harmony by means of a perfect harmonization which implies complete discordance beforehand.[64]

For Weil, the only way to restore equilibrium in the world hinges on the capacity of a person to reconstitute "harmony" in his/her life. However, the way Weil envisions reaching that goal is not by aiming towards a false state of harmony, but by pushing the subject towards the opposite, that is, to a state of "complete discordance" which she calls "decreation." "Decreation" is a process through which the subject mimics God's withdrawal and abdication of creation.[65] Like God, the subject "should renounce being something,"[66] "empty [him-/herself] of the false divinity with which [he/she was] born,"[67] and accept "not to exist."[68] By doing so, the "divine seed," the "particle of pure good"[69] that God has planted in his/her soul, grows.[70] In so doing, the whole philosophical-spiritual process envisioned by Weil is set in motion: firstly, by allowing the subject to detach him/herself from the surrounding world; secondly, by rejecting a purely materialistic concept of it; thirdly, by accepting the idea of time as "perpetuity and eternity;"[71] and fourthly, by rediscovering the divine harmony that conjoins humankind to the universe.

Finally, the third aspect that must be transformed in order to restore equilibrium is the connection that a person has with society. Even though Weil is totally aware of the dangers that exist for a person to live in a society—such as ambition, power and avarice[72]—she also realizes that a person is essentially social. For that reason, a person should struggle to help construct a good society, or at least a less evil one.[73] However, according to her there are four obstacles that are difficult in the relationship between a person and society: "our false conception of greatness; the degradation of the sentiment of justice; our idolization of money; and our lack of religious inspiration."[74] But the biggest obstacle that a person must overcome, which provides fertile ground for the growth of the four obstacles just mentioned, is the lack of balance in modern societies:

> Everybody is busy repeating, in slightly different terms, that what we suffer from is a lack of balance due to a purely material development of technical science.[75]

The disconnection between person and society has nevertheless generated a state of deception among people that has led to the awareness that our society is radically sick: "We are very proud of [our modern civilization], but we also know that it is sick. And everybody is agreed about the diagnosis of the sickness. It is sick because it doesn't know exactly what place to give to physical labor and to those engaged in physical labor."[76] Since for Weil the sickness of our civilization is deeply rooted in its foundations, she suggests that the only way to heal it radically is by creating a new spirituality. This new spirituality, instead of being based on the theoretical concepts of "reason" or "prayer" (as during the ancient and medieval periods of history) must be grounded on a certain concept of work. Work, in contrast to reason and prayer, has the capacity to transform a person radically, because it reconnects him/her with the entire universe. And by reconnecting the person to the universe, the spirituality of work is capable of destroying, from the inside, the tendency towards the immoderation of modern civilization:

> A civilization based upon the spirituality of work would give a Man the very strongest possible roots in the wide universe, and would consequently be the opposite of that state in which we find ourselves now characterized by an almost total uprootedness. Such a civilization is, therefore, by its very nature, the object to which we should aspire as the antidote to our sufferings.[77]

By transforming the concepts of time, self and work, Simone Weil provides a feasible solution to our contemporary tendency towards disequilibrium. She, in contrast to other spiritualistic thinkers who look for a perfect peace of mind to counterbalance the increasing disorder of our societies, and to some philosophers who stoically accept our situation as irreversible, looks for a philosophy with the main goal of radically transforming the tendency towards excess. For her, transformation cannot be achieved by creating a parallel mental world, or by living in a constant state of denying the surrounding reality, but by destroying the very root of our problem: the human tendency to live in an imaginary time, to create an imaginary ego, and to build an imaginary society. For if a person is capable of inverting that tendency by paying attention to the present, by renouncing the demanding impulses of the self and by cultivating a spiritual relation with the surrounding world, that person is already on his/her way towards a new existence: an existence that is grounded in this world, and is capable of generating order in it. For, according to Weil, an ordered life is the *condition of existence* for an equilibrated society, "an ordered universe . . . for an ordered body, and an ordered body for a spirit united to flesh."[78]

Notes

[1] GG[I], 231.
[2] Richard Kearney, *Modern Movements in European Philosophy* (Manchester and New York: Manchester University Press, 1986), 1.
[3] Ibid., 1–2.
[4] Ibid., 1.
[5] Ibid., 6.
[6] Leaving aside Marx, Weil mentions Lagneau, Alain and Husserl as contemporary philosophers who have some connection with her philosophy in *Quelques réflexions autour de la notion de valeur*, Oe, 125. About her philosophical preferences during her studies, see Simone Pétrement, *Simone Weil: A Life*, trans. Raymond Rosenthal (New York: Pantheon Books, 1976), 69. About her rejection of Nietzsche see SS, 231–2. Editors' note: About her relationship with Bataille, see Chapter 11.
[7] See FW, 288; Miklos Vetö, *La Métaphysique religieuse de Simone Weil* (Paris: Vrin, 1971), 148; and Pétrement, *Simone Weil*, 405.
[8] NB, 457.
[9] NB, 499.
[10] NB, 457.
[11] IC, 24.
[12] IC, 31.
[13] IC, 46.
[14] Plato, *The Republic* 493a–d.
[15] IC, 86.
[16] IC, 86.
[17] IC, 39.

18 GG[I], 216.
19 WG[I], 129.
20 FLN, 304.
21 GG[I], 216.
22 IC, 86.
23 I am following the analysis of Henry Leroy Finch, *Simone Weil and the Intellect of Grace*, ed. Martin Andic (New York: Continuum, 1999), 19–20.
24 Ibid., 20.
25 Ibid., 20.
26 Ibid., 20.
27 Ibid., 21.
28 Ibid., 20.
29 FLN, 30.
30 FLN, 29.
31 FLN, 50.
32 FLN, 50.
33 See FLN, 16. Editors' note: *See also* Chapter 14.
34 FLN, 38.
35 FLN, 59.
36 FLN, 59.
37 See FLN, 335.
38 WG[I], 61.
39 WG[I], 62.
40 SL, 137.
41 WG[I], 62.
42 WG[I], 126.
43 See IC, 89–91.
44 GG[I], 78.
45 See FLN, 78–9.
46 WG[I], 74.
47 WG[I], 74.
48 FLN, 240–41.
49 NB, 438.
50 See SE, 13–14.
51 See GG[I], 79.
52 IC, 193.
53 FLN, 79.
54 FLN, 297.
55 GG[I], 80.
56 See FLN, 234.
57 Pétrement, *Simone Weil*, 406, (Oe, 126).
58 FLN, 18.
59 FLN, 16.
60 GG[I], 65.
61 Oe, 124; AL, 405.
62 GG[I], 71.
63 GG[I], 76.

[64] NB, 539.
[65] See FLN, 140–42.
[66] GG^I, 79.
[67] GG^I, 80.
[68] GG^I, 78.
[69] NB, 401.
[70] See SN, 181–83.
[71] NB, 216.
[72] See GG^I, 216.
[73] See GG^I, 223–25.
[74] NR, 219.
[75] NR, 98.
[76] NR, 299.
[77] NR, 98–9.
[78] NB, 130.

Chapter 2

Simone Weil and the Ethic of (Im)moderation

A. Rebecca Rozelle-Stone

So the question is not whether we will be extremists, but what kind of extremists we will be. Will we be extremists for hate or for love? Will we be extremists for the preservation of injustice or for the extension of justice?
— Rev. Dr Martin Luther King, Jr[1]

Introduction

Simone Weil's most fundamental and thoroughgoing critique of modern society is its immoderation and disequilibrium.[2] Her meaning could not be more apparent when she writes, for example: "Modern life is given over to immoderation. Immoderation invades everything: actions and thought, public and private life . . . There is no more balance anywhere."[3] In our time, Weil's critique is echoed by contemporary cultural critics, including Raj Patel (with his book *Stuffed and Starved*,[4] an indictment of the excesses of the global food network); Bill McKibben (especially in his book *Deep Economy*,[5] a challenge to the philosophy of endless economic expansion); Cornel West (who warns against the rise of American imperialism and its extremes in *Democracy Matters*);[6] and Susan Bordo (in *Unbearable Weight*,[7] her scathing analysis of Western culture's unbalanced attitudes towards bodies, femininity and consumption), among many others.

Bordo, for instance, in recognizing that "the body is not only a *text* of culture" but also "a *practical*, direct locus of social control," argues that the anorexic's body is only a crystallization of a broader cultural ethos that idealizes an extreme of hyper-slenderness and bodily control. Yet this is a culture[8] that encourages indulgence and impulsiveness (for example material expenditure and sexual relations) in addition to the contrary—restraint and self-management (as in dieting and women's eating, in particular). This is a society of extremes which at both ends (asceticism and gluttony) reflects the poles of advanced consumer capitalism. Bordo explains:

> On the one hand, as producers of goods and services we must sublimate, delay, repress desires for immediate gratification; we must cultivate the work ethic. On the other hand, as consumers we must display a boundless capacity to capitulate to desire and indulge in impulse; we must hunger for constant and immediate satisfaction. The regulation of desire thus becomes an ongoing problem, as we find ourselves continually besieged by temptation, while socially condemned for overindulgence.[9]

Her point, of course, is that we find ourselves in a "double bind," torn in two mutually exclusive directions. Though coming from a different context, Weil captured the sense of this existence when she said: "Our life is impossibility, absurdity. Everything we want contradicts the conditions or the consequences attached to it, every affirmation we put forward involves a contradictory affirmation, all our feelings are mixed up with their opposites."[10] As in our own time, food and diet "are central arenas for the expression of these contradictions", so it is no surprise that these extremes have been *embodied,* as in the case of the coexistence of anorexia and obesity in our contemporary society.[11] The bulimic person, though, best represents the inscription of the contradiction in one body and therefore "emerges as a characteristic modern personality construction," the embodiment of "the unstable double bind of consumer capitalism."[12] That is, the bulimic is locked into the terrible cycle of unrestrained consumption followed by the most severe purging. Bordo argues that treating these "disorders" as purely medical problems tends to disguise the broader cultural ethos, involving politics, economics and aesthetics, that conditions and nourishes the various behaviors. Moderation is seen as a sign of weakness and lack of commitment in a proudly consumerist culture, despite our lip service to the contrary.

It is troublesome, then, to recognize that the major criticisms of Simone Weil have been aimed at her own immoderate life in its degree of asceticism, the manner of her death,[13] the unqualified, hyperbolic language in which she spoke and wrote, and the radical philosophies of purity and suffering that she espoused. Robert Coles notes that "some of [Weil's] remarks are prideful, melodramatic, even absurdly self-indulgent."[14] Depicting her as something of a self-indulgent ascetic, he writes:

> [Weil] exerted so much domination over so many of her impulses or urges that the words *discipline* and *self-control* hardly do justice to the reality of her daily life. She could do without sleep, without food . . . She had no sex life. It is said that she cringed when touched. She cared little, it seemed, about clothes, and she took poor care, in general, of her body. Such behavior, obviously, appeased some voice in her, gave some autocrat dwelling within her cerebral hemispheres considerable satisfaction.[15]

If true, this appraisal of Weil's life is problematic for her philosophy, for the extreme measures of self-denial, by Coles' account, turn out to be self-serving and hence masochistic in nature. Coles admits that words like "masochism" quickly come to mind when thinking about Weil, although "psychological explanations have a way of being all too static; they don't do justice to the mind's lively, ever fluctuating rhythms."[16] Nevertheless, the question that remains to be answered is whether Weil is guilty of her own charge of "immoderation." Were not her actions (for example joining the Spanish Civil War, and refusing to eat when she was weak and dying of tuberculosis) indicative of a lack of psychical and emotional proportion? Were not her hyperbolic and cutting words, whether expressed orally to others or written down, reflective of that "world in which nothing is made to man's measure," where "everything is disequilibrium"?[17] Isn't her philosophy paradoxically *excessive* in its self-denial?

It is this conflict I seek to address in the following pages, in the particular context of Weil's relationship to consumption: Why did she turn away from eating—both literally and figuratively? I think that the charge of extremism against Weil is not entirely unfounded or invalid, but as the Reverend Dr Martin Luther King, Jr noted, the real question is about the orientation of her extremism. Two main points need to be analyzed in light of this recognition, then, in order to understand the ethical implications of her immoderation: first, the character of Weil's renunciation and the form of nourishment she did allow herself; and secondly, the tension or disparity between the *experience* of imbalance and the *reality* of imbalance. In exploring these fundamental questions about Weil's orientation and its relation to consumption, I hope to demonstrate not that Weil was moderate, but that her immoderation is of an entirely different kind than that which characterizes our contemporary society.

Feeding on Light

In one of her many letters to Father Joseph-Marie Perrin in 1942, Weil wrote the following: "It is perhaps not inconceivable that in a being with certain natural propensities, a particular temperament, a given past, a certain vocation, and so on, the desire for and deprivation of the sacraments might constitute a contact more pure than actual participation."[18] This statement has much in common with her ideas about a "purifying atheism"[19] which may prevent an idolatrous and self-centering attachment to an imagined God. The sheer physicality of the sacraments in this context, however, yields additional meanings and implications beyond the renunciation of imaginings about God, for Weil frequently wrote using metaphors of eating, consumption, hunger and satiation. "Here below," Weil had said, "to look and to eat are two different things. We have to choose one or the other. They are both called loving. The only people who have any hope of salvation are those who occasionally stop and look for a time, instead of eating."[20] But what did Weil mean by "eating"? Is it hyperbolic of her to suggest that it precludes "looking"? And how could "looking" save us?

To begin, it befits this investigation to note the alliance and close etymology of the words "consume" and "consummation." "Consume" comes from the Latin *consumere*, "to use up, eat, or waste," or more literally, "to take beneath/under." Our modern definition is not a stretch from its origin and has a mostly negative connotation: "To use up, destroy, squander, devour, engross, absorb completely." In other words, it is to take an other (person, thing, etc.) and assimilate it/him/her into myself; to consume is to possess. "Consummation," on the other hand, has a more positive denotation and connotation, meaning "completion, end, perfection; a summing up, finishing, fulfilling." It comes from the Latin *consummare* and means "a summing-up," or "the highest taken together." But like *consumere*, it is often used to describe an event in which there are no more "loose ends," and it implies the finality of an event. Consummation, one might say, makes its undergoer *sated*; there is often consummation in consumption. It is this last characterization which will prove to be most important when analyzing Weil's disposition towards food and its renunciation.

We find that in the religious ritual of the Eucharist[21] (the participation in which Weil was questioning), these two significations merge for those partaking: *When there is physical consumption, there is simultaneously spiritual consummation.* However, we need to consider that the reception of the Eucharist is just that: a *reception*, not a *consumption*, properly speaking. That is, while there is a literal consuming of the elements, they are remembered as having been offered, as gifts, from God.[22] The religious attitude dictates that they are not objects merely *taken* or *appropriated* of one's own initiative, for we do not (or at least *should not*) crassly *take* gifts, but should open ourselves and be receptive to their "givenness," as French phenomenologist Jean-Luc Marion would say. Let us briefly examine this notion to come to a better understanding of the sort of "consumption" that ideally occurs in the Eucharist.

Marion declares that a "new model of givenness will come from the gift,"[23] and he has this to say about what constitutes a *gift*:

> The gift, to be given, must be lost and remain lost without return. In this way alone does it break with exchange, where one gives only to have it repaid (with a marginal profit) . . . [I]t is a question of the pure and simple loss involved in giving with abandon . . . Hence the paradox: the gift must be lost for me, but not for everybody. It's necessary that an Other receive it and definitely deprive me of it.[24]

From Marion's description of a gift, we see that detachment is a necessary ingredient of graciousness; otherwise, when one is attached (even to the intended beneficiary), what one engages in is not properly *giving*, or benefaction, or charity, but some sort of controlled economic exchange. A person who is attached to the gift they are giving never really gives it. Giving results in a pure loss for the giver, as Marion says. In addition, if one is attached to the other who receives, there is necessarily a return to self in the so-called giving; "investment" would be a more appropriate descriptor. Real charity or love, on the other hand, would *compel* the giving and release the "givee," such that, ironically, the act of charity would not even be recognized as such by the giver. Weil cites the disciples in this respect: "Lord, when saw we thee enhungered, and fed thee? or thirsty, and gave thee drink?"[25]

But since we are the supposed *recipients* of the Eucharistic offerings, what is the disposition proper to *this* station? Crucially, the "givee" must not seek the gift, for then it becomes an imposition on the would-be giver and is *caused*, enters into a realm of economics, and ceases to be a gift, as such. Gifts are, by definition, beyond the bounds of our control and manipulation. Weil offers an eloquent description of the nature of this sort of offering, coming down to one who does not seek it:

> With all things, it is always what comes to us from outside freely and by surprise, as a gift from heaven, without our having sought it, that brings us pure joy. In the same way, real good can only come from outside ourselves, never from our own effort . . . Thus effort truly stretched toward goodness cannot reach its goal; it is after long, fruitless effort which ends in despair, when we no longer expect anything, that, from outside ourselves, the gift comes as a marvelous surprise.[26]

However, returning to the context of the Eucharist, what does this refusal-to-seek-the-gift mean for the *Pater Noster* request, "Give us this day our daily bread," and in general, for any supplication to God? Weil tells us simply that the request for "daily bread" should be interpreted as a request for Christ, and that "our consent to his presence is the same as his presence."[27] Now, aside from the question of what exactly the presence of Christ means, especially for one who does not subscribe to Christianity or religion in general,[28] there is the issue of seeking out this supernatural bread, which she says is a necessity for us. Recall that Weil herself acknowledged that a refusal of the sacraments might constitute a purification. Nevertheless, she also admitted, "We should ask for this [supernatural] food." And, even more controversially, "At the moment of asking, and by the very fact that we ask for it, we know that God will give it to us."[29] Is this not a suggestion that we should seek out the gift of spiritual consummation, and furthermore, that it will be guaranteed? And if so, is this not an orientation towards consumption of the worst kind where we would be drawn into an economy of exchange, and a paradigm of consumerism with spiritual goods?

The answer is that in asking for supernatural bread, in asking for "Christ," that is, one is actually *consenting* to the orientation where one can be still with the void. What is "the void"? According to Weil, *le vide*, or "void," is constitutive of our true nature and is experienced as asymmetry or lack of equilibrium or vacuum, but we continually try to escape that experience by positing various fillers. Since unpleasant situations tend to recall to us this finite and unbalanced nature, the imagination is always at work, building up a false sense of security, and with it a false ego. For instance, Weil tells us, "Like a gas, the soul tends to fill the entire space *which is given it*," but "not to exercise all the power at one's disposal is to

endure the [given] void. This is contrary to all the laws of nature."[30]
We are prone, that is, to *take* the Eucharistic bread as something simply
edible, substantive, filling and consoling. It is extremely difficult to *receive*
it, void intact.

Again, this endurance of the void carries with it a feeling of imbalance
or asymmetry, and necessarily involves suffering. Indeed, Weil writes that
void is best described as "the anguished experience of lack of balance."
But loving truth entails enduring the void, because it *is* who we are and
it *reminds* us of who we are.[31] In this way, "the search for equilibrium
is bad because it is imaginary."[32] Since, in Weil's understanding, we are
constituted by void, or are "hungry," we grasp for consolations that will
provide the illusion of being "full" and complete. Not surprisingly, we
are often successful in these endeavors. In such cases, we lose consciousness of our void altogether, and this is further reinforced by the earthly
successes and privileges we may have acquired. (It is thus harder for
those who are more prosperous to understand their true nature as finite,
created beings than for the materially poor and afflicted.)

But, importantly, one should not carry out an active search or ask for
the void. Weil warns, "We must not seek the void, for it would be tempting God if we counted on supernatural bread to fill it. We must not
run away from it either."[33] This point is crucial for differentiating Weil's
philosophy from one that embraces the extreme of masochism. First,
she thought that there was no such thing as true masochism, as when
she wrote, "What excites masochists is only the *semblance* of cruelty,
because they don't know what cruelty is."[34] That is, pain that is sought
out and enjoyed can only be pain in the most superficial, physical
sense. Suffering cruelty is something that renders one really passive and
vulnerable. Second, Weil was *not* advising a life that is analogous to that
of the contemporary anorexic; given her philosophy, anorexia and obesity, for example, would not be "opposites." Succumbing to either implies
an orientation to the horizontal, natural plane; even anorexia would
not constitute a real renunciation.[35] With a willed deprivation (which
amounts to seeking the void), there is no real appreciation of hunger as
such because pride (and sometimes social prestige) accompanies the
seeming self-mastery. As Weil writes, "One might choose no matter what
degree of asceticism or heroism, but not the cross," which would carry
one beyond the will.[36] The burden of the cross brings with it no popular
support, and it negates the active will.

Our asking for the supernatural bread, then, is not a *seeking* of
the void, but is a consent to its formerly unrecognized presence and the

accompanying isolation when it "gives itself." It is the sort of request that precludes selfishness precisely because the "reward" is not compensatory in the usual way; it is not consoling, and it is not self-confirming; it demands that we wait.[37] Weil explains this character of the supernatural reward by making reference to the Gospel of Matthew: "That is why we read in the Gospel, 'I say to you that these have received their reward.' There must be no compensation. It is the void in our sensibility which carries us beyond sensibility."[38] What is being requested, then, is the ability to endure the emptiness; that is, the petition for the sacraments is actually the petition for an *increased capacity for attentiveness and patience*. Interestingly, then, the Weilienne posture of receptivity known as attentiveness involves a perpetual quest for its own improvement and extension; rather than becoming more assured of one's powers of attention via attending to the world, one would recognize, more and more, the "hunger" that is at the heart of one's being.

We know that, in fact, Weil often disallowed herself physical consummation through consumption, but she still more disallowed herself any form of spiritual consummation. In the same way that religious sacraments are confused with social ceremonies ("an intoxicating mixture which carries with it every sort of license"),[39] love is often confused with consumption. This is not to say that we are to refrain from love, but instead we should make every effort to refrain from consumptive attitudes and actions so that love may be possible. Weil writes, "A gambler is capable of watching and fasting almost like a saint," but "there is a great danger in loving God as the gambler loves his game," which is to say, with attachment and a consumptive demeanor.[40] To love something is to simply desire its existence independently of ourselves, and of our intrusions and interferences. Hence hunger or "the void" is necessary for love. Contrary to our modern self-help mantras that insist on one's own fulfillment/satisfaction/health in order to love another, Weil radically declares that the prerequisite to real love is void, hunger, renunciation of consumption, and even renunciation of consummation. Love is, in fact, distance, or rather, the "consent to distance."[41]

Indeed, Weil thinks that by "remain[ing] quite still" we actually unite ourselves with that which we desire.[42] It is this way with the supernatural, for instance: we do not dare make the approach, but paradoxically, in this way it is possible to be closest. She writes,

God and humanity are like two lovers who have missed their rendezvous. Each is there before the time, but each at a different place, and they wait and wait and wait. He stands motionless, nailed to the spot for the whole of time. She is distraught and impatient. But alas for her if she gets tired and goes away. For the two places where they are waiting are at the same point in the fourth dimension. . .[43]

It is understandable that one should not turn away from the supernatural, but why should one not actively approach it? Weil's answer to this question is also one that can be gleaned from literature: Any time distance is traversed, desire (i.e., hunger) seems to be conquered. Anne Carson noted this phenomenon, in reflecting on the poems of Sappho: "A space must be maintained or desire [Eros] ends."[44] This is the truth that Emily Dickinson expresses in the last stanza of her poem, "I Had Been Hungry": ". . . so I found/ that hunger was a way/ of persons outside windows,/ the entering takes away."[45] But this is precisely the danger. For Weil, approaching the supernatural is unlike approaching an object. This approach is characterized by having been subjected to "the cross," and thus having accepted hunger, be it literal or metaphorical. Weil reminds us of the significance of such hunger: "The eternal part of the soul feeds on hunger."[46]

What this means is that for us as finite, fallible creatures, our hunger for the "supernatural bread" is of utmost importance, for ethical attention follows desire. Weil writes, "Desire alone draws God down. He only comes to those who ask him to come; and he cannot refuse to come to those who implore him long, often, and ardently."[47] This is a desire deprived of a proper *object*, for objects turn the hunger into a *means*. When the desire becomes a means to an end, we forget our limitations and in turn begin to use others as fillers and props for our egos: "God is not present, even if we invoke him, where the afflicted are merely regarded as an occasion for doing good."[48] The emphasis here is on the vertical orientation, not on any object of desire. Weil offers us, therefore, a challenge to "love on empty," writing:

A man has all he can do, even if he concentrates all the attention of which he is capable, to look at this small inert thing of flesh, lying stripped of clothing by the roadside. It is not the time to turn his thoughts toward God. Just as there are times when we must think of God and forget all creatures without exception, there are times when, as we look at creatures, we do not have to think explicitly of God . . . There are times when thinking of God separates us from him.[49]

The vertical orientation means an abstinence from any opiate or food that can even be named "God," for such a thing would always be an idol and would give a sense of self-sufficiency. This hunger also enables us to live justly, for as Weil warns, "Our hatred, our indifference, are anthropophagous, too."[50] There is, then, only one form of ethical "feeding": the reception of supernatural bread, or what Weil elsewhere calls the "feeding on light."

To give us a better sense of Weil's particular understanding of "feeding on light," it is helpful to return to and examine her orientation towards the religious ritual of the Eucharist and the attendant receptivity in the context of, particularly, the female mystics of the medieval era. Garnering some insight into this phenomenon in this particular era will also permit us to grasp the sense of this rarefied "feeding" and the immoderate ethic that arises from it.

We should first acknowledge that *if* there were fulfillment to be found in Eucharistic devotion, it could not be thought of as fulfillment in the ordinary sense for the devotees. Many female mystics of the medieval era, for instance, viewed their receiving as serving.[51] That is, being a symbol of Christ's humanness and thus ours, the Eucharist, when eaten, was a "fusing with Christ's hideous physical suffering," and therefore, "the Christian not so much *escaped* as *became* the human," states Caroline Walker Bynum on the religious experiences of women in the medieval era and the Middle Ages.[52] Bynum goes on to say that in late medieval Catholicism, the Eucharist "encapsulated two themes:" "an audacious sense of closeness to the divine (Christians ate Jesus!) and a deep fear of the awfulness of God (if one ate without being worthy, one ate one's own destruction!)"[53] Hence the consummation of consuming the host should be grasped as *paradoxical*: it was not nourishment of the soul simply and easily come by, but the experience of a blessing, *imbued with fear and trembling*.

Primary examples of this paradoxical consummation can be found in female devotees of the late twelfth century. By this time, "imitation of Christ" (*imitatio Christi*) had come to mean something almost literal, affecting especially the Eucharist. "Margaret of Cortona and Lukardis of Oberweimar became one with the Crucifixion *rather than* simply remembering or pitying Christ's suffering" in their partaking of the Communion.[54] Margaret of Ypres submitted to "extreme self-flagellation" in order to join with Christ; indeed, her act was called a *recordatio* (a "remembrance"), but as we can imagine, this term took on new and heightened meaning.[55] External or inward stigmata seemed to follow so naturally from the reception of the Eucharist that, as Bynum puts it, "One [*became*] Christ's crucified body in *eating* Christ's crucified body."[56] In other words, in partaking of the Eucharist, one *eats void*. Contemporaries of the women on whom stigmata appeared did not question these manifestations because the predominant view of the time was that the Eucharist *is* Christ. Recall, too, that this is reflective of Weil's stance: "Christ is our bread," she wrote in explaining the *Pater Noster* supplication, "Give us this day our daily bread."[57] Thus, union with Christ—the consummation—did not entail a departure from suffering into a realm of tranquillity; but it was quite the opposite.

But why do we "need" this "food," which paradoxically seems to be an anti-food (an emptiness)? To begin with, Weil explicitly states that "we should not ask for earthly bread," where earthly bread represents all manner of void-fillers, alternative sources of energy and incentives for action, such as "money, ambition, consideration, decorations, celebrity, power, [and even] our loved ones."[58] The reason these sources of energy, or "other wages," should be regarded with caution is that we ourselves are able to find and secure them, and this gives us "the illusion" that our being "carries the principle of its preservation within itself."[59] Again, even an intentional program of asceticism or anorexia carries with it these "other wages"; one cannot seek out actual hunger, but can and should come to recognize its presence. Weil describes the danger inherent in forgetting our *innate* hunger (or void):

> The soul knows for certain only that it is hungry. The important thing is that it announces its hunger by crying. A child does not stop crying if we suggest to it that perhaps there is no bread. It goes on crying just the same. *The danger is not lest the soul should doubt whether there is any bread, but lest, by a lie, it should persuade itself that it is not hungry.* It can only persuade itself of this by lying, for the reality of its hunger is not a belief, it is a certainty.[60]

Thus the crying, which is to say the supplication, is *morally* important, for it represents an attitude that recognizes the reality of our privation and our inability to be self-sufficient; it counteracts every tendency towards egoism, which is the very source of our modern excesses. That "lie" that says we are not "hungry," is for Weil the beginning of selfishness and hence evil. She writes,

Attitude of supplication: I must necessarily turn to something other than myself, since it is a question of being delivered from self. Any attempt to gain this deliverance by means of my own energy would be like the efforts of a cow that pulls at its hobble and so falls onto its knees.[61]

As we have mentioned, there is one remedy, according to Weil, for the irresistible turning to "earthly breads" that accompanies the feeling of void: "a chlorophyll conferring the faculty of feeding on light" or, simply put, strength to continue to endure the void.[62] This supernatural bread is, again, nothing tangible. In fact, it may very well be silence: "It is when from the innermost depths of our being we need a sound which does mean something, when we cry out for an answer and it is not given us, it is then that we touch the silence of God."[63] Often, however, we attempt to convert this form of the supernatural bread into something tangible, something we can consume; the temptation to create an idol is nearly irresistible. As Weil said, "In my particular case, in order to be born of water and the spirit, I must abstain from the visible water."[64] But naturally, we fool ourselves in attempting to make the supernatural something that is visible or that can be consumed in the sense of appropriation. As Weil writes, "The supernatural is light itself: If we make an object of it, we lower it."[65] Perhaps consumption of "light," or "supernatural bread," or "void," is Weil's answer to a society that thoughtlessly and unjustly consumes everything in view; but how could such an orientation which "tears our very entrails"[66] be recommended as an antidote to a world already prone to extreme reactions and destructive solutions?

Balance from Felt Imbalance

For Weil, our destructiveness arises not from a preservation and recognition of the void, but from its opposite: the only fault for humanity is the "incapacity to feed upon light, for where capacity to do this has been lost all faults are possible."[67] She suggests that a capacity for attention—i.e., leaving the void open—may eventually be lost entirely, after continued obedience to satiation of the self. Like a species which, after years of migration deeper into a cave, has evolved eyes which would find the sun unbearable, so too, the person who has grasped after earthly energies for so long will shun light like a bat and perceive it as a great evil. The consent to feed on light and the renunciation of horizontal consolations is *experienced* as imbalance and disequilibrium; it is felt as a literal *impossibility*, especially for one accustomed to continuous consumption. Weil observes and experiences the hunger within herself as also being devoid of "the principle of rising."[68] That is, she says that only by directing her attention toward something real and something better than herself can she be "really raised up." She makes clear that this attention or "thought direction" is not to be confused with a psychological "suggestion":

> If I say to myself every morning, "I am courageous, I am not afraid," I may become courageous, but with a courage which conforms to what, in my present imperfection, I imagine under that name, and accordingly *my courage will not go beyond this imperfection. It can only be a modification on the same plane, not a change of plane.*[69]

The change of plane calls for "the supernatural," but the supernatural encompasses what, on a natural level, is considered impossible and extreme. The experience of feeding on light, then, is one of real loss and deprivation, but this is only because for so long we had become accustomed to illusions of self-sufficiency, even royalty.

Indeed, Weil tells us that we carry around an "imaginary royalty of the world,"[70] of which we are supposed to strip ourselves via *decreation*. In fact, this "stripping" does not alter the actual constitution of a person because the aggrandizement was illusory in the first place. Stripping those illusions away does not constitute real deprivation; instead, it is the basis for establishing genuine harmony and balance. For example, in *Pedagogy of the Oppressed*, Paulo Freire explains that oppressors experience any challenge to their power and unearned privilege as an oppression in itself. We know, of course, that removing the ability to dominate does not constitute an injury, but actually opens a space for true balance and harmony among all humans. Freire writes:

> Conditioned by the experience of oppressing others, any situation other than their former seems to [the oppressors] like oppression. Formerly, they could eat, dress, wear shoes, be educated, travel, and hear Beethoven; while millions did not eat, had no clothes or shoes, neither studied nor travelled, much less listened to Beethoven. Any restriction on this way of life, in the name of the rights of the community, appears to the former oppressors as a profound violation of their individual rights—although they had no respect for the millions who suffered and died of hunger, pain, sorrow, and despair.[71]

Therefore, by stripping away the imaginary royalty, one is returned to the recognition of his/her inherent void in decreation. In this way, the void is also the explanation for the imperative to decreate. What is needed, then, is that the void be accepted, or endured, because this is synonymous with the embrace of Truth. More specifically, this endurance entails rejection of earthly rewards, for again, they tend to distort our perception of ourselves by causing us to forget our inherent lack. As Weil puts it:

> The necessity for a reward, the need to receive the equivalent of what we give. But if, doing violence to this necessity, we leave a vacuum, as it were, a suction of air is produced and a supernatural reward results. It does not come if we receive other wages; it is this vacuum which makes it come. It is the same with the remission of debts (and this applies not only to the harm which others have done us but the good which we have done them). There again, we accept a void in ourselves.[72]

Clearly, the endurance of the void is also required for genuine forgiveness and charity so that in either case, a burden is not placed on the other. But more often than not, rewards are greedily sought out and accepted, burdens are displaced on others, suffering is deflected, revenge is enacted, grudges are clung to, and distractions are welcomed—in short, the void is not endured so that imbalance is not felt. In all such cases and numerous others, we have negation of void—*a-voidance*—and this is what produces actual immoderation and imbalance in the world.

To bring about real harmony, on the other hand, decreation is required, but this renunciation of self may, as we have said, consist in attentiveness, "an energy which arrests. The power to stop."[73] As we have seen, though, such "negative efforts" are often the most difficult. Alan Watts, describing Zen communities, especially the Soto and Rinzai, similarly describes the importance of this solitary "sitting and looking," despite the fact that the Western mentality considers it absurd and inefficient:

> It may seem both strange and unreasonable that strong and intelligent men should simply sit still for hours on end. The Western mentality feels that such things are not only unnatural but a great waste of valuable time, however useful as a discipline for inculcating patience and fortitude. Although the West has its own contemplative tradition in the Catholic Church, the life of "sitting and looking" has lost its appeal, for

no religion is valued which does not "improve the world," and it is hard to see how the world can be improved by keeping still. Yet it should be obvious that action without wisdom, without clear awareness of the world as it really is, can never improve anything.[74]

Furthermore, Watts adds, the best "contributions" to a world in turmoil such as ours may take a negative form; that is, the eating of the void can be understood as non-interference, sitting quietly, refusing to add to the chaos that already exists. Moreover, the "negative effort" of attentiveness and decreation is paradoxically creative.

Consider Weil's example of looking at an afflicted other, which is also a perfect example of the refusal to consume:

> One of two [humans] is only a little piece of flesh, naked, inert, and bleeding beside a ditch; he is nameless; no one knows anything about him. Those who pass by this thing scarcely notice it, and a few minutes afterward do not even know that they saw it. Only one stops and turns his attention toward it. The actions that follow are just the automatic effect of this moment of attention. The attention is creative. But at the moment when it is engaged it is a renunciation . . . The man accepts to be diminished by concentrating on an expenditure of energy, which will not extend his own power but will only give existence to a being other than himself, who will exist independently of him. Still more, to desire the existence of the other is to transport himself into him by sympathy, and as a result, to have a share in the state of inert matter which is his.[75]

We see here that creative *attention*, which is really a decreation, causes me to be transported *into* the afflicted Other, rather than the reverse which is caused by the imagination: transporting the unconsenting Other into *me*. Thus, loving and attending to the Other means that we accept diminishment of our egos, for it is a necessary consequence any time we are truly open to the reality of other persons. In this loving, we also detach ourselves from any possible return from the being we love. According to Weil, loving our neighbor means being able to ask him, "What are you going through?" "It is a recognition the sufferer exists," she contends, "as a man, exactly like us, who was one day stamped with a special mark by affliction."[76] In other words, to love is to embrace the void/hunger of another without filling it and without forgetting one's own "hunger."

Hunger *is* our universal reality, as we have seen: "The danger is not lest the soul should doubt whether there is any bread, but lest, by a lie, it should persuade itself that it is not hungry. It can only persuade itself of this by lying, for the reality of its hunger is not a belief, it is a certainty."[77] Though we may not think we wish to possess the being we approach, the distance is necessary to maintain our humility before her, and hence our love for her. For again, we must love in an other what is real, which is to say, *their* void, or hunger. Weil writes, "To be able to love in our neighbor the hunger that consumes him and not the food he offers for the appeasement of our own hunger—this implies a total detachment. It implies that one renounces feeding on man and wants in the future to feed only on God."[78] We can clearly see this position in Weil's thought on friendship, too: "To desire friendship is a great fault . . . Friendship is not to be sought, not to be dreamed, not to be desired; it is to be exercised (it is a virtue)."[79] When we understand this, we can renounce loving "like cannibals" and cease looking for our neighbors' "companionship, their words, their letters . . . [their] comfort, energy, and stimulation," and instead "love in all men either their desire or their possession of God."[80] Such love is a "looking" (rather than an eating) that is inherently good because it is a forgetfulness of self and a renunciation of any "nourishment" that the other may possibly be for me.

Thus, it is imperative that we allow ourselves to be penetrated by the reality of the world and the cries for justice, refusing the temptations of temporary consolation that would be provided by seeking (an inherently imaginary) equilibrium. In acts of justice, "there is nothing analogous to muscular effort; there is only waiting, attention, silence, immobility, constant through suffering and joy."[81] Such an orientation amounts to a turning away from the self in the course of enduring the void, and enduring the void for Weil means loving truth. In such a scenario, there is no experienced return to self, and therefore no reciprocity or natural balance. The Weilienne ethic, or idea of justice, consists in bearing the weight of the entire universe, for "in emptying ourselves we expose ourselves to all the pressures of the surrounding universe."[82] When we have done this, Weil says, we have "throw[n] away the counterweight," and by this immoderate act, have made real balance possible for the universe.

While recognizing that consumption is a necessary part of natural human existence, I would argue (with Weil) that nevertheless, we should strive towards a supernatural conception of harmony defined by the renunciation of the consumptive *posture*, and experienced as disequilibrium. As Andrea Nye summarizes:

> The just soul does not exercise her power in controlling, punishing, or forgiving; she *renounces* whatever power over others she might exercise.

The virtuous person refrains from commanding where she has the power to command. She does not take the oppressed in hand, lecturing to them, caring for them, organizing and providing for them; she turns away from such manipulative involvement . . . seeing in [others] the humanity they are in danger of losing.[83]

But we sense an entitlement and a "right" not-to-suffer, not-to-feel-the-void. This hunger is only maintained by our (re)orienting openly and honestly to what *is*, where the self recedes into the background as a consequence. Real moderation never entails self-preoccupation, for they are antithetical movements. Instead, in wholly "looking" at what exists presently, we *love* because we have been eclipsed. Love requires this reality of our eclipse and the painfully shining present, but this "direction" that is immoderate love is "impossible," and hence is on the supernatural plane.

Immoderate, "impossible" love is, however, as necessary for living the *good life* as natural consumption is necessary for maintaining physical survival. Weil would align herself with Socrates, who asked his friend Crito, simply but profoundly, "We should attach the highest value, shouldn't we, not to living, but to living well?"[84] Clearly, this reorienting towards the good life over physical life is itself risk-filled. To release power in recognizing hunger is analogous to letting go of the handle of a sword, and as Weil reminds us, releasing the handle of the sword may mean that we find ourselves quickly at the point. In the end, what is remarkable is that the acceptance of *experienced or felt disequilibrium* is precisely the condition for harmony and balance in human affairs. In other words, when we do not deflect suffering back onto the universe—whether through revenge, venting, or causing another to feel indebted to us—but we truly receive the broken bread (i.e., the suffering) of an other, we chip away at the unjust imbalances and unholy excesses that are so predominant in our world.

Notes

[1] Martin Luther King, Jr, "Letter from Birmingham City jail," in *A Testament of Hope: The Essential Writings and Speeches of Martin Luther King, Jr*, ed. James M. Washington (New York: HarperOne, 1990), 298.

[2] Editors' note: See Chapter 1.

[3] GG[1], 211.

[4] Raj Patel, *Stuffed and Starved: The Hidden Battle for the World Food System* (Brooklyn, NY: Melville House Publishing, 2007).

⁵ Bill McKibben, *Deep Economy: The Wealth of Communities and the Durable Future* (Oxford: Henry Holt, 2007). The ongoing economic crisis has been rightly attributed to the excesses of Wall Street and the unrestrained impulses of average American citizens who have been, for some time, living on credit. Weil saw this tendency in her own context: "Since credit is the key to all economic success, saving is replaced by the maddest forms of expenditure" (OL, 115).

⁶ Cornel West, *Democracy Matters: Winning the Fight Against Imperialism* (New York: Penguin Books, 2004).

⁷ Susan Bordo, *Unbearable Weight: Feminism, Western Culture, and the Body* (Berkeley: University of California Press, 1995).

⁸ Bordo is referring primarily to American popular culture in the late twentieth century.

⁹ Bordo, *Unbearable Weight*, 199.

¹⁰ GGⁱ, 148.

¹¹ Bordo, *Unbearable Weight*, 199, 201. The Center for Disease Control (CDC) and National Center for Health Statistics have determined that (as of 2006) 66 per cent of U.S. adults are either overweight or obese, while 34 per cent are actually obese. "New CDC Study Finds No Increase in Obesity Among Adults; But Levels Still High," by the Centers for Disease Control and Prevention. www.cdc.gov/nchs/pressroom/07newsreleases/obesity.htm (accessed on 9 July 2009). We are a consuming nation, not just of food, but also of natural resources, entertainment, drugs, and material goods in general.

¹² Bordo, *Unbearable Weight*, 201.

¹³ F. C. Ellert writes, "Out of compassion for her captive and undernourished fellow-countrymen, [Weil] insisted upon limiting herself to the meagerest kind of diet that proved harmful to her already frail system. Nine months after her arrival in England the statement of her death was recorded in a sanatorium in Ashford, Kent. The cause of her death: undernourishment and pulmonary tuberculosis (suicide, according to one doctor's report)." OLⁱ, vii.

¹⁴ Robert Coles, *Simone Weil: A Modern Pilgrimage* (Woodstock, VT: SkyLight Paths Publishing, 2001), 112.

¹⁵ Ibid., 117–18.

¹⁶ Ibid., 115.

¹⁷ OLⁱ, 108.

¹⁸ WG, 55.

¹⁹ Editors' note: See Chapter 4.

²⁰ FLN, 286. For another excellent article on this topic, see Claire Wolfteich, "Attention or destruction: Simone Weil and the paradox of the Eucharist," *The Journal of Religion*, Vol. 81, No. 3 (July 2001): 359–76.

²¹ Editors' note: See also Chapter 3.

²² Although according to the English translation of Matthew 26.26 (NRSV), Jesus says in the Last Supper as he breaks the bread, "*Take, eat*; this is my body," (emphasis mine) we must note the difference in taking following an *offer* to take from the provider, and the uninvited and self-initiated taking that often leads to greed and gluttony.

²³ Jean-Luc Marion, *Being Given: Toward a Phenomenology of Givenness*, trans. Jeffrey Kosky (Stanford: Stanford University Press, 2002), 74.

[24] Ibid., 86.

[25] GG¹, 93; Matthew 25.37–9.

[26] GG¹, 94. Emmanuel Gabellieri offers an elucidating discussion of the "refusal of the gift" in Chapter 8, "Décréation et Donation," of his book *Être et Don: Simone Weil et la Philosophie* (Paris: Éditions Peeters, 2003).

[27] WG, 220.

[28] Editors' note: Again, see also Chapter 4.

[29] WG, 221.

[30] GG¹, 55. (Emphasis mine.)

[31] "To love truth means to endure the void" (GG¹, 56).

[32] GG¹, 51.

[33] GG¹, 68.

[34] FLN, 260.

[35] As Bordo argued, too, anorexia and obesity are at different ends of the same spectrum rooted in the same societal tendency, arising out of the extremes of capitalist culture. Cf. Bordo, *Unbearable Weight.*

[36] GG¹, 140.

[37] There is an excellent book which draws heavily upon Weil's writings on waiting, called, appropriately, *On Waiting* by Harold Schweizer (New York: Routledge, 2008).

[38] GG¹, 69. Matthew 6.2.

[39] GG¹, 218.

[40] GG¹, 103.

[41] GG¹, 115.

[42] GG¹, 206.

[43] GG¹, 141.

[44] Anne Carson, *Eros: The Bittersweet* (USA: Dalkey Archive Press, 2000), 26. For instance, here is a stanza from one of Sappho's more well-known poems, expressing the "reach" of desire: "Ah, the sweet apple that reddens at the tip/ of the branch on the topmost limb,/ and which the pickers forgot—or could not reach." *Sappho: The Poems*, trans. Sasha Newborn (Santa Barbara, CA: Bandanna Books, 2000), 12.

[45] Emily Dickinson, *Selected Poems*, ed. Christopher Moore (New York: Gramercy Books, 1993), 26.

[46] FLN, 286.

[47] WG, 111.

[48] WG, 150.

[49] WG, 151.

[50] FLN, 285.

[51] Caroline Walker Bynum, *Fragmentation and Redemption* (New York: Zone Books, 1991), 138.

[52] Ibid., 44.

[53] Ibid., 45.

[54] Ibid., 145.

[55] Ibid., 145.

[56] Ibid., 146.

[57] WG, 220.

58 WG, 221.

59 GG[1], 47.

60 WG, 210. (Emphasis mine.)

61 GG[1], 47.

62 GG[1], 47.

63 GG[1], 166.

64 WG, 86.

65 GG[1], 185.

66 GG[1], 166.

67 GG[1], 48.

68 GG[1], 152.

69 GG[1], 152 (emphasis added).

70 GG[1], 57.

71 Paulo Freire, *Pedagogy of the Oppressed*, trans. Myra Bergman Ramos (New York: Continuum, 2003), 57.

72 GG[1], 55–6.

73 NB, 96.

74 Alan Watts, *The Way of Zen* (New York: Vintage Books, 1989), 154–55.

75 WG, 147.

76 WG, 115.

77 WG, 210.

78 FLN, 286. I think Weil would agree with Richard A. Cohen, who, in describing the ethics of Emmanuel Levinas says this: "One is not called on to 'love thy neighbor *as* oneself,' according to the biblical precept, as if self-love preceded other-love and were the measure of other-love. Rather, the proper formulation of Levinas' thought is more extreme, an infinite demand never satisfied even in its fulfilment: to 'love thy neighbor *is* oneself.'" Richard A. Cohen, "Introduction: Humanism and anti-humanism—Levinas, Cassirer, and Heidegger," in Emmanuel Levinas' *Humanism of the Other* (Chicago: University of Illinois Press, 2006), xxvii.

79 GG[1], 116.

80 FLN, 284.

81 WG, 194.

82 GG[1], 144.

83 Andrea Nye, *Philosophia: The Thought of Rosa Luxemburg, Simone Weil, and Hannah Arendt* (New York: Routledge, 1994), 99.

84 Plato, *Crito* 48b, trans. David Gallop in *Defense of Socrates, Euthyphro, and Crito* (Oxford: Oxford University Press, 1997).

Chapter 3

The Supernatural as Remedy to Totalitarian Regimes: Simone Weil on Sanctity and the Eucharist

Marie Cabaud Meaney

In 1943 Simone Weil writes in her essay "Human personality": "In all the crucial problems of human existence the only choice is between supernatural good on the one hand and evil on the other."[1] There is no middle ground for her. One cannot simply be naturally good; this is a contradiction in terms. To follow a merely natural sense of justice, of right and wrong, will turn one into an idolater and make one an easy prey to any totalitarian system. Acknowledging the supernatural is therefore necessary to avoid further man-eating regimes and genocides. Without the supernatural, one simply follows the inner dynamic of *pesanteur* and becomes an easy victim of force, either as oppressor or oppressed.[2] Therefore Weil wrote about the significance of the supernatural in her essays for the Free French Government and in her articles criticizing Marxism, among others, since she knew that no lasting peace could be achieved without it. If Weil is right, her analysis is of the utmost importance for present times. The hope that after the fall of the Third Reich and of the Soviet Union another widespread totalitarian regime can be avoided is empty if merely based on the belief in progress, hope in man's good nature, or the conviction that learning from the past would be sufficient. By excluding the supernatural, by continuing the process of secularization, humanity is inevitably drifting towards the next bloodthirsty regime. Instead, the supernatural must become the focus again; following its radical demands to their logical conclusion means becoming a saint. In turn, saints become the supernatural's most powerful witness since they are, according to Weil, its most visible expression. The Eucharist, in contrast, is its most hidden form; both are tightly linked since the saints have to nourish themselves on this supernatural bread and be transformed into Eucharists themselves. Thus after looking at the origin of

secularization, and at the supernatural as well as the natural, I will analyze these two manifestations of the supernatural as the greatest counter-
forces to temporal Messianism.

The Renaissance at the Root of Secularization

Though human nature continually shies away from the supernatural since
it means death-to-self (as will be seen in the next point), an historical shift
occurred during the Renaissance which initiated the process of secularization. As Weil points out in her article "The Romanesque Renaissance,"
the Renaissance made man the measure of all things, instead of God.[3] We
are reaping the fruits of this humanism now, for: "The errors of our time
are the result of Christianity minus the supernatural element. This is due
to *laïcisme* (secularization), and in the first place, to humanism."[4]

The Renaissance's mistake was not its return to ancient Greek culture,
but doing so at the expense of Christianity, thinking wrongly that the two
were opposed.[5] In reality, Christianity and Greek culture are identical in
an important way, since both know about the nature and reign of force,
yet do not worship it—as Weil claimed in her article "The 'Iliad,' or the
poem of force," where she wrote: "The Gospels are the last and most
marvelous expression of Greek genius, as the *Iliad* is its first expression."[6]
This startling statement makes sense in light of her definition of force.

Force reigns supreme; it turns human beings into *choses* (things) by
exposing them to death, fear of death, or slavery. Nobody can escape it,
neither oppressor nor oppressed; for even the oppressors need to follow
its rules, as Machiavelli observed so astutely, in order to maintain their
power, given that force is not infinite and nobody can control all circumstances.[7] Marx recognized the mechanics of force in class struggle, but
failed to see that the supernatural or grace could affect it.

Thus the greatness of the *Iliad* and the Gospels for Weil is their capacity
to grasp the nature of force, yet not to be subjugated by it: For the temptation is either to admire it, to deny it, or to think it can be eliminated.
The Nazis, embracing the Nietzschean idea of the *Übermensch*, admired it;
but so did the French, with their nationalism and colonialism. Only
those who have entered the realm of the supernatural, only the saints
(and geniuses who write masterpieces like the *Iliad*) are capable of
understanding and withstanding the temptation of force:

It is only by entering into the transcendent, the supernatural, the truly
spiritual that man can rise above the social. Up till then, in fact, and

whatever one may do about it, the social is transcendent with respect to man. It follows, then, that the only possible protection open to man is that those who are upon the road to sanctity should fulfil [*sic*] a recognized social function.[8]

Thus the saints are absolutely essential to the health and even survival of society, which otherwise would become engulfed by force in its most barbaric and totalitarian manifestations.

The Renaissance failed to learn from ancient Greece and Christianity their clear perception of force. To recognize force's pervasive nature, however, is key to understanding the necessity of redemption. An outside power, namely grace, is required for this recognition. The Renaissance, because of this oversight, focused on the human rather than on the divine. Furthermore, just as every pre-Roman culture had its own revelation, according to Weil, so Greece had "the revelation of human misery, of God's transcendence, of the infinite distance between God and man."[9] It attempted to bridge the gulf between God and man by means of religion, philosophy, art and science. Except for its religion, we have inherited these bridges from Greece. Yet, under the influence of the Renaissance: "We have built them up [these bridges] much higher. But we believe now that they were made to live in. We are unaware that they are only there to be passed across; we do not know, if we crossed over, whom we should find on the other side," namely God Himself.[10] Thus the Renaissance failed to understand the core of Greek culture and successfully banned the supernatural from common life, hence setting the stage for a society without God, of which the Third Reich and the USSR were the consequences.

However, it seems a big jump to move from a still very Christian Renaissance to the anti-Christian ideologies of Nazism and Communism.[11] What are the reasons for this downward spiral?

The Human Condition: From the Pull of Gravity to the Great Beast

The most important reason is human nature. To describe the human condition, Weil likes to cite Plato's allegory of the cave: "The image of the Cave makes us clearly perceive that man's natural condition is darkness, that he is born and lives and dies in it unless he turns towards a light which falls from a place beyond the sky."[12] In her essay "God in Plato," she discusses the allegory at length. Human beings live a lie by taking the shadows cast against the wall for reality; tragically, they are not even aware of it.[13] However, someone or something else can tell them about another reality and free them from their chains. Getting up and moving around is painful for limbs atrophied by passivity.[14] There is therefore a great temptation to avoid this painful yet cathartic experience, for it requires a complete transformation:[15] "But whereas we can turn our eyes in a new direction without or almost without using the body, it is not so as regards the soul. The soul cannot turn its eyes in a new direction without turning entirely in that direction."[16] This conversion is a violent and painful process. It means going through a dark night of the soul, for one's inner eyes, so to speak, are blinded by the unaccustomed light.

What this detachment from the familiar world of shadows stands for is the detachment from the sensible world, from one's idols which fill one's inner void and give one energy.[17] It means death-to-self, which is only complete once the soul has let go of everything. Only the saint has achieved this degree of detachment; only the saint has gone through the darkness of the cave without giving up hope, despite the blinding rays of the sun. And only the saint goes back into the cave "so as to shed upon this world, upon this earthly life, a reflection of the supernatural light."[18]

But why are human beings in the cave in the first place? According to Weil's interpretation of Plato, it is clear that they are born punished.[19] Those who remain in the cave and believe that the shadows are real, live a lie. They cannot know reality, they cannot even know themselves. What they see, since it is fabricated, cannot reflect the good. Thus "it would be impossible to set a greater distance between [their] universe and God," for unbeknownst to themselves, they are separated from the good.[20] Hence they are the slaves of force, and don't even recognize it.

Out of touch with reality and thus the truth, the prisoners in the cave can be easily misled if only someone knows how to feed their desires and avoid irritating them. Having become part of a mass, they are guided by the *Zeitgeist* and are an easy prey to opportunistic, charismatic leaders. In his *Republic*, Plato calls this new entity which they now form *le gros animal* ("the great beast").[21] Only those who have been outside the cave, only the saints, should be their guides, for they alone can tell them about a reality that is beyond their restricted world, namely the supernatural. The saints do so in words, or better, by bearing witness through who they are. For "the unique supernatural fact in this world is holiness itself

and what lies near to it."[22] The saints are the embodiment of the supernatural, and the greatest witness to its existence. But what exactly is the
supernatural, according to Weil?

The Supernatural

In her "Draft for a statement of human obligations," Weil describes the
supernatural in the following words:

> There is a reality outside the world, that is to say, outside space and
> time, outside man's mental universe, outside any sphere whatsoever
> that is accessible to human faculties. Corresponding to this reality, at
> the centre of the human heart, is the longing for an absolute good, a
> longing which is always there and is never appeased by any object in
> this world.[23]

Hence the supernatural is not a mere continuation, or simply another
dimension of the natural. It is a different kind of reality Weil is talking
about here, just as Pascal's order of charity is worlds apart from the
orders of power and genius.[24] As he and Weil point out, one cannot
simply move from a lower level to a superior one by one's own strength,
from the natural to the supernatural, from being a ruler to being a saint.
Weil explains this in "Forms of the implicit love of God":

> There are people who try to raise their souls like a man continually
> taking standing jumps in the hopes that, if he jumps higher every day,
> a time may come when he will no longer fall back but will go right up
> to the sky . . . We cannot take a single step toward heaven. It is not in
> our power to travel in a vertical direction.[25]

The natural cannot reach the supernatural of its own accord; it takes the
descent of the supernatural to open up this dimension to human beings,
as Weil's mystical experiences had taught her.

Though Weil cannot make this descent happen, she can confront the
reader with the supernatural, state it as a fact, point to it as something to
be acknowledged.[26] Yet the "experience of the transcendent: this seems
a contradiction in terms, and yet the transcendent can only be known
through contact, since our faculties are unable to construct it."[27] Even if
one's intelligence and senses cannot reach it, the human heart can, in its

longing for an absolute good.[28] Thus one needs to be attuned to one's heart, acknowledge its deepest desires, and realize that nothing finite can ever satisfy its infinite longing, as St Augustine stated in his *Confessions*: "our hearts are restless till they rest in Thee."[29] Thus Weil writes in her *Cahiers*: "Nothing on this earth is really an object for the desire that is in me . . . [T]here must be something in Reality which possesses at least the same valor as this desire."[30] The heart is therefore much more than the center of passions and of feelings; it has a cognitive dimension, which Pascal pointed out: "The heart has its reasons which reason itself does not know."[31]

Ultimately, it takes faith to recognize the supernatural's existence; "to be able to study it [the supernatural] as such, one must first of all be capable of discerning it. Faith is therefore necessary."[32] Faith opens one's eyes to the supernatural which, on the one hand, is minuscule—"the share of the supernatural here on earth is that of secrecy, silence, the infinitely small"[33]—and yet on the other hand is infinitely vaster than this world.[34] Though the supernatural is like a mustard seed, the smallest of all seeds, and works like yeast in invisible ways, in reality it encompasses the universe.[35] It is its "true centre, which is not in the middle, which is not in space and time, which is God."[36] Thus God is the supernatural and God is Love. So whenever one witnesses an act of true love or encounters a saint, God Himself becomes palpable; the supernatural breaks through the natural and becomes visible, at least to the eye of faith.

Yet, if faith is required, how can the supernatural ever become discernible to the non-believer? For Weil admits explicitly in her article "Is there a Marxist doctrine?" that the supernatural, since it "escapes the human faculties, cannot, by definition, be either verified or refuted."[37] However, it cannot be left out of account either, as she shows in her analogy of the blind islanders cut off from the world, who have no concept of light. Since light "offers no obstacle, exerts no pressure, is weightless, cannot be eaten," these islanders cannot experience it directly; yet "by it alone the trees and plants reach towards the sky in spite of gravity" and "by it alone seeds, fruits, all the things we eat, are ripened."[38] Thus light needs to be included in a coherent account of reality. Similarly, one can know the existence of the supernatural at least by its consequences, for example true justice or *caritas*—which are accessible to our faculties, as Weil states, even if the supernatural itself is not. Furthermore, mystical experiences, as well as the consensus among the mystical doctrines of every religion, indicate the supernatural's existence.[39] Finally, she adds to ways of knowing about the supernatural the *reductio ad absurdum* of theories which exclude it, and whose "absurdity can be verified both by reasoning and by experience," Marxism being one of them.[40]

Thus a number of mistakes can be made vis-à-vis the supernatural: one is to deny its existence, and subsequently to miss what is at the very heart of reality. Another is to believe that the supernatural is simply the continuation of the natural, and therefore to fail to see that they are in conflict.[41] In any case, the supernatural issues heroic demands: from abandoning one's idols, to sacrificing one's life for its sake.[42]

Secularism is therefore a comfortable option, making one blind to the dramatic choice at the heart of every human life. In his *Divine Comedy*, Dante relegates those who refused to make a choice to the vestibule of hell. If the vestibule was already well populated in Dante's time, where does this leave us? For this secularism is the scourge of modernity. The neutrality that secularism claims to promote is a lie, and lulls one into a false sense of security. As Weil writes in *l'Enracinement*: "It is certain that neutrality is a lie. The laic (anti-clerical) system is not neutral." For "if children are brought up not to think about God, they will become Fascist or Communist for want of something to which to give themselves."[43] Ultimately, secularism cannot get rid of man's essential need for the divine; instead, it encourages him to seek an *Ersatz*, and thus sets him up for idolatry in its modern form, namely ideology, as promoted by totalitarian regimes.[44]

However, Weil does not say that nature in the sense of the cosmos is opposed to the supernatural—only sinful nature dragged down by *pesanteur*, or self-will which does not want to die to itself and thus flees the light of the supernatural.[45] Otherwise nature is ordered towards the supernatural in Weil's thought, as Emmanuel Gabellieri points out in *Être et don*.[46] Gabellieri refers in particular to Weil's idea of mediation, that reality is determined by *rapport* (by relationship), by number or, put differently, by the *logos*. As Weil writes in her *Cahiers*: "The Word is the light which comes with every being."[47] Therefore the human condition cannot be understood except in light of Christ who is the *eidos*, the paradigm for man.[48]

It is therefore a serious mistake to believe that man can be understood independently from his supernatural origin and destiny. He is like a tree needing light from the sky to give him energy in order to grow strong roots in the ground, as Weil explains in "Human Personality." Or rather, as she adds, he is rooted in the sky.[49] Thus the supernatural is man's firm foundation, which alone gives him the strength to resist the *Zeitgeist*. In contrast, ideological systems such as Communism and Nazism cut man off at his roots by denying the existence of our true foundation, thus letting him starve and wither away, for the *Ersatz*-nourishment that the ideologies offer cannot feed him. Hence, as Weil pointed out, Marxism—standing for all ideologies here—rather than religion is an opiate, promising a fulfillment which only God can give.[50]

On the one hand, the supernatural seems elusive. It is infinitely small and operates in secrecy.[51] Weil often uses Christ's parables to speak about the workings of the supernatural. It is like a mustard seed which, though the smallest, grows so high that the birds of the sky find shelter in it. On the other hand, it is accessible to human beings, even the most mediocre, in the form of three mysteries present in every human life, as she writes in *Intuitions Pré-chrétiennes*: firstly beauty, secondly the "work of pure intelligence applied to the contemplation of theoretic necessity" and its incarnation in work, and finally "those flashes of justice, of compassion, of gratitude" in everyday life.[52] Therefore, "there is no possibility of a profane or natural life being innocent for man here below."[53] Thus there is no escape, no excuse and certainly no possibility of compromise.

The supernatural issues a call to every person, a call to conversion, or to *retournement* as Weil preferred to term it. It cannot be ignored without leading to injustice, disaster and moral self-destruction. Though no human being can convert another, he can at least turn him towards the supernatural: "What a man can do for another man is not to add something to him, but to turn him towards the light that comes from elsewhere, from above."[54]

The Saints and the Eucharist

The saints are perhaps the most important way of making the prisoners in the cave aware of another reality. They can give them a taste of the truth.[55] Hence Weil saw them to be of the utmost significance, especially during her times: "The world needs saints who have genius, just as a plague-stricken town needs doctors."[56] As in an epidemic, extreme evil calls for extreme measures, namely great holiness paired with genius. This new holiness would be analogous to a "new revelation of the universe and of human destiny," for "it is the exposure of a large portion of truth and beauty hitherto concealed under a thick layer of dust."[57] Saints briefly lift the veil from the world we live in, to reveal the existence of the supernatural. They open the door Weil writes about in her poem

"*La Porte*," which we cannot break down by our own efforts, yet behind which is a luminous space, different from the expected meadows and flowers, but which "satisfie[s] the heart, and washe[s] the eyes almost blind beneath the dust."[58]

The saints are unconventional, not because they are anarchists driven by the desire to undo the current order, but because they obey only the truth. Instead of following the *Zeitgeist*, they are in touch with the true, unchangeable center of the universe, namely God Himself.[59] Thus they are the only ones with a fixed anchor, while other human beings are swept along by opinion and become part of the "great beast." To others the saints may seem like fools, for they follow divine laws rather than common sense. To the world they seem to be wearing a fool's cap, while in reality they are adorned with a crown since: "any man who is in contact with the supernatural is essentially king, for he represents the presence in society, in the form of something infinitely small, of an order transcending the social order. But the position that he occupies in the social hierarchy is absolutely of no importance at all. He is a centre of gravity in that position . . . It is his presence alone which is infinitely, transfinitely great."[60]

This kind of royalty excludes pride, for it despises force. Hence humility is its cloak, which appears like foolishness but is in reality wisdom, since it sees through the paraphernalia of the world in order to embrace the Cross. Humility is only explainable in terms of the supernatural, for "to humble oneself is supernatural, moral gravity is opposed to it."[61] There is no natural incentive to be truly humble, since it means death to self. "Humility is the only entirely supernatural virtue, that is to say one to which no natural virtue that imitates it corresponds."[62] Hence, either humility is supernatural or it is a vice disguised as a virtue, such as Uriah Heep's hypocritical and self-serving lowliness in Charles Dickens' *David Copperfield*. In contrast, God's selfless humility becomes apparent in His kenotic incarnation and crucifixion.

But God's humility also reveals itself in the Eucharist, which is perfectly appropriate to a God of love who desists from the use of all force: "God can only be present in secret here below . . . His presence is more complete inasmuch as it is more secret."[63] The fact that one cannot know about God's presence in the Eucharist other than through faith is therefore no argument against it. Instead, it confirms its authenticity for it corresponds to God's humble withdrawal, which allows for human freedom and goes against all display of prestige.

Though the Eucharist is a convention established by God,[64] this does not make it any less real, for "a convention with God is more real than any reality."[65] To turn it merely into a symbol rather than acknowledging it as God's real presence means doing away with its mystery; this deserves condemnation as heresy, Weil thinks—strong words from someone who was so critical elsewhere of the Church's *anathema sit*.[66] But this convention allows even more for God's humble secrecy; for there is nothing in a piece of bread that would point to it being God.[67]

However, though it takes faith or supernatural love to recognize God's presence in the Eucharist,[68] its impact on the soul is verifiable. For God's absolute purity alone is capable of destroying evil in the soul.[69] Only adoration, by which man fixes "his full attention upon perfect purity," is able "by a process of transference, to destroy a part of the evil that is in him. That is why the Host is really the Lamb of God which takes away sin."[70] Hence its effect on the soul is palpable, and even painful: "The real presence of God is determined by the revolt of the entire mediocre part of the soul. The presence of God cuts the soul in two, the good to one side, the evil to the other. It is a sword. Nothing else has this effect. This presence can therefore be ascertained."[71] Adoration thus means being slowly transformed, purified and sanctified.[72]

There is, then, a strong link between sanctity and the Eucharist.[73] Saints must (almost by definition) be adorers of God in the Eucharist. Furthermore, transubstantiation and sanctity are analogous, for "sanctity is a transmutation like the Eucharist."[74] The saints must become Eucharists themselves, to be fed to the suffering since they are living Christs: "Man no longer lives for himself, but Christ lives in him; his flesh has become the flesh of Christ, and the afflicted eat it."[75]

This presupposes, however, that the saints have not fed on the wrong kind of food, namely on idols. Resistance to the "wrong food" is very difficult, for it means bearing the inner emptiness without filling it with these pseudo-absolutes. As Weil writes: "Men exercise their imaginations in order to stop up the holes through which grace might pass, and for this purpose, and at the cost of a lie, they make for themselves idols . . . If one conceives of them as relative, there is a void."[76] She adds, "And then the source of energy can only be supernatural bread. (We need some every day)." Otherwise, "idolatry is . . . a vital necessity."[77]

Preserving the void means embracing the Cross, for one must bear the emptiness coming from the absence of one's idols and the suffering that entails.[78] Through this suffering, one gains wisdom and becomes "a centre of gravity in that position,"[79] as quoted above. One's soul is like a scale, and though "the scales tip every way . . . a nail . . . fixes the centre. Therefore the register is true. The nail does not indicate any figure, but because of the nail the pointer marks accurately."[80] Suffering, i.e. the nail, makes it possible for the scales to be accurate. The saints, having embraced the Cross and abandoned all idols, have thus become one of the only firm points in a society otherwise storm-tossed by ideologies. They point us to the supernatural which is the true center of the universe.

The Eucharist is therefore the manna that leads one through that inner desert and on that painful, steep path out of the cave. It is the fruit from the tree of life that human beings were barred from eating once they had fallen, that has now been given to them, growing on the tree of the Cross. It alone can burn away all sin and mediocrity, as Weil points out; in order to do so the Eucharist, that is the Crucified Lord, needs to be adored and received.

Thus one could rephrase Karl Rahner's famous statement that "the Christian of the future will be a mystic or will not exist at all," to say that the Christian of the future will be an adorer of the Eucharist or will not exist at all.[81] Without adoration, there is no sanctity; and without sanctity, there is no protection against ideologies and totalitarian regimes.[82] Modern society needs Eucharistic adorers and saints as a plague-stricken city needs medicine. Given this, it could be that Pope John Paul II and Benedict XVI's call for Eucharistic adoration is the most radical and adequate response to the crisis of our times.[83] As Weil writes in her notebooks: "Human life is so made that many of the problems which present themselves to all men, without exception, are insoluble apart from holiness."[84] Hence sanctity is not the calling of an elect few, but a necessity for everyone; for the path of moral compromise within a comfortable, neutral, secular realm leads to evil. Christ is very harsh with the man who buries his talent in the hope that he can avoid making a decision, for decision is unavoidable. The choice is either faith or treason.[85] It depends on this choice, whether the future will hold a new totalitarian regime of apocalyptic dimensions, satisfying human beings' idolatrous desire for temporal Messianism with its false promise of a paradise on earth, or whether that can be warded off.

Notes

[1] SE, 23/EL, 29. [Reference to the English editions will be followed by additional reference to the original French version.]

[2] *Pesanteur* is the law of gravity affecting the moral realm. Following its downward pull is natural, while going against it can only be explained by grace.

[3] SE, 47/EHP, 78.

⁴ NB, 502/OC VI.3, 201.

⁵ SE, 47/EHP, 78. However, Weil distinguishes between two different kinds of Renaissance, an earlier one like the Romanesque period or Occitan civilization uniting the spirit of ancient Greek culture with Christianity, and a later one which she criticizes (NR, 295/E, 254; SE, 47/EHP, 78).

⁶ IC, 52/OC II.3, 251.

⁷ IC, 86-87/SG, 90; OL, 236/OEL, 170.

⁸ NB, 286/OC VI.2, 397.

⁹ SE, 46/EHP, 77.

¹⁰ SE, 46/EHP, 77.

¹¹ For Weil's critique of Nazism see, for example, her article "The great beast" (SE, 89–140) and of Marxism, see her articles contained in *Oppression and Liberty*.

¹² SE, 53/EHP, 84.

¹³ SN, 108/SG, 101.

¹⁴ SN, 109/SG, 102.

¹⁵ SN, 109–10/SG, 102.

¹⁶ SN, 108/SG, 101.

¹⁷ SN, 106/SG, 98; CS, 112.

¹⁸ SN, 112/SG, 106.

¹⁹ SN, 108/SG, 100.

²⁰ SN, 108/SG, 101.

²¹ SN, 99/SG, 89.

²² NR, 264; E, 226.

²³ SE, 219/EL, 74.

²⁴ Blaise Pascal, *Pensées and Other Writings*, trans. Honor Levi (Oxford: Oxford University Press, 1995), No. 339, 86–7.

²⁵ WG¹, 127/AD¹, 191. See also PSO, 135.

²⁶ That Weil is an apologist of the supernatural was the conclusion to my book, *Simone Weil's Apologetic Use of Literature: Her Christological Interpretations of Ancient Greek Texts* (Oxford: Oxford University Press, 2007). As Emmanuel Gabellieri points out, no philosopher since Maurice Blondel, apart from Weil, has investigated the supernatural as a philosophical concept. See Emmanuel Gabellieri, *Être et don: Simone Weil et la philosophie* (Leuven: Peeters, 2003), 530.

²⁷ NB, 242/OC VI.2, 343.

²⁸ SE, 219/EL, 74.

²⁹ Augustine, *Confessions*, trans. F. J. Sheed (Indianapolis, IN: Hackett Publishing Company, 1993), Book I, §1, 3.

³⁰ NB, 562/OC VI.3, 277.

³¹ Pascal, *Pensées and Other Writings*, No. 680, 158.

³² NB, 226, 344/OC VI.2, 324, 469.

³³ OL, 166/OEL, 217.

³⁴ NB, 400/OC VI.3, 84–5.

³⁵ IC, 3/IPC, 12; SE, 218/EL, 108.

³⁶ SN, 183/PSO, 104.

³⁷ OL, 167/OEL, 231.

³⁸ OL, 166/OEL, 231.

[39] OL, 166/OEL, 231.

[40] OL, 167/OEL, 232. Her critique of Marxism in "Is there a Marxist doctrine?" is along those lines; despite its materialism Marxism presupposes a purpose to history, namely the rule of the proletariat, which cannot be explained by a materialist worldview (OL, 164–5/OEL, 227–8).

[41] SE, 23/EL, 29. To think the supernatural is simply the continuation of the natural leads to a secular faith, described in the following way by H. Richard Niebuhr, as "*a God without wrath [who] brought men without sin into a kingdom without judgment through the ministrations of a Christ without a cross*" (H. Richard Niebuhr, *The Kingdom of God in America,* [Hanover, NH: Wesleyan University Press, 1988], 193).

[42] For further elaboration of this point, see my chapter on Antigone, in Meaney, *Simone Weil's Apologetic Use of Literature,* 77–114.

[43] NR, 90, 91/E, 82, 83.

[44] Another mistake would be to think the supernatural should suppress the natural order instead of transforming it. Weil is critical of a totalitarian spirituality as embodied, in her eyes, in Gothic art. In contrast, Occitan civilization is her ideal, for therein the supernatural does not crush the profane (SE, 48/EHP, 79). Thus in "L'Articulation entre le surnaturel et le social chez Simone Weil," Birou rightly emphasizes that Weil does not advocate escapism; instead she wants the supernatural to illuminate and penetrate society (Alain Birou, "L'Articulation entre le surnaturel et le social chez Simone Weil," *Cahiers Simone Weil* Vol. VIII, No. 1 [1985], 58–9).

[45] WG[1], 111–2, 126–7/ADI, 166–7, 190–1.

[46] Gabellieri, *Être et don,* 326.

[47] NB, 226/OC VI.2, 324.

[48] NB, 284; OC VI.2, 394. Thus Gabellieri claims that the human condition, because of its essential openness to the supernatural, should be called "transnatural" (Gabellieri, *Être et don,* 531).

[49] SE, 23/EL, 29–30.

[50] OL, 165/OEL, 229.

[51] OL, 166/OEL, 230.

[52] IC, 196/IPC, 165.

[53] IC, 196/IPC, 165.

[54] SN, 105/SG, 97.

[55] In "Morality and literature," Weil speaks about sanctity and the experience of absolute evil as the only ways of breaking through the fictional world we build around ourselves (SE, 161–2 and *Cahiers Simone Weil* Vol. X, No.4 [1987], 350–51).

[56] WG[1], 51/AD[1], 82.

[57] WG[1], 51/AD[1], 81.

[58] PSO, 12.

[59] For this reason, Maria Clara Lucchetti Bingemer writes in "Simone Weil et Albert Camus" that "a saint is an 'ex-centric' person, since it is always the Other that leads him" (Maria Clara Lucchetti Bingemer, "Simone Weil et Albert Camus: Sainteté sans Dieu et mystique sans Église," *Cahiers Simone Weil* XXVIII, No. 4 [2005], 365–86 [my translation]).

[60] NB, 481/OC VI.3, 180. See Weil's famous reflections on fools in her next-to-last letter to her parents: "Everybody... is unaware that what they [Shakespeare's fools] say is true. And not satirically or humorously true, but simply the truth. Pure unadulterated truth—luminous, profound, and essential" (SL, 200/EL, 256).

[61] NB, 218/OC VI.2, 314.

[62] NB, 275/OC VI.2, 384. See also SN, 101/SG, 91.

[63] WG¹, 122, 123/ADI, 183, 184.

[64] OC VI.4, 170; PSO, 137.

[65] OC VI.4, 170.

[66] OC VI.4, 175.

[67] WG¹, 121–2/AD¹, 182–3. In "Quelques observations sur la pensée de Simone Weil concernant l'Eucharistie," Jean Guitton emphasizes the link between God's love and His secrecy, becoming increasingly pronounced from His creative act, to His Incarnation and the Eucharist (Jean Guitton, "Quelques observations sur la pensée de Simone Weil concernant l'Eucharistie," *Cahier Simone Weil* Vol. V, No.1 [1982], 20–21).

[68] NB, 295, 308/OC VI.2, 417, 432.

[69] WG¹, 124/AD¹, 186.

[70] WG¹, 123/AD¹, 184–5. See also: WG¹, 124–5/AD¹, 186–7, and PSO, 140–1.

Interestingly, in her "Théorie des sacraments," Weil speaks of the purifying effects of daily communion, while in "Forms of the implicit love of God" she writes of those in terms of attention directed towards the Eucharist, in other words of adoration (PSO, 141; WG¹, 123–5/AD¹, 184–7). But even in the first text, she moves towards a description of that attention/adoration and of its spiritual significance (PSO, 142–5).

Adoration is ultimately a form of watchful waiting, a loving focus on the absolute good. It is an attitude of total obedience towards the good, not getting distracted by fatigue, hunger, discouragement, or even the news that the master the servant is waiting for is dead.

[71] OC VI.4, 349.

[72] Weil spent hours in adoration; this was not simply for lack of being able to receive the Eucharist, though she greatly desired it as well (PSO, 151). Claire Wolfteich confirms in her article, "Attention or destruction: Simone Weil and the paradox of the Eucharist," the importance of adoration or "looking" before eating in Weil's thought (Claire Wolfteich, "Attention or destruction: Simone Weil and the paradox of the Eucharist," *The Journal of Religion* 81, No. 3 [July 2001], 369). Anyway, Communion itself must be an act of adoration, as Ratzinger writes in *God is Near Us* (Joseph Cardinal Ratzinger, "The presence of the Lord in the Sacrament," in *God Is Near Us: The Eucharist, The Heart of Life*, ed. Stephan Otto Horn and Vinzenz Pfnür, trans. Henry Taylor [San Francisco: Ignatius, 2003], 74–93).

[73] Weil likes to emphasize the connection between manual labor and the Eucharist. The farmers, by working in the fields, sacrifice their energy to produce wheat and grapes offered at Mass. But more generally speaking, one's work, if offered as a sacrifice, turns one into a Eucharistic offering (PSO, 25; NB, 78–9/OC, VI.2, 62).

[74] OC VI.4, 123.

[75] OC VI.4, 302–3. Thus Ann Loades' critique (in her article, "Eucharistic sacrifice: Simone Weil's use of a liturgical metaphor") of Weil's Eucharistic understanding as being self-destructive misses the point (Ann Loades, "Eucharistic sacrifice: Simone Weil's use of a liturgical metaphor," *Religion and Literature* 17, No. 2, 43–54). Weil's focus, as Wolfteich shows, is not on the destruction of the body (which Weil does not consider evil), but on the person's egoistic self which the Eucharist can burn away (Wolfteich, "Attention or destruction," 368).

[76] NB, 145/OC VI.2, 151.

[77] See also WG[I], 147/AD[I], 221–2; OC VI.4, 404.

[78] NB, 135/OC VI.2, 136.

[79] NB, 481/OC VI.3, 180.

[80] FLN, 151/OC VI.4, 195.

[81] Karl Rahner, *Concern for the Church* Vol. 20, Theological Investigations, trans. Edward Quinn (New York: Crossroad, 1981), 149.

[82] Weil comments in "A propos du Pater" about needing this supernatural bread every day: "for when our actions only depend on earthly energies, subject to the necessity of this world, we are incapable of thinking and doing anything but evil" (WG[I], 147/AD[I], 222).

[83] For example, in his encyclical *Ecclesia de Eucharistia* from April 2004 John Paul II writes about the importance of adoration (no. 10). See: John Paul II, *Ecclesia de Eucharistia* (17 April 2003); http://www.vatican.va/holy_father/special_features/encyclicals/documents/hf_jp-ii_enc_20030417_ecclesia_eucharistia_en.html (accessed on 17 January 2009). Pope Benedict XVI saw the significance of starting his pontificate during the year of the Eucharist, as he pointed out himself in his first statement on 20 April 2005. See: Benedict XVI, "First message of His Holiness Pope Benedict XVI at the end of the Eucharistic concelebration with the members of the College of Cardinals in the Sistine Chapel," No. 4 (20 April 2005); http://www.vatican.va/holy_father/benedict_xvi/messages/pont-messages/2005/documents/hf_ben-xvi_mes_20050420_missa-pro-ecclesia_en.html (accessed on 17 January 2009).

[84] NB, 611/OC VI.3, 339.

[85] IC, 196/IPC, 165.

Chapter 4

Christianity and the Errors of Our Time: Simone Weil on Atheism and Idolatry[1]

Mario von der Ruhr

Introduction

In his 1985 book on philosophy and atheism, the Canadian thinker Kai Nielsen, a prolific writer on the subject, wonders why the philosophy of religion is "so boring," and concludes that it must be "because the case for atheism is so strong that it is difficult to work up much enthusiasm for the topic."[2] Indeed, Nielsen even regards most of the contemporary arguments for atheism as little more than "mopping up operations after the Enlightenment"[3] which, on the whole, add little to the socio-anthropological and socio-psychological accounts of religion provided by thinkers like Feuerbach, Marx and Freud, as any "reasonable person informed by modernity" will readily acknowledge.[4] On this view, the answer to Kant's question—"What may we hope?"—does not gesture towards a resurrection and personal immortality, but instead to the death of religious discourse itself:

> I think, and indeed hope, that God-talk, and religious discourse more generally, is, or at least should be, dying out in the West, or more generally in a world that has felt the force of a Weberian disenchantment of the world. This sense that religious convictions are no longer a live option is something which people who think of themselves as either modernists or post-modernists very often tend to háve.[5]

A construal like this, which views religious belief as a phenomenon whose philosophical examination has been pretty much concluded, and which may therefore be handed over to the social scientist for general historio-graphic and anthropological archiving, certainly makes it hard to see what the philosopher of religion could have to contribute to the subject that, far from being "boring," would constitute a clarification of what is involved in the religious form of life. Moreover, given Nielsen's construal, it seems unlikely that this sort of clarification would even be recognized as such, even by those who, unlike Nielsen, are religious believers.

However, the latter are likely to object that Nielsen's indictment of religious discourse is itself the product of problematic assumptions about the nature of religious belief, on the one hand, and the requirements of philosophical inquiry, on the other. The claim that the case for atheism is "so strong" as to make religious convictions passé, for example, seems to imply, not only that both attitudes or forms of life are answerable to some Archimedean standard of intelligibility and rationality, but also that the logical relation between religious belief and atheism must be roughly analogous to that between the affirmation of a proposition and its negation. Indeed, Nielsen thinks it obvious that, when religious believers affirm that there is a God, or that God created the world,

> they . . . believe that [these] are *factual* assertions: that is to say that they have truth-values. It is a *fact* that there is a God; it is a *fact* that he created the world; it is a *fact* that he protects me and the like.[6]

But since all factual claims must, on Nielsen's view, be subject to public verification or falsification, and "if we cannot even say what *in principle* would count as *evidence* against the putative statement that God created the world, then 'God created the world' is devoid of factual content."[7] Thus, the believer's avowal purports to assert a fact when, ironically, it does not even have a truth-value.[8]

If this analysis adequately characterizes religious utterances *en gros*, then it looks as if the believer is, indeed, guilty of a semantic sleight of hand, in which the very conditions of a meaningful assertion are suspended no sooner than they have been acknowledged, thus turning the believer into what Oscar Wilde would have described as "an adept in the art of concealing what is not worth finding."[9]

That this conclusion would, however, be as hasty as Nielsen's identification of the truth-valued with the factual, and as unwarranted as his assumptions about what believers *must* mean by assertions whose surface grammar resembles that of empirical propositions, has been forcefully argued by the late D. Z. Phillips. In fact, Phillips has provided a detailed response to Nielsen in *Wittgensteinian Fideism?*[10] This response owes much of its inspiration to the works of Ludwig Wittgenstein and Simone Weil, two thinkers who not only shared a deep religious sensibility, but who rightly sensed that positivist or emotivist analyses of that sensibility were just as crude as the charge that all atheists suffer from an idolatrous aberration of the intellect.

Nielsen's own attitude towards Wittgenstein and Weil is guarded and skeptical. While he admits that Wittgenstein's remarks on religion, for example, are "suggestive," he still dismisses them as "too fragmentary and apocalyptic in tone to be much more than exasperating hints,"[11] and thus as not being of much use in the debate. On the contrary, he finds that a Wittgensteinian conception of religion "yields an utterly devastating view for Christianity," because it turns religion into

a form of life that cannot be shown to have any superior rationality, authenticity, or justifiability to other incommensurable forms of life. But that is precisely what anyone who regards himself as a Christian, in any tolerably orthodox sense, cannot accept . . . With such Wittgensteinian friends, the Christian philosopher might remark, who needs enemies.[12]

Nielsen is, of course, right to caution the Christian thinker against false prophets in the philosophy of religion, but then a similar warning could be issued against those atheists whose condescending caricatures of religion undermine the very humanist cause they are ostensibly trying to defend. Moreover, the claim that "tolerably orthodox" Christian philosophers should be able to demonstrate the "superior rationality" of their religious convictions over alternative perspectives on life, seems to me neither warranted, nor defensible.

While it is true that, for such believers, *fides* and *ratio* form a symbiotic relationship in which the former can be inspired, helpfully expounded, and deepened by the latter—for example, in natural and systematic theology—and while they may regard their faith as the deepest and most appropriate response to the existential questions that trouble them, they would surely not be so naïve as to think that they could rationally demonstrate the superiority of that response to atheists like Schopenhauer, Nietzsche, or Kai Nielsen.

Indeed, it is precisely because such an undertaking would be as formidable as that of trying to persuade a miser to be generous, on the miser's *own* terms, that Plato's depiction of Socrates' exchanges with the power-hungry orators in the *Gorgias*, for example, can emerge as a realistic and truthful account of what would be involved in the kind of persuasion that informed a radical reorientation of the spirit. In presenting us with a dialogue that does *not* culminate in an epiphanic ending for any of Socrates' interlocutors, Plato is not so much revealing Socrates' dialectic labours to be futile—in fact, as genuine expressions of concern for the spiritual welfare of his fellow citizens, they never are—as he is drawing attention to both the (psychological) obstacles that may get in the way of seeing things from Socrates' perspective, and the limits of *rational justification*. Far from giving offence to orthodox Christians, these limits are clearly acknowledged in their emphasis on the need for revelation, and summarized in the dictum *credo ut intelligam*.[13]

Readers who have been struck by the close philosophical kinship between Wittgenstein and Simone Weil will not be surprised to learn that Nielsen views the latter with a mixture of admiration and incomprehension. On the one hand, he admits that he is impressed by the starkness of Weil's thought—on the subject of *hubris*, for example[14]—granting that it "has insight" and acknowledging that it is "sensitive to *some* of the conceptual perplexities" that also occupy his own thinking about religion. Indeed, Nielsen finds that his disagreements with her seem to arise from a shared universe of discourse:

> Miss Weil is not, after all, to me like the Azande with his witchcraft substance. We both learned "the language" of Christian belief; only I think it is illusion-producing while she thinks that certain crucial segments of it are our stammering way of talking about ultimate reality.[15]

Then again, Nielsen has to confess, "What she can understand and take as certain, I have no understanding of at all," and indeed, he writes that Weil "blithely accepts what [he finds] unintelligible," so that, apart from momentary flashes of agreement, "a very deep gulf separates [them]."[16] In what follows, I will not engage with Nielsen's assessment of Wittgenstein and Weil, but rather I will look at some of what Weil herself has to say about atheism and its relation to religious belief, not only for the sobriety her reflections bring to the polemical exchanges that have come to dominate much of the current debate about religion, but because of the impartiality with which she exposes the practitioners of idolatry on *either* side of the divide. In addition, her thought calls for the continuation of precisely the kind of dialogue that, in her own time (especially from 1934 to 1938) brought together such staunchly anticlerical movements as the 'Popular Front,' and Christian thinkers like Yves Congar, Jacques Maritain, Jean Daniélou, and Henri de Lubac.[17]

Idolatrous Atheists and Idolatrous Christians

In *Gravity and Grace*, a series of notebook entries compiled by her friend Gustave Thibon after her death, Simone Weil claims that "[the] errors of our time come from Christianity without the supernatural,"[18] and that the influences of secularism and humanism are the primary causes of this development. What she means by "supernatural" in this context is not "metaphysical," however, but rather a certain purity of character or motive, one that is uncontaminated by self-regarding desires or sentiments. Thus, Mother Teresa's love of the poor and afflicted, for example, could be described as supernatural, whereas a love directed solely at what is pleasing, attractive, or lovable, would count as "natural" love. As for the "errors of our time," Weil's catalogue includes blind faith in technological and economic progress;[19] the prevalence of narrowly utilitarian conceptions of the good;[20] the idolization of religious, social or political bodies and institutions;[21] an uncritical deference to science as the only paradigm of true knowledge and understanding;[22] debased notions of compassion and gratitude;[23] a "mutilated, distorted, and soiled" sense of beauty (for example in art, music, architecture or litera-ture);[24] the proliferation of pseudo-spiritualities;[25] a growing rift between secular life and religious practices;[26] the degradation of the sacraments to merely external rituals;[27] and an ever-growing skepticism about "man's supernatural vocation."[28] Now, even though Weil believes that secularism and humanism are the prime causes of these social ills, she also insists that a certain kind of atheism, far from undermining belief in God, may actually serve to deepen it.[29] If this is so, then the relation between religious faith and atheism is far more complex than the ready counterpos-ing of terms like "believer" and "atheist" in ordinary discourse about religion might suggest, and merits further investigation. What, then, does Weil have to say about the two kinds of atheism—the one which is directly antithetical to the Christian faith, and that which may contribute to its purification?

As she sees it, the former is typically materialist in orientation and therefore idolatrous, taking as its object not only material goods[30] but aspirations towards power, fame, and other variants of prestige. In addition, such idolatry may include the desire to attain absolute goods (justice, equality, liberty, and so on) through revolutionary change wrought by a worldly power:

> Atheistic materialism is necessarily revolutionary, for, if it is to be directed towards an absolute good here on earth, it has to place it

in the future. In order that this impetus should have full effect there must therefore be a mediator between the perfection to come and the present. This mediator is the chief—Lenin, etc. He is infallible and perfectly pure. In passing through him evil becomes good.[31]

In the *Notebooks*, Weil calls the revolutionary activist's faith in progress "the outstanding atheistic idea," but of course she does not mean by this that it would be a waste of time to work towards the realization of a just society. Such an attitude would betray precisely the kind of un-Christian fatalism and quietism that Weil herself never tired of combating, whether in her writings, in the classroom, or on the factory floor. The point of her remark is rather that the propagation of the "progress" in question may be grounded in *hubris* and fuelled by idolization of an individual (Lenin, Hitler), a collective (the proletariat), or an abstract process (History). As Weil puts it:

Even materialists place somewhere outside themselves a good which far surpasses them, which helps them from outside, and towards which their thought turns in a movement of desire and prayer. For Napoleon it was his star. For Marxists it is History. But they place it in this world, like the giants of folklore who place their heart (or their life) inside an egg inside a fish in a lake guarded by a dragon; and who die in the end. And although their prayers are often granted, one fears they must be regarded as prayers addressed to the devil.[32]

To take another instance of idolatry, Weil is also struck by the frequent combination of such unholy self-transcendence with the overly zealous reverence for science, or *scientism*. Her examples of this alliance include the French atheist Félix Le Dantec (1869–1917), and a well-known gang of anarchist terrorists:

In France, people question everything, respect nothing; some show a contempt for religion, others for patriotism, the State, the administration of justice, property, art, in fact everything under the sun; but their contempt stops short of science. The crudest scientism has no more fervent adepts than the anarchists. Le Dantec is their saint. Bonnot's *bandits tragiques* took their inspiration from him, and the greatest hero among them, in the eyes of his comrades, was nicknamed "Raymond la Science."[33]

Weil is by no means opposed to scientific or technological progress *per se*, which would be an absurd position to take, nor does she reject automation if this would bring genuine relief to the worker. Her concern is rather with the crudely positivist gospel of writers like Le Dantec, whose ready dismissal of religious belief in *Athéisme* (1907) ends up doing just as great a disservice to the cause of science, as it does to atheism.[34]

At this point, it would be tempting to conclude that the religious believer exemplifies the exact opposite of the atheist as here described, but Weil, ever suspicious of deceptively simple dichotomies, instead proceeds to show that the expression "religious believer" is no less problematic and obscure than the label "atheist." Indeed, she tells us that the latter provides a mirror in which the former can see the reflection of their own spiritual deformities. For while it is true that "[e]very atheist is an idolater—unless he is worshipping the true God in his impersonal aspect," there is (as yet) no reason for the believer to congratulate themselves on her own moral and spiritual rectitude, because, as Weil insists in the *First and Last Notebooks*, "The *majority* of the pious are idolaters."[35] Her verdict is grounded, not only in personal encounters with fellow Christians, including priests and other leading representatives of institutionalized religion, but in her belief that, like any social collectivity, the Church is prone to idolatrous self-adulation and, in this regard, is no different from the worldly revolutionary movements that it has traditionally opposed.[36] Even her friend and spiritual mentor Father Perrin, she thought, was not immune from the subtly suggestive powers of the religious institution of which he was himself a member. Reflecting on Perrin's attitude towards the affliction of those who are outside the Church, for example, she tells him:

It also seems to me that when one speaks to you of unbelievers who are in affliction and accept their affliction as a part of the order of the world, it does not impress you in the same way as if it were a question of Christians and of submission to the will of God. Yet it is the same thing.[37]

Weil's comment reveals something about the subtle ways in which the believer's spiritual loyalties may be remodeled or directed away from their original object, with unwitting discrimination marking the early stage of a progressively deepening idolatry. Looking back at the history of her own country, Weil finds that even as well-intentioned a Christian as Cardinal Richelieu (1585–1642), prelate and minister to Louis XIII, was not immune to the allure of stately power, and that he presents a good example of a Christian who failed to see that "the welfare of the State is a cause to which only a limited and conditional loyalty is owed."[38] The attempt to make the Church a department of the state is, for Weil, just as misguided as the Church's use of the Inquisition as a means of eradicating heresy, since both involve an idolatrous worship of a (political or religious) collective.

Equally alarming, for Weil, is the tendency of such misdirected loyalties to make the citizen, whether atheist or believer, a willing accomplice in the state's wider political designs, including the colonization of foreign cultures and, as far as the Church is concerned, missionary expeditions:

> The more fervent secularists, freemasons, and atheists approve of colonization . . . as a solvent of religions, which in fact it is . . . French colonization does indeed disseminate some Christian influence and also some of the ideas of 1789; but the effect of both is comparatively slight and transitory. It could not be otherwise, given the method of propagating those influences and the vast discrepancy between our theory and our practice. The strong and durable influence is that of unbelief or, more accurately, of scepticism.[39]

If the religious believer is prepared to condemn the militant atheist's use of colonization as a "solvent" of religion, then how can they condone the Church's missionary ventures if these have similarly deleterious effects, both materially and spiritually? Readers familiar with the *Letter to a Priest* will recall Weil's personal response to that question: her confession that she would "never give even as much as a sixpence towards any missionary enterprise;"[40] her belief that, far from having Christianized the African and Asian continents, such enterprises merely "brought these territories under the cold, cruel and destructive domination of the white race;"[41] her disappointment at the Church's failure to condemn punitive expeditions to avenge the missionaries it had lost;[42] and her conviction that these missions have caused the irretrievable loss of valuable sources of spiritual illumination.[43]

Weil's concern for these uprooted cultures and peoples, and her opposition to colonization and Christianization by force, are rooted in her understanding of Christ's own mission, and the *manner* of his encounter with those who did not (yet) believe:

[It] was in any case never said by Christ that those who bring the Gospel should be accompanied, even at a distance, by battleships. Their presence gives the message a different character; and when the blood of the martyrs is avenged by arms it can hardly retain the supernatural efficacy with which tradition endows it. With Caesar as well as the cross, we hold too many aces in our hand.[44]

It is clear to Weil that, insofar as the cross is crucially important for an understanding of Christ, it must also inform the believer's conception of her relation to God. Among other things, this means that "[one] may not debase God to the point of making Him a partisan in a war,"[45] whether in the Old Testament, by the Church of the Middle Ages,[46] or in Jeanne d'Arc's letters to the King of France.[47] Indeed, contemplating even a short excerpt from one of these letters, one finds it difficult not to agree with Weil that, in spite of the saintly aspects of her character, "there is something essentially false" about her story, something bound up with *prestige*.

I am sent by God, the King of Heaven, to chase you one and all from France . . . If you refuse to believe these tidings from God and the Maid, when we find you, we shall strike you and make a greater uproar than France has heard for a thousand years . . . And know full well that the King of Heaven will send the Maid more strength than you could muster in all your assaults against her and her good men-at-arms. We shall let blows determine who has the better claim from the God of heaven.[48]

The pertinence of Weil's observations for religious fundamentalism, especially the more militant and fanatical kind, need hardly be pointed out. For her, all atrocities conducted in the name of God or any other deity constitute a *reductio ad absurdum* of any pretensions to religious witness, an ironic lapse into the very idolatry that is ostensibly being attacked. Here, the atheist who worships God "in his impersonal aspect," that is, who lives just as much in the *spirit* of Christ as Weil herself was doing until she discovered the truth of the Cross, is surely at one with the believer (who does not use religion as a bulwark for the ego).

But isn't the *language* of religious belief—that is, talk of divine creation, original sin, angels and saints, incarnation, intercessionary prayer, atonement, grace, eternal life, and so on—so radically at odds with the terms in which atheists would couch their experience of the world that it would be seriously misleading to amalgamate the two? Surely, isn't someone who engages in "God-talk" *ipso facto* expressing a different conception of reality from someone who does not?

Weil is not denying that the world of a Christian like Francis of Assisi is radically different from that of an atheist like Arthur Schopenhauer, nor is she asking us to let the Stoic detachment and self-effacing attitude of the latter make us oblivious to the wider conceptual framework of which it forms a part. But she is asking how much, if anything, a speaker's employment of religious vocabulary can reliably reveal about his attitude to life and the world at large. Even Félix Le Dantec begins his book *Athéisme* with a dedication (to his mentor Alfred Giard) in which he resorts to the very language whose meaning his book is designed to undermine:

> *Dieu merci, mon cher maître (voilà, je l'avoue, un début bizarre pour un livre sur 'l'athéisme', mais il faut bien parler français), Dieu merci, l'on n'est plus brûlé aujourd'hui pour ses opinions philosophiques; on n'a plus besoin d'héroïsme pour dire ce que l'on pense.*[49]

When Dantec insists that one must, after all, "speak French," he is, of course, merely generalizing about a common practice in any language whose historical development involves religious associations, as the casual use of expressions like "Thank God!" "For Christ's sake!" "Jesus!" "Bloody hell!" or "I'll be damned!" readily illustrate. Nor should Dantec, descended as he was from a devout Catholic family in the Bretagne, be reprimanded for preferring the more emphatic "*Dieu merci*" to "*heureusement*" or, even worse, advised to consult an *index verborum prohibitorum* compiled especially for atheists like him. And while Dantec's linguistic habits are part of, perhaps even reinforce, the kind of profanation in which religious symbols become mere fashion accessories and holy sacraments are diluted into a "lifestyle option," they neither intend to deceive, nor are they mistaken for a religious confession.

However, there are other and more sinister examples of God-talk, by comparison with which Dantec's "*Dieu merci*" seems trivial and harmless. Consider, for instance, Heinrich Himmler (1900–1945) and the Nazi Party's modifications of the Catholic baptismal, burial, and other public rites which they envisaged for the new Reich. In proposing "improvements" for these practices, Himmler recognized the inevitable resistance of religious devotees in his parents' generation:

Please! *Jawohl!* One cannot change people of seventy. There is no point in upsetting the peace of mind of people of sixty or seventy. Destiny does not require that, nor our own ancestors of the earliest times— who merely want us to do it better in the future.[50]

It was not long before Himmler and his fellow *Gruppenführer* did begin to do it "better," by instituting new birth or name-giving ceremonies in which a "sponsor" would hand the child a silver birth tankard from which it could drink as it was growing up, and solemnly declare: "The source of all life is *Got* . . . From *Got* your knowledge, your tasks, your life-purpose and all life's perceptions flow. Each drink from this tankard be witness to the fact that you are *Got*-united."[51] Commenting on the Nazis' use of the word "*Gott*," the Himmler biographer Peter Padfield rightly points out that "[the] word was given only one 't' in the transcription, allegedly the old Germanic spelling, but it was chiefly useful, probably, to distinguish the SS God from the conventional Christian *Gott*."[52]

Simone Weil's reaction to this example would, I believe, have at least three points. First, she would agree with Padfield that it illustrates a defilement—in every sense of the word—of God's name. Second, she would ask us to recall the equally idolatrous demeanor of the Ancient Romans, and draw our attention to various structural analogies between their thinking and Nazi ideology. In fact, *The Need for Roots* contains a highly illuminating remark in which she does exactly that:

[The Romans] felt ill at ease in their all too vulgar idolatry. Like Hitler, they knew the value of a deceptive exterior of spirituality. They would have liked to take the outer coverings of an authentic religious tradition to act as a cloak for their all too visible atheism. Hitler, too, would be pleased enough to find or found a religion.[53]

Third, her thoughts would linger on the 19-year-old Himmler's profession of undying loyalty to the Catholic faith, noticing both its ironic and, considering the rest of Himmler's biography, more tragic aspects.[54] In this context, one is not only reminded of Saint Peter's betrayal of Christ, but of Weil's penetrating comments on its genesis:

St Peter hadn't the slightest intention of denying Christ; but he did so because the grace was not in him which, had it been there, would have enabled him not to do. And even the energy, the categorical tone he employed to underline the contrary intention, helped to deprive him of this grace. It is a case which is worth pondering in all the trials life sets before us.[55]

Unlike St Peter's betrayal of Christ, Himmler's betrayal of the Catholic faith was neither acknowledged nor atoned for, the cult of the *Führer* drawing him ever further away from the God of his father.

"Purifying" Atheism and Orthodox Christianity

In light of Weil's observations about (idolatrous) atheism, her harsh verdict even on the spiritual condition of the faithful—"the majority of the pious are idolaters"—and her conviction that, unless our faith is deep, we ourselves will be "creating by contagion men who believe nothing at all,"[56] her assessment of our relation to the Cross must appear both sobering and disheartening.

If her diagnosis is accurate, then how are "our diseased minds"[57] to be cured of these ills, and what role could a "purifying" atheism play in this cure? Weil's answer must be pieced together from remarks scattered across her oeuvre, and since her whole way of thinking is inimical to systematizing and theorizing, one must not expect a comprehensive and unified account of the matter. Even so, the general direction of her thought may be summarized as follows:

(i) Apart from the idolatrous kind discussed above, there is a species of atheism that purifies the notion of God by, for example, purging it of anthropomorphism and thus highlighting the nature and radical otherness of God's being:

> A case of contradictories which are true. God exists: God does not exist. Where is the problem? I am quite sure that there is a God in the sense that I am quite sure my love is not illusory. I am quite sure that there is not a God in the sense that I am quite sure nothing real can be anything like what I am able to conceive when I pronounce this word. But that which I cannot conceive is not an illusion.[58]

The atheist rejects belief in a personal God, whether He be conceived as a giant policeman in the sky, an entity whose existence and whereabouts might be determined by empirical evidence, or a being who might be held to account for his actions, who might get angry and vengeful, or change over time, and so on.[59] For Weil, proper contemplation of the atheist's rejection of such a god can give the believer a deeper understanding of what "God" means (or rather, does *not* mean), and is therefore to be welcomed.

(ii) Purifying atheism gives its complete assent to the necessity governing the visible world *without*, however, mistaking the order of that world for a proof of God's non-existence.[60] This attitude not only mirrors the *amor fati* of the Stoics, but is analogous to the Christian believer's loving acceptance of God's will:

> Whatever a person's professed belief in regard to religious matters, including atheism, wherever there is complete, authentic and unconditional consent to necessity, there is fullness of love for God; and nowhere else. This consent constitutes participation in the Cross of Christ.[61]

When Weil speaks of necessity, she has in mind the impersonal and mechanical relations of cause and effect in the physical world, as well as the psychological propensities that characterize us in our interactions with each other. It is an important part of her understanding of creation that, even though "God has entrusted all phenomena, without any exception, to the mechanism of this world,"[62] it would nevertheless be wrong to conclude from this that suffering is specifically sent to particular individuals as ordeals. Rather, "[God] lets Necessity distribute them in accordance with its own proper mechanism."[63] Human suffering, in other words, must not be justified or explained (away) by God's arbitrary interference in his own creation. Instead, it should be seen as an ineliminable part of the material "veil" between God and man, one whose mechanism expresses a kind of obedience to the divine will. Weil uses the example of a shipwreck to illustrate her thought:

> The sea is not less beautiful in our eyes because we know that sometimes ships are wrecked by it. On the contrary, this adds to its beauty. If it altered the movement of its waves to spare a boat, it would be a creature gifted with discernment and choice and not this fluid, perfectly obedient to every external pressure. It is this perfect obedience that constitutes the sea's beauty.[64]

It may be difficult to hold on to this perception of the sea when it causes the sailors difficulties or even costs them their lives, but Weil still insists that, just as a man should cherish the needle handled by his departed wife, so the material world, "on account of its perfect obedience," deserves to be loved by those who love its Master.[65]

Weil does not see in this attitude a recipe for passivity and quietism vis-à-vis human affliction, however. On the contrary, she would commend an atheist like Docteur Rieux in Camus' *La Peste* precisely for his Stoic and courageous struggles against such affliction, no matter how much they may be thwarted by forces beyond his control.[66] Like Weil, Camus had a deep appreciation of Ancient Greek culture and civilization; he was familiar with, and highly respectful of, Christian thought, even writing a Master's thesis on "Christian metaphysics and neoplatonism." He supported political activism without placing his faith in the revolutionary movements of his day, and he counted among his best friends such thoughtful and serious believers as the poet René Leynaud, a Resistance comrade who would be executed by the Germans in 1944, and Jean Grenier, who had been a fellow student at the University of Algiers.[67] Moreover, Camus always thought of his atheism as an entirely *personal* affair, not as the only tenable conclusion to be drawn from sober and analytical philosophical reflection. As he emphasized in a speech at the Dominican monastery of Lautour-Maubourg, in 1948: "I wish to declare . . . that, not feeling that I possess any absolute truth or any message, I shall never start from the supposition that Christian truth is illusory, but merely from the fact that I could not accept it."[68]

(iii) The purifying atheist does not believe in his own, continued existence beyond the grave—or what the late D. Z. Phillips has aptly called "a transcendentalized version of 'See you later,'"[69]—but instead views the world he inhabits as a home. As Weil puts it:

Not to believe in the immortality of the soul, but to look upon the whole of life as destined to prepare for the moment of death; not to believe in God, but to love the universe, always, even in the throes of anguish, as a home—there lies the road toward faith by way of atheism.[70]

On Weil's account, the idea of death as complete annihilation is preferable to a belief in the soul's temporal progression beyond the grave because it highlights the significance of *life*, of what the individual becomes, and of what she will (eternally) remain when her life has expired. "The thought of death," Weil says, "gives a colour of eternity to the events of life. If we were granted everlasting life in this world, our earthly life, by gaining perpetuity, would lose that eternity whose light shines through it."[71] Thus, an atheist who takes this attitude towards death will not be indifferent to the way her life goes, but will instead want to prepare herself for the final hour, similarly to the way in which a believer would prepare for it by "dying" to the world and detaching herself from all that might get in the way of her salvation. Both would agree on the significance of a life's narrative unfolding one way rather than another, and on what it would mean to speak with any depth about the meaning of death.

(iv) Our atheist will reject false consolations, including the hope of future compensations for sufferings undergone and losses sustained in the past. Contrary to common assumptions about the psychological "benefits" of religious belief, Weil takes the view that "religion, in so far as it is a source of consolation, is a *hindrance* to true faith,"[72] and that this is also why the atheist's rejection of such hopes *may* reveal a deeper appreciation of human suffering and bereavement. These must not be cheapened or absorbed into a general theory in which their meaning is diluted—something that theodicists are unwittingly doing as they grapple with the problem of evil—but recognized for what they are. In his moving memoir *A Grief Observed*, C. S. Lewis captures well the spirit of Weil's own thinking on the subject. Contemplating the loss of the woman he loves, Lewis records:

> You tell me, "she goes on." But my heart and body are crying out, come back, come back . . . But I know this is impossible. I know that the thing I want is exactly the thing I can never get. The old life, the jokes, the drinks, the arguments, the lovemaking, the tiny, heartbreaking commonplace. On any view whatever, to say, "H. is dead," is to say, "All that is gone." It is a part of the past. And the past is the past and that is what time means, and time itself is one more name for death, and Heaven itself is a state where "the former things have passed away." Talk to me about the truth of religion and I'll listen gladly. Talk to me about the duty of religion and I'll listen submissively. But don't come talking to me about the consolations of religion or I shall suspect that you don't understand.[73]

(v) Atheists or "infidels" who are free from self-adoration, whose relation to their fellow men is marked by pure compassion, and whose love demands nothing in return, are, in Weil's view, "as close to God as is a Christian, and consequently know Him equally well, although their knowledge is expressed in other words, or remains unspoken."[74] As we saw in connection with Himmler, the use of religious symbols or utterances no more vouches for true, Christian discipleship, than their absence from a person's life and thought signifies the opposite. If "infidels" exhibit supernatural virtue, then, as Weil rightly insists, "such men are surely saved."[75]

A good illustration of the kind of atheism Weil has in mind here is provided by the literary character of Axel Heyst, in Joseph Conrad's novel *Victory*. While Heyst's restless travels and conscious avoidance of close personal attachments suggest an uprootedness and anxiety that do not entirely fit Weil's requirement that one love the universe "as a home," and even though Heyst's general conception of the world bears a much closer resemblance to the pessimistic outlook of a Schopenhauer than it does to that of an agnostic humanist, he nevertheless responds to his neighbor's plea for help with an admirable spontaneity and generosity, expecting nothing in return. Conrad draws our attention to these traits early on in *Victory*, as Heyst is approached by an acquaintance called Morrison, who is about to lose his livelihood—an old brig—unless he can pay the fine that will keep it from falling into the hands of the Portuguese authorities. Having just described his predicament to Heyst, Morrison adds:

> Upon my word, I don't know why I have been telling you all this. I suppose seeing a thoroughly white man like you made it impossible to keep my trouble to myself. Words can't do it justice; but since I've told you so much I may as well tell you more. Listen. This morning on board, in my cabin, I went down on my knees and prayed for help. I went down on my knees![76]

The ensuing exchange, apart from touching on the notion of prayer, also reveals much about the character of Morrison's relation to God:

> "You are a believer, Morrison?" asked Heyst with a distinct note of respect.
> "Surely I am not an infidel."
> Morrison was swiftly reproachful in his answer, and there came a pause, Morrison perhaps interrogating his conscience, and Heyst reserving a mien of unperturbed, polite interest.
> "I prayed like a child, of course. I believe in children praying—well, women, too, but I rather think God expects men to be more self-reliant. I don't hold with a man everlastingly bothering the Almighty with his

silly troubles. It seems such cheek. Anyhow, this morning I—I have never done any harm to any God's creature knowingly—I prayed. A sudden impulse—I went flop on my knees; so you may judge—"[77]

Heyst's response to Morrison's confession is unhesitating and generous: "Oh! If that's the case I would be very happy if you'd allow me to be of use!" he tells the latter, leaving him greatly bewildered by this unexpected offer. Such things do not, in Morrison's experience, happen very often, so this must either be a miracle and Heyst has been sent from God, or it is a case of deception and Heyst is, in fact, an emissary from the Devil. But Morrison's fears are soon allayed:

"I say! You aren't joking, Heyst?"

"Joking!" Heyst's blue eyes went hard as he turned them on the discomposed Morrison. "In what way, may I ask?" he continued with austere politeness.

Morrison was abashed.

"Forgive me, Heyst. You must have been sent by God in answer to my prayer. But I have been nearly off my chump for three days with worry; and it suddenly struck me: 'What if it's the Devil who has sent him?'"

"I have no connection with the supernatural," said Heyst graciously, moving on. "Nobody has sent me. I just happened along."

"I know better," contradicted Morrison. "I may be unworthy, but I have been heard. I know it. I feel it. For why should you offer—"

Heyst inclined his head, as from respect for a conviction in which he could not share. But he stuck to his point by muttering that in the presence of an odious fact like this, it was natural.[78]

Atheists, Believers, and Divine Judgment

Looking back on Weil's remarks about atheism and idolatry, some of her Christian readers might well agree with her condemnation of the first, idolatrous kind of atheism, and yet wonder whether her attempted *rapprochement* between the "purifying" type of atheist and the Christian believer does not come at too high a price, even for those who are prepared to give their atheist neighbors a sympathetic hearing. After all, Axel Heyst is not—despite the phonetic similarity and certain aspects of his demeanor—an incarnation of Christ, someone who could truly *save* a man like Morrison, not just from bankruptcy, but from despair over his suffering, or over the point of his life as a whole. Heyst's gesture may have led Morrison to place his trust in this particular man, Axel Heyst, and perhaps it has even restored his faith in humanity at large, but none of this seems to cut to the *core* of his religious convictions. Imagine, for the moment, a Morrison who, instead of being helped by Heyst, is callously dismissed by him, subsequently losing his precious brig to the Portuguese and, through no fault of his own, receiving the kind of beating that leaves the victim permanently crippled in body and soul. Would even the most compassionate atheist be able to offer an innocent sufferer like Morrison any *hope* that will speak to his need for the restoration of justice? And would such hope, if it could be given, not have to involve the kind of consolation Weil would reject? The question is pertinent because of the light its answer would shed, not merely on the atheist's (or Axel Heyst's) conceptual distance from the believer, but on Simone Weil's relation to orthodox Christianity. Suppose further that we asked a character like Morrison, for example, how he had managed to retain his faith in the face of all the injustices he had endured, and he replied as follows:

> This innocent sufferer has attained the certitude of hope: there is a God, and God can create justice in a way that we cannot conceive, yet we can begin to grasp it through faith. Yes, there is a resurrection of the flesh. There is justice. There is an "undoing" of past suffering, a reparation that sets things aright. For this reason, faith in the Last Judgment is first and foremost hope.[79]

Would Morrison's belief in the resurrection of the flesh be just as clear an instance of "false consolation" as his belief in an "undoing" of past suffering? Would it not depend on how these beliefs informed Morrison's life and thought more generally—for example, whether they deepened his love of his neighbors, or cheapened his sense of what their affliction meant to them? And couldn't Weil agree that an adequate elaboration of the affirmation "*Spes mea in Deo*" should contain the thought that

> Grace does not cancel out justice. It does not make wrong into right. It is not a sponge which wipes everything away, so that whatever someone has done on earth ends up being of equal value . . . Evildoers, in the end, do not sit at table at the eternal banquet beside their victims without distinction, as though nothing had happened.[80]

While I do not think that Simone Weil would have an unequivocal response to these questions—she was not a dogmatist, either philosophically or religiously—the general tenor of her answer is disclosed in two remarks concerning the resurrection. One of these occurs in a letter to her Dominican friend Father Perrin, written shortly before her departure from Marseille, on 16 April 1942:

> Once I have gone, it seems to me very improbable that circumstances will allow me to see you again one day. As to eventual meetings in another world, you know that I do not picture things to myself in that way. But that does not matter very much. It is enough for my friend-ship with you that you exist.[81]

The second appears in correspondence with the French priest Father Couturier, to whom she wrote in the autumn of the same year:

> [If] the Gospel omitted all mention of Christ's resurrection, faith would be easier for me. The Cross by itself suffices me.[82]

In an interview, Albert Camus once confessed that, while he had a deep sense of the sacred, he did not believe in a future life.[83] It is because, for him, untiring revolt against affliction and suffering do *not* come with the prospect of a future life and rewards in heaven, that Weil would think herself closer to him than to many of her fellow Christians. Their faith, she would insist, has yet to be purified through an encounter with just such an atheist.

Notes

[1] I am very grateful to Mr John Kinsey, Dr Ieuan Lloyd, Prof. Anthony O'Hear, and the audience who attended a presentation of this paper on 27 February 2009 at the Royal Institute of Philosophy in London, for their generous and helpful comments.

[2] Kai Nielsen, *Philosophy and Atheism* (New York: Prometheus, 1985), 224.

[3] Ibid.

[4] Ibid., 224–5.

[5] Kai Nielsen, "Can anything be beyond human understanding?" in Tim Tessin and Mario von der Ruhr (eds), *Philosophy and the Grammar of Religious Belief* (London: Macmillan, 1995), 179–80.

[6] Kai Nielsen and D. Z. Phillips, *Wittgensteinian Fideism?* (London: SCM Press, 2005), 31. (My emphasis.)

[7] Ibid.

[8] Ibid.

[9] Oscar Wilde, "The decay of lying," in *Complete Works* (London: Collins, 1983), 973.

[10] Nielsen and Phillips, *Wittgensteinian Fideism?*

[11] Kai Nielsen, *An Introduction to the Philosophy of Religion* (London: Macmillan, 1982), 45.

[12] Nielsen, *Philosophy and Atheism*, 223–4.

[13] Now, whether a Wittgensteinian analysis of key Christian concepts might nevertheless cause just such offence, is an altogether different matter which I will not pursue here, save to note the following: On the one hand, even the more orthodox Catholics among, for example, D. Z. Phillips' commentators, agree that his account must not be understood as a unified theory of religious discourse, but that it represents a broad spectrum of philosophical positions and perspectives that range from the strictly orthodox to the 'heretical.' In addition, such commentators contend that this is also what one would expect of a philosopher like Wittgenstein who sees himself as a disinterested grammarian of *Lebensformen* (forms of life) and their distinctive, though by no means unrelated, conceptual and linguistic frameworks.

Thus, as the Thomist scholar Brian Davies has pointed out in a recent, critical reappraisal of Phillips' work, much of it can simply be read as a straightforward attack on anthropomorphism, and his account of God-talk, in particular, as an unqualified endorsement of Aquinas' doctrine of divine simplicity—i.e., the view that God is not an object among objects, but unique, non-spatial, causally unaffected, changeless, etc.—according to which God's existence is *not* properly described as a "fact" that might, for instance, lend itself to *a posteriori* investigation. If Phillips is theologically out of line here, then, as Brian Davies rightly insists, so is Thomas Aquinas (Cf. Brian Davies, "Phillips on belief in God," *Philosophical Investigations*, Vol. 30, No. 1 [July 2007], 219–44, esp. 229–30), whose place in the history of biblical scholarship is hardly that of a non-traditionalist or revisionist. This is not to deny that there are features of Phillips' account of religion from which the orthodox believer would rightly withhold the *imprimatur*, including a construal of immortality according to which "[eternity] is not an extension of this present life, but a mode of judging it . . . not *more* life, but this life seen under certain moral and religious modes of thought" (D. Z. Phillips, *Death and Immortality* [London: Macmillan, 1972], 49). But then, as has already been pointed out, Phillips' work was never intended as an exercise in religious apologetics to begin with, nor should he be criticized for diverging from official Church doctrine when alternative understandings of immortality, prayer, covenant, the idea of a chosen people, etc., seem to him deeper, both philosophically and spiritually. For a critical assessment of Phillips' view, see Mario von der Ruhr, "Theology, philosophy, and heresy: D. Z. Phillips and the grammar of religious belief," in Andy Sanders (ed.), *D. Z. Phillips' Contemplative Philosophy of Religion* (London: Ashgate, 2007), 55–75.

[14] Nielsen and Phillips, *Wittgensteinian Fideism?*, 197.

[15] Ibid., 31.

[16] Ibid., 30.

[17] For an excellent discussion of this dialogue and its aftermath, see Stephen Bullivant, "From 'Main Tendue' to Vatican II: The Catholic engagement with atheism 1936–1965", in *New Blackfriars* Vol. 90, No. 1026 (March, 2009): 178–88.

18 GG, 115.

19 GG, 162.

20 NR, 539.

21 SE, 53.

22 NR, 237.

23 WG, 162–3.

24 WG, 162–3.

25 NR, 273.

26 IC, 151. See also NR, 118.

27 FLN, 295.

28 SE, 47.

29 "There are two atheisms of which one is a purification of the notion of God" (GG, 114).

30 NB, Vol. 1, 144.

31 GG, 173–4.

32 FLN, 308.

33 NR, 236.

34 Félix Le Dantec, *Athéisme* (Paris: Flammarion, 1907). The following remark is characteristic of Dantec's outlook: « *Je crois à l'avenir de la Science: je crois que la Science et la Science seule résoudra toutes les questions qui ont un sens; je crois qu'elle pénétrera jusqu'aux arcanes de notre vie sentimentale et qu'elle m'expliquera même l'origine et la structure du mysticisme héréditaire anti-scientifique qui cohabite chez moi avec le scientisme le plus absolu. Mais je suis convaincu aussi que les hommes se posent bien des questions qui ne signifient rien. Ces questions, la Science montrera leur absurdité en n'y répondant pas, ce qui prouvera qu'elles ne comportent pas de réponse.* » Quoted at http://agora.qc.ca/mot.nsf/Dossiers/Scientisme (accessed on 18 Feb 2009).

35 FLN, 308. (My emphasis.)

36 WG, 54.

37 WG, 95.

38 NR, 115. For a different interpretation of Richelieu's motivations, see D. P. O'Connelli, *Richelieu* (London: Weidenfeld and Nicolson, 1968). Among other things, the author argues that, contrary to appearances, "Richelieu's policy was not so much to make the Church a department of the state, as to make France a theocracy, with the church interlocked with the state and permeating secular activity with its moral authority" (139).

39 SE, 197.

40 LP, 18.

41 LP, 17.

42 LP, 18.

43 LP, 19.

44 SE, 197.

45 NB, Vol. 1, 55.

46 NB, Vol. 2, 502.

47 NB, Vol. 1, 25.

48 *The Trial of Joan of Arc*, trans. and ed. Daniel Hobbins (Cambridge, MA: Harvard University Press, 2005), 134–5.

49 Dantec, *Athéisme*, 1: "Thank God, my dear Maître (there, I admit it, a strange opening for a book on 'atheism,' but one had better speak French), thank

God that we are no longer burnt for our philosophical opinions, that it no longer requires heroism to say what one thinks." (My translation.)

50 Peter Padfield, *Himmler. Reichsführer – SS* (London: Macmillan, 1990), 172.

51 Ibid., 174.

52 Ibid., 175.

53 NR, 273.

54 Take, for instance, the following diary entries made over a period of 20 years: "Come what may, I shall always love God, pray to Him and adhere to the Catholic Church and defend it, even if I should be expelled from it" (Padfield, *Himmler*, 3; entry in Himmler's diary, dated 15.12.1919); "[All] that there was and is on this earth was created by God and animated by God. Foolish . . . people have created the fable, the fairytale, that our forefathers worshipped gods and trees. No, they were convinced, according to age-old knowledge and age-old teaching, of the God-given order of this whole earth, the entire plant- and animal-world" (ibid., 176); and "No, . . . don't talk to me about this sort of hunting. I don't care for so crude a sport. Nature is so wonderfully beautiful, and every animal has a right to life" (ibid., 351). Taken on their own these remarks seem to reflect different aspects of a continuous and admirable devotion to the Catholic faith, including the firm belief in a divinely ordained natural order in which animals are accorded a prominent place. Unfortunately, Himmler underwent a major transformation, from fervent profession of Catholicism (1919) to wholesale rejection of Christian ritual (1936): "I should like to say some things about all the festivals, all the celebrations in human life, in our life, whose Christian forms and style we cannot accept inwardly, which we can no longer be a party to, and for which, in so and so many cases, we have not yet found a new form" (ibid., 172). Having attended his own father's Catholic funeral in the previous year, Himmler admitted that he had merely done so out of respect for his father's beliefs, even though he did not share them himself: "I myself, in my personal case, have acted in that way. My father was—according to the tradition of our family—a convinced Christian, in his case a convinced Catholic. He knew my views precisely. However, we did not speak on the religious issue . . . I never touched on his convictions and he did not touch on mine" (Ibid.).

55 NR, 180–1. See also FLN, 161.

56 SE, 197.

57 NR, 266.

58 GG, 114.

59 OL, 168.

60 NR, 266.

61 IC, 184.

62 NB, Vol. 2, 361.

63 WG, 73.

64 WG, 129.

65 WG, 128.

66 Weil died too young (1943) to have read *La Peste* (1947), but it is worth noting that, when Camus himself began to read Weil's work while on a lecture tour in New York, in 1947, he was so impressed by it that he soon began to publish

it in his *Collection Espoir,* a book series he had founded with Gallimard. Over the years, nine volumes of Weil's work would appear in this series. Camus' interest in Weil is, perhaps, not surprising when one considers the intellectual affinities between the two authors.

67 James Woelfel, *Albert Camus on the Sacred and the Secular* (Lanham, MD: University Press of America, 1987), 25.

68 Quoted in ibid., 27.

69 D. Z. Phillips, "Dislocating the soul," in *Can Religion Be Explained Away?*, ed. D. Z. Phillips (London: Macmillan, 1996), 247.

70 NB, Vol. 2, 469.

71 FLN, 275.

72 GG, 115. (My emphasis.)

73 C. S. Lewis, *A Grief Observed* (San Francisco: Harper, 2001), 24–5.

74 LP, 22. See also LP, 20.

75 LP, 20. See also FLN, 84.

76 Joseph Conrad, *Victory* (Oxford: Oxford University Press, 1986), 65.

77 Ibid.

78 Ibid., 67.

79 Benedict XVI, *Saved in Hope* (San Francisco: Ignatius Press, 2008), 90.

80 Ibid., 92.

81 WG, 59.

82 LP, 34.

83 Quoted in Woelfel, *Albert Camus*, 18.

Chapter 5

"To Make Known This Method": Simone Weil and the Business of Institutional Education

Christopher A. P. Nelson

We work our jobs
Collect our pay
Believe we're gliding down the highway
When in fact we're slip slidin' away.[1]

In the third and final part of her work, *The Need for Roots*— subtitled "The Growing of Roots"—Simone Weil writes the following:

> To want to direct human creatures—others or oneself—towards the good by simply pointing out the direction, without making sure that the necessary motives have been provided, is as if one tried, by pressing down the accelerator, to set off in a motor-car with an empty petrol tank. Or again, it is as if one were to try to light an oil lamp without having put in any oil. This mistake was pointed out in a celebrated passage that has been read, re-read and alluded to over and over again for the last twenty centuries. In spite of which, we still go on making it.[2]

The "celebrated passage" to which Weil is referring is almost certainly Matthew 25.1–13, commonly referred to as the parable of the wise and foolish virgins. That text reads as follows:

> At that time [i.e., the second coming of Christ] the kingdom of heaven will be like ten virgins who took their lamps and went out to meet the bridegroom. Five of them were foolish and five were wise. The foolish

ones took their lamps but did not take any oil with them. The wise, however, took oil in jars along with their lamps. The bridegroom was a long time in coming, and they all became drowsy and fell asleep. At midnight the cry rang out: "Here's the bridegroom! Come out to meet him!" Then all the virgins woke up and trimmed their lamps. The foolish ones said to the wise, "Give us some of your oil; our lamps are going out." "No," they replied, "there may not be enough for both us and you. Instead, go to those who sell oil and buy some for yourselves." But while they were on their way to buy the oil, the bridegroom arrived. The virgins who were ready went in with him to the wedding banquet. And the door was shut. Later the others also came. "Sir! Sir!" they said. "Open the door for us!" But he replied, "I tell you the truth, I don't know you." Therefore keep watch, because you do not know the day or the hour.[3]

However, given the context of the above passage from *The Need for Roots*—a delineation and discussion of the variety of "means of education"[4]—another and equally celebrated passage from the canon of Western literature may well spring to mind:

If this [i.e., the just completed "allegory of the cave"] is true, then, we must conclude that education is not what it is said to be by some, who profess to put knowledge into a soul which does not possess it, as if they could put sight into blind eyes. On the contrary, our own account signifies that the soul of every man does possess the power of learning the truth and the organ to see it with; and that, just as one might have to turn the body round in order that the eye should see light instead of darkness, so the entire soul must be turned away from this changing world, until its eye can bear to contemplate reality and that supreme splendour which we have called the Good. Hence there may well be an art whose aim would be to effect this very thing, the conversion of the soul, in the readiest way; not to put the power of sight into the soul's eye, which already has it, but to ensure that, instead of looking in the wrong direction, it is turned the way it ought to be.[5]

That a given passage from one or another of Weil's writings should effectively recall one or another passage from the New Testament, along with one or another passage from the dialogues of Plato, is not surprising. In the present case, the unifying thread or common concern—whether rendered metaphorically, parabolically, or allegorically—is the diagnosis of a certain kind of mistake. This mistake, as both Weil and Plato make explicit, bears particularly upon the enterprise called "education." But a mistake in education can only be diagnosed and treated as such relative to some working conception of the nature and significance of education itself. In the case of Plato, this is provided for the most part in the *Republic*, the *Meno*, and the *Laws*—although the reader will be hard pressed to find a Platonic dialogue in which the issue of education is not invoked in some way or another. Weil's unique contribution to this discussion is provided in her "Reflections on the right use of school studies with a view to the love of God"[6]—an essay which is most fruitfully approached and understood with all three of the above passages in mind.

A Synopsis of Weil's "Reflections"

As Aristotle states rather more directly than his predecessor and teacher, "Every art and every inquiry, and similarly every action and choice, is thought to aim at some good; and for this reason the good has rightly been declared to be that at which all things aim."[7] Accordingly, as education is counted as an item (somewhere) in the preceding catalog, it too aims at some good, and principal among the tasks of any philosophy of education is to offer some account of this good. The philosophy of education espoused in Weil's "Reflections" is no exception to this general rule. The highest good, according to Weil, is "contact with God."[8] As Weil will go on to explain, although this mystical "contact" is explicable in two seemingly different senses as one emphasizes one or the other of the two great commandments—to love God absolutely, and to love one's neighbor as oneself[9]—its "substance" is one and the same thing.[10] In either case, what is called upon is the faculty of "attention," and the "real object" of school studies is, according to Weil, the exercise and development of this faculty. Cultivation of the faculty of attention is the relative or instrumental good at which school studies aim, vis-à-vis the ultimate or highest good conceived alternately as prayer and neighbor-love.[11] The *telos* of school studies is attention, and the *telos* of attention is contact with God.

Consequently, Weil proposes that considerations regarding tastes and/or aptitudes are virtually irrelevant vis-à-vis the true *telos* of the educational experience.[12] To take a strategically selected example: whether the student loves or hates geometry, whether the student does well or poorly in geometry, indeed whether or not the student is any closer to solving a given geometrical proof after an hour of work, the student who has been attending to the problem, as such, has sown the seeds of the fruit eventually reaped elsewhere.[13] As common as it may be for students to be advised according to a determination of the particular school subjects that they happen to "like" and/or happen to be "good at," such considerations can all too easily become detrimental distractions. In cases where a student happens to have a taste for a particular school subject, the danger arises of mistaking this otherwise instrumental end—the study of a particular subject—as an end in itself. In cases where a student happens to have an aptitude for a particular school subject, the danger arises of finding one's way through a problem or exercise without having to tap one's faculty of attention in any but the most superficial sense. To be sure, students who happen to like and/or have a natural ability for a given school subject may find opportunity enough to exercise their attention. Taste and aptitude are not necessarily barriers to attention— but neither are they its facilitators.

Conceived in this light, the point of school studies is not to grasp the truth, but rather to acquire "a greater aptitude for grasping" the truth.[14] And while faith that one's efforts of attention will bear fruit remains "the indispensable condition,"[15] Weil identifies two further conditions to be observed in this regard. First, students must make "increasing the power of attention . . . the sole and exclusive purpose of [their] studies."[16] Second, students must "take great pains" to carefully consider their academic faults and failures.[17] The latter—the contemplation of our own "stupidity"[18]—is, at least relative to the former, rather easy to enact. As Weil puts it, "it is enough to wish to do so."[19] The former, however, is more difficult, and Weil spills more than a little ink in the attempt merely to say what this power of attention is not. It is not, for instance, a muscular effort;[20] nor is it will power;[21] nor is it the dutiful application of oneself to a given task.[22] It is an effort, "the greatest of efforts perhaps, but it is a negative effort."[23]

Positively stated, attention is a kind of suspension, detachment, or emptiness of thought.[24] The opposite of attention is thus not what one might initially and reasonably suppose, namely, something like active ignorance, or neglect, or disregard—rather, the opposite of attention [*attention*], this "way of waiting [*attendre*] upon truth,"[25] is searching, seeking, seizing. Indeed, and as a more or less readily verifiable corollary, all academic errors, mistakes, missteps, etc. are, according to Weil, a result of "seiz[ing] upon some idea too hastily,"[26] "set[ting] out to seek for" the gift of truth,[27] "go[ing] out in search of" a solution,[28] etc. The effort consists in the attending; the negative consists in the waiting. The connection between the two is well preserved in the French. And if it is permissible to indulge another play on words in this regard, Emma Crauford affords a further recognition when she translates Weil's formulation of the master's directive to his slave, "*Prépare mon repas et sers-moi,*"[29] as: "Prepare my meal, and wait upon me."[30] To attend is to wait, and to wait is to serve.

Now, to be sure, the derivation of a philosophical insight from a mere play on words—and a play involving two languages, no less—may well test a critical reader's patience. Indeed, Plato's seemingly whimsical *Cratylus* may well spring to mind in this connection. The connection is entirely apropos, as it poses the very question: Can something like an ostensibly superficial play on words be borne upon a deeper undercurrent, animated by and revelatory of a deeper purpose? In the present case an affirmative answer is not out of the question as Weil actually proceeds in the final pages of her "Reflections" to attend to that principal dimension of Christian service, "the love of our neighbor."[31] Love of our neighbor, writes Weil, "is first of all attentive."[32] Emptied of all selfish concerns, it is a way of looking, of listening, of waiting, of asking: "What are you going through?"[33] Or, in the original French: "*Quel est ton tourment?*"[34] Such a way of looking, listening, and waiting—such a suspension of self, detachment from self, and emptiness of self—is admittedly difficult to achieve and still more difficult to maintain. Hence the value of school studies: "provided we devote the right kind of effort to them . . . they can one day make us better able to give someone in affliction exactly the help required to save him, at the supreme moment of his need."[35] This is the substance of the love of God, and rightly used, school studies are preparatory exercises in this regard. Weil concludes: "Academic work is one of those fields containing a pearl so precious that it is worth while to sell all our possessions, keeping nothing for ourselves, in order to be able to acquire it."[36]

Packed with allusions to a variety of potent passages from the New Testament gospels,[37] such a conclusion effectively situates Weil in conversation with some estimable company. Thinkers such as Plato, Aristotle and Rousseau—and more recently Dewey, Whitehead, Freire, Postman and Noddings—come to mind, if only because of the comparably elevated estimation of the significance of education manifest in each of their writings. Simone Weil sits squarely and securely at this table. The fact that her estimation of the significance of school studies is inextricably bound up with a particular ethics, and a particular metaphysics, is beside the point—the same may be said for every other thinker at the table.

Indeed, any philosopher-of-education whose educational philosophy is not so bound up with an ethics, and a metaphysics,[38] belongs more properly and really ought to be seated, as at a crowded family gathering, at the kids' table.

Three Questions of Scope

Given the admittedly rough sketch of the philosophy of education in and according to the above synopsis of Weil's "Reflections," a trio of issues emerge pertaining to what may be referred to generically as the question of scope—i.e., the question as to the actual beneficiaries of Weil's essay. By way of anticipation, the three issues may be summarily posed in a single compound question: Is any of this relevant for teachers, nonbelievers, and/or adult students? An affirmative answer will be given in all three cases.

The first question of scope may be formulated thus: Since Weil's "Reflections" reads primarily as an encouragement to students—detailing how they should and should not approach their studies, what they should and should not expect from their studies, etc.—is there anything of practical relevance in this essay for the teacher, as such? That the essay was originally written for and presented to Father Joseph-Marie Perrin—whose assignment to Montpellier "put him into contact with students"[39]—is encouraging in this regard. Additionally, it seems altogether reasonable to suppose that any sound advice for students ought to bear some relevance for the prospective teacher. However, throughout the essay the correlative implications for teachers are left largely to the imagination of the individual reader. Perhaps this is as it should be. Nevertheless, there is a single passage in her "Reflections" in which Weil turns and directly addresses the teacher as such:

> Our first duty toward school children and students is to make known this method to them, not only in a general way but in the particular form that bears on each exercise. It is not only the duty of those who teach them but also their spiritual guides. Moreover, the latter should bring out in a brilliantly clear light the correspondence between the attitude of the intelligence in each of these exercises and the position of the soul, which, with its lamp well filled with oil, awaits the Bridegroom's coming with confidence and desire.[40]

The "method" in question is nicely elucidated in the preceding paragraph:

> In every school exercise there is a special way of waiting upon truth, setting our hearts upon it, yet not allowing ourselves to go out in search of it. There is a way of giving our attention to the data of a problem in geometry without trying to find the solution or to the words of a Latin or Greek text without trying to arrive at the meaning, a way of waiting, when we are writing, for the right word to come of itself at the end of our pen, while we merely reject all inadequate words.[41]

The question thus becomes: How shall the teacher make this method known to the student? An answer to this question will be developed in the final section, below, apropos a re-reading of the allegory of the cave suggested by the substance of Weil's "Reflections." For present purposes, it is sufficient to answer that there is a relevant message for teachers in "Reflections."

The second question of scope may be formulated thus: Since Weil's "Reflections on the right use of school studies" are explicitly qualified as "with a view to the love of God," is there anything of practical relevance in this essay for the non-believer? This question is a bit trickier than the first, and the forthcoming affirmative answer will have to be qualified in some respects. One way of angling into this question might be to take a step back and attempt to render some clear line of demarcation between the believer and the non-believer, perhaps by virtue of some such question as: What does it mean to be a Christian? One might even appeal to Weil's own relationship to institutional Christianity in this regard, although it is difficult to tell whether this would help clarify or further obscure the issue. In any case, there is a single passage in Weil's "Reflections" that comes close, or at least closer than any other, to addressing this question: "For an adolescent, capable of grasping this truth and generous enough to desire this fruit above all others, studies could have their fullest spiritual effect, quite apart from any particular religious belief."[42] The "truth" in question, as elucidated in the preceding paragraph, is that school studies, conceived as preparatory exercises, "may be of great service one day" in making us "better able" to attend to our neighbor.[43] The question thus becomes: How does it stand with this love of our neighbor, or how does the *telos* of neighbor-love stand apart from any particular religious belief? Again, an answer to this question will be developed in the final section, below, apropos a revisiting of the parable of the wise and foolish virgins suggested by the substance of Weil's "Reflections." For present purposes, it is sufficient to point to the olive branch extended across sectarian divides and answer that there is a relevant message in "Reflections" for many who would count themselves as non-believers.

The third question of scope may be formulated thus: Since Weil appears to have "school children" and "adolescent(s)" in mind in the composition of her "Reflections," is there anything of practical relevance in this essay for older, adult students—university, college, or continuing education students, for instance? In contrast to the first two questions treated above, this third question is relatively easy to handle. Aristotle provides a perfectly coherent response to this very question when he says of the potential student: "it makes no difference whether he is young in years or youthful in character; the defect does not depend on time."[44] Of course, within the context of Aristotle's argument this remark is a qualification of the conclusion that the "young" are not fit to participate in political discussions, lacking the requisite life experience with the content material of the subject, and being driven hither and thither by their passions alone. Nevertheless, the point here stands: unless it is assumed that the cultivation of the faculty of attention is something over and done with by the time that one reaches a certain age, the continued or higher cultivation of this faculty is a purpose to which continuing or post-secondary education appears perfectly suited. This is not to deny that higher education may have different aims and ends than those of primary and secondary education, but within the context provided by Weil's "Reflections" such aims and ends remain instrumental and relative vis-à-vis the ultimate and highest good. Or shall the post-secondary student and post-secondary professor be permitted the luxury of rendering their proximate educational ends and their immediate academic goals a little "less relative" according to the particulars of their own manifestly developed tastes and aptitudes? Suffice it to say, the substance of Weil's "Reflections" remains practically relevant for anyone yet to perfect the faculty of attention.

The Mistake That We Still Go On Making

Two questions remain. The first, encountered in the above treatment of the student/teacher issue of scope, was formulated as follows: "How shall the teacher make this method [of waiting upon truth] known to the student?" The second, encountered in the above treatment of the believer/non-believer issue of scope, was formulated as follows: "How does it stand with this love of our neighbor, or how does the *telos* of neighbor-love stand apart from any particular religious belief?" As promised, the first will be developed and addressed according to a re-reading of the allegory of the cave in Book VII of Plato's *Republic*, and the second according to a revisiting of the parable of the wise and foolish virgins in the Gospel of Matthew. Having thus developed and addressed these two questions, the present exercise will conclude with a little something about the relevance of Weil's "Reflections" to and for the business of institutional education—or rather, to and for teachers and students who happen to be such within the terrain of the contemporary educational scene.

How shall the teacher make this method of waiting upon truth known to the student? Socrates provides a possible answer to this very question in Book VII of the *Republic*,[45] according to which the cave-bound prisoner—the student—is forcibly freed, made to stand up, turned around, made to look at the fire, drug out of the cave, prevented from retreating back down into the cave, and further compelled to look at reflections on water and other reflective surfaces, to look at real objects, and to look at the sun. Eventually, the acclimated student has a kind of epiphany. The student now knows the Good, is now fully educated, and is now fit to serve as a philosopher-king back down in the cave. There are two things to notice with regard to this model of education. First, the idea of the philosopher as the one who knows the Good, and therefore also the true nature of ultimate reality,[46] appears to conflict somewhat with the idea of the philosopher, such as one finds in the *Apology*, as the one who, in a manner of speaking, knows that he or she does not know.[47] Second, the idea that the student is compelled through the various stages of the educational process by a teacher, while a seemingly reasonable assumption, is highly questionable insofar as Socrates appears to make a point of leaving the actual source of this compulsion an open question.[48]

The substance of Weil's "Reflections" provides one possible way of resolving both of the above problems, a resolution that consists in the idea that "the Good," conceived in terms of the comportment of human beings, is the very waiting upon the good. The end, in a sense, is the means.[49] As a result, the idea of the teacher who has "seen the sun" and subsequently seeks to reorient the student by "simply pointing" them in "the direction" of the good, "without making sure that the necessary motives have been provided"[50]—along with the idea that the "desire" required to lead "the intelligence"[51] is the kind of thing that can be provided by the application of direct, external compulsion in the form of, say, rewards and punishments—must be discarded. In its place, Weil suggests a radical alternative that, although victim to a certain ambiguity in English translation, is perfectly clear in the French. The duty of the teacher vis-à-vis the student is "*faire connaître cette méthode*"[52]—not *faire savoir cette méthode*—meaning that the teacher's first duty toward students is to make them "acquainted" or "familiar" with this method. And familiarizing or acquainting a student with something is not at all the same thing as instructing or telling them about it. While it has regrettably acquired the ring of a cliché in contemporary parlance, the petition "show me don't tell me" acquires a radical significance in this regard, as showing is something done by example—and not merely as when one works an example of a problem on the board in a classroom, but rather and more importantly as when one becomes an example.

For the teacher, this insight harbors a double significance. Take the example of a geometry teacher who, in working a problem for the benefit of the student, presumably already knows the solution to the problem and has presumably already worked this very problem several times before for the benefit of other students. In order to exemplify the method of waiting upon truth, the teacher must in a sense forget the solution—or rather, the teacher must remember the problem, must shift his or her attention to the problem as such, perhaps by asking: What makes this "problem" a problem?[53] In doing so, the teacher will also presumably realize that a problem is simply not the kind of thing that can exist in the abstract. Every problem worth the name is a problem for someone. Accordingly, the teacher is also therewith compelled to ask the student: What makes this a problem for you? And here the situation comes full circle, as the teacher is really asking the student: *Quel est ton tourment?* What is *your problem*?[54] This is how the method is made known. This is the love of our neighbor.

And so: How does it stand with this love of our neighbor, or how does the *telos* of neighbor-love stand apart from any particular religious belief? Given the above development and resolution of the question regarding the making known of this method, this second question becomes a bit more pressing. To begin with, there is something disconcerting, prima facie, about the parable of the wise and foolish virgins. As Jesus tells the story, the "foolish" virgins, upon realizing that they were nearly out of oil, asked the others: "Give us some of your oil; our lamps are going out." The others, the "wise" virgins, responded: "No . . . there may not be enough for both us and you. Instead, go to those who sell oil and buy some for yourselves." Notwithstanding the subordinate role that this particular exchange occupies within the overall narrative—the point of which appears to consist wholly in the imperative to be prepared[55]—the question might be posed as to whether or not the response of the wise virgins is commensurate with the basic Christian message. Consider the following passage, for instance: "And if someone wants to sue you and take your tunic, let him have your cloak as well. If someone forces you to go one mile, go with him two miles. Give to the one who asks you, and do not turn away from the one who wants to borrow from you."[56] It would thus appear that Jesus is saying two very different things: on the one hand, that the righteous ought never to refuse anything to someone who asks, and on the other hand—if in fact the wise virgins are intended as models to be followed—that the righteous ought not to give (any of their oil) to those who ask. The matter becomes all the more grave as one comes to grips with the stakes involved. The context of this passage is, after all, a discussion of who will and who will not be left in the lurch at the second coming.

Again, the substance of Weil's "Reflections" provides some help in navigating this seeming contradiction. The question is not whether or not the wise ought to give their oil to the foolish, but rather whether or not they *can*. And the answer, in one sense at least, is: absolutely not. On Weil's reading of this passage, or at least on the reading of this passage implied by the use to which Weil puts it, the "oil" in the parable represents the power of attention. A variety of phrases to the contrary notwithstanding—e.g., paying attention to someone, or giving someone attention—the power of attention, as such, is not the kind of thing that can be transferred from one human being to another. To press the parable, being out of oil—attention conceived as suspension, detachment, emptiness—actually entails being full of something besides oil. This is why, although one may pay attention *to* another, it is absolutely impossible to pay attention *for* another. Whether it is conceived as the love of God or as the love of our neighbor, attention is not the kind of thing that one human being can provide for another. It must be built up.[57]

So what of those who do not, as the saying goes, share the faith? That, in effect, is the question—and it is a question best handled with two hands, depending upon what exactly is meant by the qualification, "nonbeliever." On the one hand, there are those who disbelieve or actively deny one or another or even many of the doctrinal elements of the Christian religion, and yet believe and actively affirm that the "love of our neighbor" is in fact the *summum bonum* of human existence. On the other hand, there are those who disbelieve or actively deny that neighbor-love is in fact the highest good. In the case of the former, there would appear to be little if any difficulty involved in communicating the relevance of Weil's "Reflections." Indeed, given the basic agreement regarding the primacy of neighbor-love, every other subsequent dispute becomes precisely the kind of issue to which teachers and students may rightly continue to devote their attention, so long as they remain mindful of the relative status of such inquiries and discussions. With regard to the latter, however—i.e., those who disbelieve or actively deny the status of neighbor-love as the *summum bonum*—the burden shifts wholly to the side of the proponent of faith. In fact—and one may well wonder which party to the exchange has more to learn—the evangelist has but to ask one question of the disbelieving neighbor: *Quel est ton tourment?* Literally: What is your torment? To deny the ultimate goodness of neighbor-love is to say something—but what? That is the question to be posed, and the addressee of this question demands and is due our attention. This is how it stands with the love of our neighbor, apart from any particular religious belief.

With the whole of the above in mind, and in attempting at last to say something about the relevance of Weil's "Reflections" vis-à-vis the contemporary situation of the business of institutional education, a certain temptation needs to be signaled, if only the better to be avoided. In this regard, it is helpful to recall the character of Socrates, who, to borrow a line from Kierkegaard, "had his strength in making the conversation so concrete that everyone who conversed with him and intended to speak about some enormous subject or other (administration of the state on the whole, public education on the whole, etc.) was brought, before he was aware of it, to speaking about himself."[58] The temptation to speak of "education on the whole," institutional reform, and indeed even the business of institutional education as such, is of course perfectly understandable. There is much that is lamentable in the contemporary situation, especially in the United States. Christianly conceived, however—and the Christian conception parallels the above Socratic conception fairly neatly in this respect—the intention to speak about such an enormous subject ought to be checked against the spirit of the following question: "How can you say to your brother, 'Let me take the speck out of your eye,' when all the time there is a plank in your own eye?"[59]

Those with an investment in the perpetuation of the conversation about "public education on the whole" might reply that the suggested analogy fails, as it is not a brother in need of de-specking, but rather an institution or indeed an institutional system. The substance of Weil's "Reflections," however, suggests that the spirit of the admonition is still entirely to the point, and might be better formulated as Herb Brooks (coach of the 1980 United States men's Olympic hockey team) is reported to have snapped at (team captain) Mike Eruzione between periods in a game against Sweden: "You worry about your own game. Plenty there to keep you busy."[60] Indeed, a very real part of the relevance of Weil's "Reflections" for teachers is in the very reminder that they are the ones concerned, and the ones to be concerned. Whether or not there are also implications to be drawn vis-à-vis the administrative levels of institutional education is, of course, an interesting question worthy of some attention—so long as such inquiries can be kept from rivaling, supplanting or subordinating the deeper purpose of cultivating the faculty of attention.[61] And this is, in effect, the relevance of the radical, the relevance of the reminder to not forget our deeper purpose as faithful and hopeful and loving participants in the educational enterprise, for it is this very forgetfulness, whatever its form and however lofty its speech, that lies at the base of, or rather simply is, the "mistake" that "*we* still go on making."[62] To modify a remark by James Baldwin, "[students] have never been very good at listening to their [teachers], but they have never failed to imitate them."[63] The initial sting notwithstanding—reading "because" instead of "but"—there is hope signaled in this recognition. Let us not forget it.

Notes

[1] Paul Simon, "Slip Slidin' Away," *Greatest Hits, Etc.* (New York: Columbia Records, 1977).

[2] NR, 188.

[3] Matthew 25.1–13 (NIV).

[4] NR, 188.

[5] Plato, *Republic* VII 518b–d, trans. F. M. Cornford, in *The Republic of Plato* (Oxford: Oxford University Press, 1945).

[6] WG, 105–6.

[7] Aristotle, *Nicomachean Ethics* I 1094a1, trans. W. D. Ross and J. O. Urmson, in *The Complete Works of Aristotle*, ed. Jonathan Barnes (Princeton: Princeton University Press, 1995).

[8] WG, 105.

[9] See Matthew 22.34–40.

[10] WG, 114.

11 WG, 105, 115.
12 See WG, 108.
13 WG, 106.
14 WG, 107.
15 WG, 107.
16 WG, 108.
17 WG, 108–9.
18 WG, 109; cf. GG, 178.
19 WG, 109.
20 WG, 109–10.
21 WG, 110.
22 WG, 111.
23 WG, 111.
24 WG, 111.
25 WG, 113.
26 WG, 112.
27 WG, 112.
28 WG, 113.
29 AD, 95.
30 WG, 113.
31 WG, 114.
32 WG, 115.
33 WG, 115.
34 AD, 96.
35 WG, 115; cf. GG, 120.
36 WG, 116.
37 See, e.g., Matthew 7.1–6, 13.44–6; Luke 12.22–34 (cf. Matthew 6.25–34), 18.18–30 (cf. Matthew 19.16–30; Mark 10.17–31).
38 As George Grant puts it: "It is a simple fact that what actions we think to be good depend on what we think is ultimately real." Grant, "The paradox of democratic education," in *The George Grant Reader*, ed. William Christian and Sheila Grant (Toronto: University of Toronto Press, 1998), 182.
39 Simone Pétrement, *Simone Weil: A Life*, trans. Raymond Rosenthal (New York: Pantheon Books, 1976), 462–3.
40 WG, 113; cf. NR, 188; Matthew 25.1–13.
41 WG, 113; cf. GG, 120.
42 WG, 115–6; cf. WG, 107.
43 WG, 115.
44 Aristotle, *Nicomachean Ethics* I 1095a6.
45 See Plato, *Republic* VII 514a–521b.
46 Cf. Plato, *Meno* 81c–d.
47 See, e.g., Plato, *Apology* 22d–23b.
48 See, e.g., Plato, *Republic* VII 515c; cf. Jon M. Torgerson, "Socrates: outwardly a monster, all beauty within," *Metaphilosophy* 22:3 (1991), 239–50.
49 Cf. Søren Kierkegaard, *Upbuilding Discourses in Various Spirits*, trans. Howard V. Hong and Edna H. Hong (Princeton: Princeton University Press, 1993), 141.
50 NR, 188.

51 WG, 110.

52 AD, 94.

53 Cf. Gareth B. Matthews, "The career of perplexity in Plato," and Martin Andic, "Commentary on Matthews," *Proceedings of the Boston Area Colloquium in Ancient Philosophy* 13 (1997), 35–55, and 56–68.

54 Cf. Paulo Freire, *Pedagogy of the Oppressed*, trans. Myra Bergman Ramos (New York: Continuum, 1997), 105.

55 See H. H. Halley, *Halley's Bible Handbook* (Grand Rapids: Zondervan Publishing House, 1965), 447; cf. Craig S. Keener, *The IVP Bible Background Commentary: New Testament* (Downer's Grove: InterVarsity Press, 1993), 116–7.

56 Matthew 5.39–42 (NIV); cf. Luke 6.27–31.

57 Cf. Kierkegaard, *Works of Love*, trans. Hong and Hong (Princeton: Princeton University Press, 1995), 209–24.

58 Kierkegaard, *The Book on Adler*, ed. and trans. Hong and Hong (Princeton: Princeton University Press, 1998), 147.

59 Matthew 7.4 (NIV).

60 This exchange is dramatized in Scene 14 of the motion picture, *Miracle* (Pop Pop Productions, 2004).

61 For an interesting case of an educator and administrator who, much indebted to Weil, attempted to conduct such inquiries and conversations, see the writings of George Grant collected in Part 2 ("Philosophy and education") of *The George Grant Reader*, 157–203.

62 NR, 188.

63 Cf. Baldwin, *Nobody Knows My Name: More Notes of a Native Son* (New York: Vintage International, 1993), 61–2.

Chapter 6

Mystery and Philosophy

Eric O. Springsted

Does Mystery Belong in Philosophy?

In 1955, Michael Foster, a philosopher noted for his work on theology and science, delivered a set of lectures at the University of Edinburgh that were subsequently published under the title *Mystery and Philosophy*.[1] The book became a classic for many philosophers who believed that religion was important to human life and thinking, but who justifiably felt themselves beleaguered by analytic philosophy, the dominant way of doing philosophy in the English-speaking world. Analytic philosophy in itself was not anti-religious, although it was decidedly anti-metaphysical, and numerous analytic philosophers failed to see the difference between the two. But in the same year that Foster gave his lectures, *New Essays in Philosophical Theology* was published, which, using analytic philosophy, set the philosophical case against theism for the next 20 years.[2] Some alternative vision was needed and *Mystery and Philosophy* helped provide it. It did so not by taking on any specific case made against religion; instead, it exposed the deep assumptions of analytic philosophy that misunderstood biblical religion and that were ultimately incompatible with it. Even though the intellectual climate has changed since then, these are assumptions that might fairly be said to still haunt both philosophy and science today, including among friends of religion.

They were indeed assumptions, and not a philosophical doctrine. But they were all the more pernicious because it was so easy to overlook the freight that they carried. Foster pointed out two of them. First, there was "a demand for a certain kind of clarity;"[3] secondly, there was the assumption "that all thinking, and therefore all philosophical thinking, consists in solving problems."[4] The issue is not that clarity is bad, or that one should not solve problems, but rather "the belief that nothing is really puzzling and that therefore there cannot be anything unclear that we legitimately want to say."[5] In short, analysis assumed that there was no mystery in philosophy, and whatever passed by that name was simply a problem that could be solved with due diligence and rendered clear by analysis.

Foster was not the first nor the only one to notice the problem. In fact, he explicitly drew on Gabriel Marcel. Marcel, first in *Being and Having* and then in his Gifford Lectures, *The Mystery of Being*, had made the crucial distinction between a mystery and a problem.[6] The latter is capable of solution—it is a sort of puzzle; the former is not capable of solution, but gives itself infinitely. Moreover, Marcel argued, the response to a mystery is something that involves the whole person; as the ancients might have said, it involves the heart. Foster, using Marcel's work, then put his finger on how the distinction was important for unveiling a whole approach to philosophy. For most analytic philosophers, whatever was mysterious was due either to a lack of knowledge or to unclear thinking. They believed that science would fix the first, and philosophy the second. The goal of both disciplines was the same, for "the goal towards which both the scientist and philosopher are working is a state in which there will be no more mystery."[7]

Why is this a problem? It is certainly not the case that analysis of terms, concepts and arguments is bad. Theology is itself a sort of analysis. Still, it proceeds on different assumptions, and those assumptions were being dismissed out of hand. In particular, the assumptions of analytic philosophy "exclude Revelation as a source of truth *ab initio*."[8] They do so because Revelation, at least as it has been understood biblically, is a matter of God speaking – not in the sense of communicating factual information that could, in principle, be gotten by science or linguistic therapy, but in the sense that God communicates Himself and His Holiness. The appropriate response to *that* is repentance, an opening up of oneself in order to listen further. This is what mystery is about; it is not something to be solved, it is not a set of facts, but something that keeps giving itself. This is not only the biblical worldview; ancient Greeks such as Plato had it, too. Truth was something that revealed itself. That required contemplation and the attitude of wonder from thinkers. *Theoria* is looking and gazing, not a closing of the case. Analytic philosophy unconcernedly blows past all of this.

The upshot of this argument was Foster's distinguishing between mystery as a theological category and clarity as a philosophical one. He argued that the thought worlds of science and the Bible were different.

Neither should be reduced to the other, and one did not have to choose between the two; one needed to recognize the importance of both to human thinking. So if one took the difference seriously it was necessary to recognize that "part of us is captured by our Lord."[9] Thus, he proposed that in the future "the basic question will be not what is rational and what empirical, but what is human and what divine; what is in man's power to discover and what can be revealed only by God."[10]

This general position is one that bears important similarities to Simone Weil's thinking. She made explicit appeals to mystery and even gave a helpful and penetrating definition of what should count as a mystery. For this reason, understanding Foster's argument can be helpful to understanding Weil's thinking on this issue as well as setting a general context for the relevance of her use of the concept of mystery. It helps us see what sort of questions she is tackling, and that they do have connections with what other philosophers have thought. However, I also want to suggest that she went a lot farther than Foster did in treating the concept of mystery. Where and how she did so is important not only to understanding her, but to truly having a sense of what it means to live surrounded by the divine mystery. For Weil did not set philosophical clarity and theological mystery against each other (as Foster also did not), nor side by side in human life (as Foster did). Rather, she thought that if we were involved in mystery in any significant sense, we were involved in mystery at *all* points in life, even though we might not always recognize it. Thus she ultimately saw the nature of philosophical thought quite differently than any number of thinkers in the modern period. Its point for her was not ultimately to clarify things. Real philosophy was something undertaken with a sense of wonder, as Plato thought, and with an explicit recognition of mystery. Ultimately, it was something that drives beyond rationality towards an explicit divine encounter, effecting the transformation of the human by the divine.

If this is the case, then there are two additional conclusions that need to be drawn, ones that Weil herself drew. The first is one concerning the role of philosophy in a life that is surrounded by a divine mystery, and the second is a certain conception of life itself. In both of these, I want to maintain, lies a great deal of Simone Weil's radical challenge to contemporary thought. For there is a great contrast between a world that has no mystery and one that exists within the divine mystery. A world without mystery, or one where mystery is not acknowledged, is a world where technique and mastery dominate, and where contemplation and wonder retreat. It is essentially a flat world; there is little texture and there is no concern for the importance of aesthetic form, or concern for beauty as having anything to do with truth. Goodness is deduced from common principles, and is rarely a matter of striving for anything transcending. Charles Taylor, quoting Oscar Wilde, has talked about this "flatness of modern civilization which sees 'the final triumph of the Hollow Men, who, knowing the price of everything and the value of nothing, had lost the ability to *feel* or *think* deeply about anything.'"[11] On the other hand, the acknowledgment of mystery, at least the mystery of the Good, involves us in all those things. Life within an embracing mystery that balances contraries and does not obliterate them has to recognize the importance of beauty, and a striving for a non-evident and often hidden good. If there is such a mystery, then it is at least philistinism to try to eliminate it; at worst it is the manifestation of a single-minded pursuit of technique and power.

Weil's Understanding of Mystery

The most obvious place to begin is by looking at how Weil treats explicit theological mysteries. In numerous places she writes of "the mysteries of the faith"[12] which she is willing to equate with dogmas. However, it is equally apparent that she is no propositionalist with respect to theological mysteries. She is adamant that mysteries are beyond what the intellect can affirm or deny. For example, she notes that "the dogmas of faith are not things to be affirmed. They are things to be regarded from a certain distance with attention, respect and love."[13] They "are not of the order of truth but above it. The only part of the human soul which is capable of any real contact with them is the faculty of supernatural love."[14] Thus, like Foster and Marcel, she thinks that mysteries need to be approached and dealt with in a significantly different way than, say, analytic, or scholastic, or neo-scholastic philosophy tried to deal with propositions. Mysteries are not informational; instead, there is something existential about them; they engage us and draw us into involvement with them. That is where their relevance and importance lies. Thus, demanding propositional clarity about them often mistakes how they function in our lives, including our intellectual lives; demanding adherence to them as truths similar to geometrical truths is illegitimate.

Weil's very definition of a mystery underlines this sense of a living engagement. She argues that we only have hold of a legitimate mystery when, after an intellectually rigorous search, we come to an impasse and a contradiction, but also when it would seem wrong to solve the contradiction in favor of one side or the other: "the suppression of one term makes the other term meaningless and . . . to pose one term necessarily involves posing the other."[15] Far from demanding more work to solve the apparent contradiction, that intellectual impasse needs to be paid attention to; it then acts "like a lever . . . [and] carries thought beyond the impasse, to the other side of the unopenable door, beyond the domain of intelligence and above it."[16] Mysteries in this sense engage love, and not speculation.

It is fairly easy to illustrate theologically how helpful Weil's definition of mystery can be, and how it is rooted in the actual living of religious life. Consider simply a doctrine, a mystery such as the Trinity: there is one God only, yet in three distinct persons. What we know about how that doctrine arose in the early church is that, on the one hand, there was the strict monotheism of Judaism, which was also the Church's, and on the other hand, there was also the very early tendency to talk about Jesus in terms that normally belonged to God. For example, there was the practice of calling Jesus "Lord," a title normally belonging to God. Moreover, there were practices such as praying to Jesus that seemed to make him equivalent to the one and only God, and there were sayings ascribed to him that made him equal to God. He was thought to reveal God perfectly. But how can all this divinity that attaches to Jesus be possible if there is only one God? The early Church, of course, recognized the issue, and any number of people tried to solve what seemed to be the contradiction. But those solutions became the history of heresy, which favors one end of the contradiction over the other, and tries to resolve it rationally. Its failure is that in trying to make things clearer, it ends up losing a light found in the practice of worshiping one God, and Jesus Christ as His only begotten Son, God of God, light of light, true God of true God. For example, were one to solve the mystery as Arius did by suggesting that there are three persons, but that two of them, the Son and the Spirit, are not God, then one can no longer claim that God became a man and died for us; God remains at a distance, having sent a substitute to help us out. Thus, as St Gregory of Nazianzus observed of the related Eunomian heresy, by trying to say more through defining the divine nature rationally, they actually kept one from saying as much as one could. In this sense, the Nicene Creed, then, is ultimately rooted in protecting the grammar of the mystery that is rooted in the actual life of the Christian community; its only creativity was that of explicitly writing that grammar in order to protect it.[17]

Mysteries in this theological sense often have in Weil's writings a sense of being end-points to thought. Thought drives towards them, and then in front of them gives way to attention and love. But this is also where Weil begins to enter into a much broader sense of mystery, one that does not put contemporary philosophy at its side, but one that demands a much different way of doing philosophy. This happens first with respect to philosophical method, which, she thinks, ought to reflect the mystery whose appreciation is its goal; second, it determines that the value of philosophy is how it engages a thinker with questions of value.

Mystery involves something like being enlightened from gazing at what lies behind two contradictory lines of thought. It is no surprise, therefore, to discover that Weil thinks that contemplating contradiction lies at the very heart of doing philosophy. From early on, she told her students: "Method of investigation: as soon as we have thought something, try to see in what way the contrary is true."[18] This, of course, is always a good idea since it at least allows one to develop a critical faculty. But there is more to it than that for Weil. Borrowing from a suggestion Plato makes in the *Republic,* she believes that one needs to think about contradiction because it is what will ultimately allow one to emerge from a point of view. It allows us to move from a limited perspective on reality to one that is far more inclusive. Here she makes extensive use of an example taken from Greek mathematics. When the ancient Greek mathematicians discovered that certain types of lines—e.g. the diagonals of right-angled triangles—had no common measure with the lengths of the sides of those triangles, they were in a quandary since numbers were for them thought of as proportions between lengths. But here there could be no exact proportion possible, at least as long as they thought of numbers consisting only of what we call "rational numbers." However, Eudoxus in time discovered that both these irrational numbers (the diagonals) and the rational numbers could be incorporated into a system of "real numbers" which included both rationals and irrationals.[19] This "Eudoxean system" Weil thought could be carried through equally well in "psychological and spiritual matters."[20] Weil's distinctive treatments of "necessity" and of "reading" are both related to this method. For example, her discussions of "necessity" analyze the concept as having at least three different levels— brute necessity; the mathematical tissue of invariant relations of force; and finally, as what is "persuaded by Goodness" and obedient to God.[21] Each of these, furthermore, is related to a level of reading, the way by which value impresses us, as we read the world also at three different levels: at the level of individual pleasure and pain; at a second level where individual preference is left behind and one reaches a sort of Stoic acceptance of all that happens—*amor fati*; and finally, where all that happens in the world is felt, as it were, as something belonging intimately and lovingly to one's own self. There is a hierarchy to these concepts, and Weil presumes that one moves up through them by contemplating the contradictions at lower levels.

To leave it at this, however, might well leave one with the impression that Weil is engaged in a sort of idealist, Hegelian project, whereby apparent oppositions and antitheses in thought are reconciled and synthesized in a higher unity. For her, that sort of approach works best in a limited, piecemeal way that describes individual growth, and even historical, cultural workings-out of ideas. However, for Weil there is no ultimate synthesis, at least not on any level that is accessible to the intellect, or realizable in history. Mystery is the end-point of thought, as it is its beginning; it is what one casts one's gaze upon, and it is what one lovingly accepts when one *cannot* go any farther. Mystery is most apparent in the face of a well-developed intellectual pluralism. Mystery dawns as one appreciates more and more all the diverse roads of thought that one thinks.

It is for this reason that Weil points out that "all philosophical thought contains [contradictions]."[22] It does not eliminate them, and it does not, therefore, try to construct systems. At their best such systems are poetry; at their worst, "these systems are below even the level of conjecture, for conjectures are at least inferior thoughts, and these systems are not thoughts."[23] Wittgenstein, in what was perhaps a similar frame of mind, described this attempt to eliminate contradiction and find answers to all philosophical questions as a "sickness" and an "obsession" at the heart of the enterprise of philosophy. Weil, on that score, would have had no disagreement. The philosophers of any worth are those who maintain the contradictions, and do not try to solve them.

A further comparison with Wittgenstein is apt at this point, in order to reveal a better sense of what Weil is driving at. Wittgenstein famously ended his *Tractatus Logico-Philosophicus* with the comment, "Whereof we cannot speak, thereof we must be silent."[24] On one interpretation of this comment, Wittgenstein was thinking of something like the ethical or religious, even something like the mysterious givenness of the world, as what cannot be put into propositions, and that we must therefore be silent about. Wittgenstein himself tended not to talk directly about these things as such, at least not in any way that sought to *explain* them. He was ever careful to avoid what seemed to be the impossibility of drawing a line in language between the sayable and the unsayable. The respect for the distinction lay somewhere else. While Weil occasionally violates this warning, and is quite willing to talk directly about mysteries in terms that make her look like a classical metaphysician—a dangerous tendency since it allows mysteries to be invoked in ways to justify most anything— the fact of the matter is that she really is close to Wittgenstein on this issue. Her point about mysteries is that the intellect, in encountering them, can go no farther than to acknowledge that two contradictory lines of thought are both correct, and to carry out thought under the shadow of its incompleteness. Where mystery enters into the human realm is somewhere else, namely, in love and attention. Indeed, her greatest complaint about the Roman Catholic Church's approach to faith was that it made it a matter of intellectual belief. The dogmas, the mysteries of the Church she thought were not matters for the intellect at all, but things meant to be gazed on with love. She says quite plainly:

> The mysteries of faith are not a proper object for the intelligence considered as a faculty permitting affirmation or denial. They are not of the order of truth, but above it. The only part of the human soul which is capable of any real contact with them is the faculty of super-natural love. It alone, therefore, is capable of an adherence in regard to them.[25]

Thus Weil, although she talks about mysteries, does not think she is in any sense capturing them in doing so, and certainly not in language. But that one cannot capture or define them does not leave the concept of mystery as vacuous, or fuzzy beyond use. In fact, Weil thinks that we can have a very definite sense of when someone has given him or herself to a mystery. One's encounter with them is seen in the light that they shed on everything else.

This "light that they shed on everything else" needs to be described in a couple of different ways. First, there is the image of a balance that Weil uses. The supernatural, or a mystery if you will, is not an item among others that is ever put into balance with other things. It is not on the bal-ance at all. Rather, it is something like the fulcrum of the balance; it is what is outside the system of equilibrium that puts everything else in that system into equilibrium. In this sense, the person who has actually encountered mystery is not revealed by their knowledgeable words about mystery—there is no right or wrong description, and a fool or a liar might be able to say as much and as well as them. Rather, his encounter is seen in the way that he balances everything else, in the way that he puts things into relation with each other.

Just what this means can be seen in a second way of illustrating how Weil thinks of a mystery, namely, how one thinks and acts in the world. In a series of striking phrases she puts this enlightenment by mystery in these ways:

> [A] bride's friends do not go into the nuptial chamber; but when she is seen to be pregnant they know that she has lost her virginity . . . There is no fire in a cooked dish, but one knows that it has been on the fire . . . It is not the way a man talks about God, but the way he talks about the things of this world that best shows whether his soul has passed through the fire of the love of God. In this matter no deception is possible. There are false imitations of the love of God, but not of the transformation it effects in the soul, because one has no idea of this transformation except by passing through it oneself . . . According to the conception of human life expressed in the acts and words of a man I know . . . whether he sees life from a point in this world or from above in heaven . . . The value of a religious or, more generally, a spiritual way of life is appreciated by the amount of illumination thrown upon the things of this world.[26]

One's engagement with a mystery or with the supernatural is something that belongs to one's habits of the heart; it is something written in our way of being. It is in that respect something that is seen only insofar as it is incarnated, and lived in the flesh.

The Question of Depth

It starts to become clearer why the concept of mystery is so important, and how relevant it is. For the concept of mystery, and philosophy's engagement with it, is not a matter of a position, or an argument. It is not an assertion of a fact, say, that there is a God, to be argued for or against. The question that mystery poses is asked and answered somewhere other than in the intellect, although our reasoning plays a role in the process. In the end, the concept of mystery concerns the very question of depth and meaning and goodness in life, and is, despite being displayed and represented by arguments, something that lies at the very heart of the human being's activity as a living being. It is, perhaps even better put as what the question of depth and meaning and goodness *is* in human life, a question that stands behind all the rest of our subsequent reasoning.

How this is so may be seen by looking briefly at Weil's essay, "Some reflections around the concept of value,"[27] which contains numerous points that illumine Weil's thinking, particularly on what philosophy is. In doing so, I am assuming that depth and meaning and goodness can be translated into what one may call the concept of value. If so, we can then proceed to note her assertion at the outset of the essay that "the concept of value is at the center of philosophy. All reflection bearing on the notion of value and on the hierarchy of values is philosophical; all efforts of thought bearing on anything other than value are, if one examines them closely, foreign to philosophy."[28] Leaving aside here the argument of who is really a philosopher and who is not, we can simply concentrate on what Weil lays out as to how we think about value and all that it involves.

Philosophizing about value, trying to get clear about what is valuable and what is not, is very different from the pursuit of any other kind of knowledge, and involves certain deep problems. On the one hand, it is a matter of finding a means of judging between values, as the search for knowledge in other areas is also finding a means for judging. It requires comparing and contrasting different values. But this assumes that we can take a distanced, cool and hypothetical attitude to value. The problem is we cannot be indifferent on this score; "a value is something that one admits unconditionally. At the moment when it directs our actions, our system of values is not accepted with conditions or provisionally or reflec- tively; it is purely and simply accepted."[29] Thus Weil contends, with a hint of paradox, that values are "unknowable." This is simply to say that every- thing else that we know, and therefore knowledge itself, is "hypothetical" or, we might say, contingent; it depends on links to other demonstrations and other facts. So if that is what "knowable" means, then values are not knowable.

Yet, Weil goes on, one ought not to conclude that values are irrational, or mere emotional statements of idiosyncratic preference, as A. J. Ayer tried to claim was the case with ethics because ethics could not be shown to fit the epistemological principles of positivism. "One cannot give up on knowing them, for giving up would mean giving up on believing in them, which is impossible, because human life always has a direction."[30] Thus, she contends, "at the center of human life is a contradiction,"[31] a contradiction that is at the heart of the philosophical enterprise, that is, the search for value. The contradiction is that on the one hand, we need as searchers not to be prejudiced in our search; on the other hand, that we are searching at all means that we have committed to some value, and stand on it absolutely. (If we did not think it absolute, it would not really be a value for us. If we really thought it were better than what we currently accept, we would make it ours. The price of doing otherwise would be to destroy moral thinking, for we would then deliberately choose the worse over the better—because we thought it was better!)

So how do we approach value? How do we change from the worse to the better? If philosophy were simply a matter of presenting arguments and devising ethical systems, we would probably have little hope of it doing anything for us on this score. For the most part, it would simply be rather sophisticated advocacy, or poetics, or simply sophistry. So even though we do not give up on reason or argument, a very different sort of attitude is required, a different sort of reflection, one that demands detachment. This detachment is radical, and it is a radical openness. "Detachment is a renunciation of all possible ends without exception, a renunciation which puts a void in the place of the future just as the imminent approach of death does."[32]

For numerous reasons, Weil sees this detachment as something that borders on the miraculous, and as a matter of grace. For example, it has to be the supreme value, but in order to be that, all other values have to be set aside already. But what at least is clear is that philosophy as Weil wants to take it, namely as a search for transforming value, is not an accumulation of knowledge, but a radical disposition to knowledge. It is a matter of attention, which she famously defines as demanding detachment and availability. It is a willingness to live with the contradictions of life, and not to force them, just as Wittgenstein argued that we should not force the grammar of one way of speaking about the world upon another. What the world is, is in all the ways we have spoken about it, and we should not choose one grammar over another. That restraint is not logical, it is moral, for it is a matter of respecting what is given to us. Thus we are to gaze upon the world, and wait upon it in order to be transformed, in order to move from the worse to the better, from the mediocre to the excellent, from the nice to the good. As Foster had argued with respect to the somewhat narrower question of biblical revelation, what is required here is an attitude that lets us be spoken to, and an attitude where our listening takes into our hearts what we hear, and lets it change us and transform us. Any other attitude is simply moving within the confines of our own reading.

A Philosophical Life

I have already suggested some ways in which the concept of mystery is important in the contemporary world. Our obsession with technique and method, and the resulting flatness, the monodimensional aspect this obsession gives to life, are reasons enough to take the concept of mystery seriously in philosophical life. But in concluding I want to confine myself to saying something more about this idea of transformation, of moving towards greater depth and meaning. In doing so, just as I relied on another philosopher, Michael Foster, to introduce the issues surrounding the concept of mystery, so I now want to rely on another to help illustrate this issue of depth and to locate it.

In his recent work, *A Secular Age*, Charles Taylor has examined from just about every perspective possible what it means to say that we live in a secular age. In the end, it is not a matter of saying that belief and the religious have actually disappeared. However, belief can no longer be assumed and religion is questioned as a matter of course. We just don't think any more that it cannot be questioned, and even if we are of the committed faithful, we are not surprised and shocked by our friends and relatives who might think differently. Now, a good part of Taylor's exposition is dedicated to explaining how this has come about. In part it has been because science has, indeed, contested certain religious claims. But science, Taylor has argued, is not solely responsible for the secular turn of mind. Religions themselves have contributed more and more to it, as they defended themselves against criticism by moving in a more and more immanentist direction. They bought the viewpoint of their critics, and ceased to look to their own original transcendent and transforming core. For example, one well-rehearsed way of defending Christianity is to talk of its civilizing effects, of what it has contributed to the culture—in short, to talk about it largely as a form of crowd control. As Taylor points out, the transcendent aspect, the deep moral challenge of biblical religion, is lost in this interpretation. Or, spirituality becomes "excarnated" in Taylor's phrase: "the steady disembodying of spiritual life, so that it is less and less carried in deeply meaningful bodily forms, and lies more and more 'in the head.'"[33] The challenge to any deep transformation of life is lost; in "identifying the Christian life with a life lived in conformity with the norms of our civilization, we lost sight of the further, greater transformation which Christian faith holds out, the raising of the human life to divine (*theiosis*)."[34]

Often when people first encounter Weil, they do so with respect to her extraordinary biography. The more and more that I consider Taylor's comments, the more and more I have come to realize how important the extraordinary and even bizarre elements of Weil's life are as showing the depth of her life. They indicate, as Susan Sontag suggested many years ago, a seriousness about life that is sadly lacking in a monodimensional world. Sontag suggested that while admiring this seriousness, we do not need to follow her example.[35] In numerous particulars, perhaps not. I think Weil herself knew that there was a certain pathology in some of her aspirations. But that should not blind us to the fact that her own thinking was not "excarnated"; it really is an example of living a philosophical life. The philosophical life, which is what a serious life lived in a world surrounded by mystery is, is always an extraordinary life, and one that will never fit into the common unexamined goals set out by method. A serious life, a philosophical life, is one that is revealing of the great depth and goodness that is open to the human spirit if only it will let itself be spoken to, and if only it will look attentively.

Notes

[1] Michael Foster, *Mystery and Philosophy* (Westport, CT: Greenwood Press, 1980; London: SCM Press, 1957). Citations are from the Greenwood Press edition.

[2] A. Flew and A. MacIntyre, eds. (London: Macmillan, 1955). To be sure, the volume contained essays by able defenders of religion. Yet, it still seems that even they were responding to a formidable case laid against religion, and that the burden of proof was being laid on them.

[3] Foster, *Mystery and Philosophy*, 11.

[4] Ibid., 18.

[5] Ibid., 17.

[6] See *Mystery of Being* (South Bend: Gateway, 1950) Vol. I, "Reflection and Mystery," 211–2.

[7] Foster, *Mystery and Philosophy*, 20.

[8] Ibid., 27.

[9] Ibid., 88.

[10] Ibid.

[11] Charles Taylor, *A Secular Age* (Cambridge: Harvard University Press, 2007), 734.

[12] E.g., in *Letter to a Priest* § 26, 27, 28; NB, 238–9.

[13] GTG, 113.

[14] GTG, 118.

[15] SWW, 110.

[16] SWW, 110; FLN, 131.

[17] Obviously, this is said from the assumption that this is true.

[18] GTG, 93.

[19] For a fuller discussion of this see my *Christus Mediator: Platonic Mediation in the Thought of Simone Weil* (Chico: Scholars Press, 1983); E. O. Springsted,

"Contradiction, mystery and the use of words in Simone Weil," in *The Beauty that Saves*, ed. J. Dunaway and E. O. Springsted (Macon: Mercer University Press, 1996); and Vance Morgan, *Weaving the World* (Notre Dame: University of Notre Dame Press, 2005).

[20] NB, 162.

[21] See my "Théorie weilienne et théorie platonicienne de la necessité," *Cahiers Simone Weil* Vol. IV, No. 3 (1981).

[22] "Reflections autour de la notion de la valeur," OC IV.1, 59.

[23] "With respect to the completed systems constructed with the intention of eliminating all the essential contradictions of thought, we see that they do have value, but only as poetry" (OC IV.1, 60).

[24] *Tractatus Logico-Philosophicus* (London: Routledge & Kegan Paul: 1961), 151.

[25] GTG, 118.

[26] FLN, 145–8.

[27] This essay, which we have already quoted, has only recently been published in French and has not been translated. Its existence has, though, not been a secret. The chief reason it would seem that it has not been published until recently is that it was not a completed essay.

[28] OC.IV.1, 54.

[29] OC IV.1, 55.

[30] OC IV.1, 55.

[31] OC IV.1, 55.

[32] OC IV.1, 57.

[33] Taylor, *A Secular Age*, 771.

[34] Ibid., 737.

[35] Susan Sontag, "Simone Weil," in *Against Interpretation* (New York: Farrar, Straus & Giroux, 1961), 50.

Part Two

Radical World

Chapter 7

Miracles and Supernatural Physics: Simone Weil on the Relationship of Science and Religion

Vance G. Morgan

Fact and Value

Given the proliferation in the last several years of publications concerning the relationship of science and religion, it is hard to imagine that Simone Weil, writing 60 years ago, would have much to contribute to this important discussion. It is my aim in this essay to argue that Weil's frequent remarks on the relationship between science and faith are not only important, but also provide a timely contribution to the current debate by describing a metaphysical framework for the discussion entirely different than those generally preferred by current participants in the dialogue.

Writing during the last few months of her life, in the midst of World War Two, Weil argues that "the modern conception of science is responsible, as is that of history and that of art, for the monstrous conditions under which we live, and will, in its turn, have to be transformed, before we can hope to see the dawn of a better civilization."[1] In our contemporary world, science and religion have become almost entirely disconnected, producing not only a vacuum where values once existed, but also an intense psychological and intellectual distress.

The absolute incompatibility between the spirit of religion and that of science . . . leaves the soul in a permanent state of secret, unacknowledged uneasiness . . . The most fervent Christians express every hour of their lives judgments, opinions, which, unknown to them, are based on standards which go contrary to the spirit of Christianity. But the

most disastrous consequence of this uneasiness is to make it impossible
for the virtue of intellectual probity to be exercised to the fullest extent
. . . The modern phenomenon of irreligion among the population can
be explained almost entirely by the incompatibility between science
and religion.[2]

In Weil's estimation, the response to many contemporary crises must be
rooted in a reawakened understanding of the necessary connection
between true science and religion. "The remedy is to bring back again
among us the spirit of truth, and to start with in [sic] religion and science; which implies that the two of them should become reconciled."[3]

Fast forward to the present. Bookstores are full of books and periodi-
cals that would seem to be the bearers of good tidings; the relationship
of science and religion has never been more *en vogue*. It appears that on
some level a real dialogue between science and religion is going on.
What is the nature of that dialogue, however? Does our current intellectual fascination with the relationship of science and religion respond, at
any meaningful level, to Weil's call for a reconciliation between religion
and science?

I suspect not. As one example of a contemporary approach to the relationship between science and religion, consider one of the late Stephen
Jay Gould's final publications, a short book entitled *Rocks of Ages*. This
book is of particular interest because Gould, one of the most highly
respected scientists of his generation, was a self-described agnostic Jew
who had "great respect for religion."[4] Gould begins the book as follows:

I write this little book to present a blessedly simple and entirely conventional resolution to an issue so laden with emotion and the burden
of history that a clear path usually becomes overgrown by a tangle of
contention and confusion. I speak of the supposed conflict between
science and religion, a debate that exists only in people's minds and
social practices.[5]

Gould's "blessedly simple" resolution of this conflict proposes a "central
principle of respectful noninterference"[6] between religion and science.
This "noninterference" should be "accompanied by intense dialogue
between the two distinct subjects, each covering a central fact of human
existence."[7] Gould calls his noninterference principle the "Principle of
Non-Overlapping Magisteria" (NOMA), with "magisterium" defined as
"a domain where one form of teaching holds the appropriate tools for

meaningful discourse and resolution."[8] As Gould describes it, "NOMA represents a principled position on moral and intellectual grounds, not a merely diplomatic solution,"[9] advocating a continuing "mutual humility" amongst both scientists and religious thinkers.

At its core, the NOMA principle is rooted in the distinction between fact and value, between what is the case and what ought to be the case.

> The net, or magisterium, of science covers the empirical realm: what is the universe made of (fact) and why does it work this way (theory). The magisterium of religion extends over questions of ultimate meaning and moral value. These two magisteria do not overlap, nor do they encompass all inquiry . . . To cite the old clichés, science gets the age of rocks, and religion the rock of ages; science studies how the heavens go, religion how to go to heaven.[10]

Just as one cannot play the game of baseball according to the rules of cricket (and vice versa), so the players of the games of science and religion must respect the independence, even sanctity, of games radically different from their own. "If religion can no longer dictate the nature of factual conclusions residing properly within the magisterium of science, then scientists cannot claim higher insight into moral truth from any superior knowledge of the world's empirical constitution."[11]

Gould is honest enough to admit (in a footnote) that his unquestioning assumption that fact and value must be sharply separated looks like a blatant example of assuming what needs to be proven in "an old and difficult topic."[12] Whether or not such a sharp distinction can or should be drawn between fact and value is precisely the philosophical issue that must be addressed when investigating the relationship of science and religion. Despite, however, his allowing that "if an academic outsider made a similarly curt pronouncement about a subtle and troubling issue in my field of evolution or paleontology, I'd be pissed off,"[13] Gould argues that fact and value are so different in kind that the governing magisteria for each, science and religion, must adopt mutual stances of "respectful noninterference."

Simone Weil clearly would have rejected such a conclusion concerning the relationship of science and religion. In *The Need for Roots*, she asks: "How should there be any opposition or even separation between the spirit of science and that of religion? Scientific investigation is simply a form of religious contemplation."[14] Weil insists that we must begin with the conviction that there is a foundational unity to truth that cuts across all seemingly impenetrable barriers between perceived magisteria. One page prior to the above quote, Weil writes that

> The spirit of truth can dwell in science on condition that the motive prompting the scientist is the love of the object which forms the stuff of his investigations. That object is the universe in which we live. What can we find to love about it, if it isn't its beauty? The true definition of science is this: the study of the beauty of the world.[15]

Weil would agree with Gould that a value-free conception of scientific inquiry is undoubtedly the favored paradigm in our contemporary world. This conception, however, is highly problematic.

> Since the Renaissance . . . the very conception of science has been that of a branch of study whose object is placed beyond good and evil, especially beyond good; viewed without any relation either to good or evil, but especially without any relation to good . . . Facts, force, matter, isolated, considered singly, without reference to anything else—there is nothing here that a human mind can love.[16]

Weil frequently warns that we divorce fact sharply from value at our extreme peril. Science cannot simply restrict itself to gathering and analyzing data for the purpose of manipulating future experience; the effort of understanding human experience is value-laden from the start.

> All thought is an effort of interpretation of experience, and experience provides neither model nor rule nor criterion for the interpretation; it provides the data of problems but not a way of solving or even of formulating them. This effort requires, like all other efforts, to be oriented towards something . . . [Man] cannot do without values. For all theoretical study the name of value is truth.[17]

According to Weil, "present-day scientists have nothing in their minds, however vague, remote, arbitrary, or improbable, which they can turn towards and call it truth."[18] Given that science has become the contemporary oracular authority, the notion of truth itself has disappeared. Since something must fill this vacuum, since human effort must be directed towards something, the purpose of science becomes utility and power—a dangerous prospect.

Utility becomes something which the intelligence is no longer entitled to define or to judge, but only to serve. From being the arbiter, intelligence becomes the servant, and it gets its orders from the desires. And, further, public opinion then replaces conscience as sovereign mistress of thoughts, because man always submits his thoughts to some higher control, which is superior either in value or else in power. That is where we are today.[19]

Without overestimation, it can be said that Weil's overriding concern in her lifelong thinking on science was to consider how science might be reconceived in such a way as to repair the devastating rupture between fact and value.

My primary concern in this paper is to investigate what happens to the relationship between science and religion if one refuses, as Weil does, to separate them into distinct magisteria. Gould argues effectively that both religion and science can survive and even thrive if they are kept apart, arguing at the same time that the failure to keep them separate opens us to the likelihood that both domains will be irreparably damaged. The history of what happens when religion and science are not kept separate would seem to justify Gould's concerns. Weil, however, will argue that science and religion can indeed be unified if we pay close attention to what both science and religion really are. The heart of her position can be revealed through an investigation of miracles.

Science and Miracles

In her Marseille notebook, Simone Weil writes that "the stories about miracles confuse everything."[20] In an era in which "the scientific conception of the world predominates,"[21] there is no place for miracles. Hence in the minds and hearts of many religious persons, for whom miracles supposedly play a foundational role in terms of belief, a schizophrenic cognitive split results. One possible way to address this split, prescribed by Gould, is to embrace it as reflective of incommensurable magisteria. Miracles have an important place in the magisterium of religion, but no place in the magisterium of science. Weil, however, argues in *The Need for Roots* that "the problem of miracles only causes difficulty between religion and science because it is badly presented. To present it properly, it is necessary to give a definition of a miracle."[22]

Many contemporary thinkers believe the definitive philosophical treatment of the topic of miracles is contained in Section X of David Hume's *An Enquiry Concerning Human Understanding*. Hume writes that

> A miracle is a violation of the laws of nature; and as a firm and unalterable experience has established these laws, the proof against a miracle, from the very nature of the fact, is as entire as any argument from experience can possibly be imagined.[23]

Stephen Jay Gould expands this definition slightly to reveal clearly why miracles have the potential to "confuse everything" when considering the relationship of science and religion. Gould defines a miracle as "a unique and temporary suspension of natural law to reorder the facts of nature by divine fiat."[24] Those who believe in miracles defined in this way are projecting a belief from religion into science in a way that has great potential to violate the independence of both magisteria.

Weil argues that this standard definition of miracles is essentially meaningless:

> To say that [a miracle] is a fact contrary to the laws of nature is to say something completely devoid of significance. We do not know what the laws of nature are. We can only make suppositions in regard to them. If the laws we suppose are contradicted by facts, it shows that our supposition was at any rate in part erroneous.[25]

This pronouncement is surprising, to say the least. The task of science, after all, is through regular observation and continual experimentation to progressively and precisely describe the laws that underlie the behavior of the physical world. Because we believe that science has largely accomplished this task, we are uncomfortable with miracles; by definition, miracles are a violation of what we believe we know best, the laws of nature. On what basis, then, can Weil possibly dismiss our confidence in scientific inquiry by saying that "we do not know what the laws of nature are"?

Simply put, Weil is challenging contemporary science's hubristic assumption that it has so clearly identified the laws of nature that it can confidently dismiss reports of any events that appear to violate these laws. Writing 40 years after Weil, Thomas Nagel describes such "scientism" as follows:

> At its most myopic [scientism] assumes that everything there is must be understandable by the employment of scientific theories like those

we have developed to date—physics and evolutionary biology are the current paradigms—as if the present age were not just another in the series . . . Too many hypotheses and systems of thought in philosophy and elsewhere are based on the bizarre view that we, at this point in history, are in possession of the basic forms of understanding needed to comprehend absolutely anything.[26]

The hubristic response to reported events that violate the laws of nature is a denial that the reports are true, since we already "know" what the laws of nature are. Weil, however, asks us to take an entirely different attitude towards such reports. Rather than rejecting a miracle as a violation of the laws of nature, we must embrace such an event as pointing towards a necessary expansion of our understanding of what these laws are.

Few thinkers have ever been more convinced than Weil that we live in an entirely law-governed universe. Miracles are not violations of these laws; instead, they are crucially important reminders that our knowledge of the laws of nature is incomplete. When we encounter reports of miracles, such as in the Gospels, we should approach these reports with the same scientific rigor as we approach reports of less rare phenomena. Weil suggests that "one could find in the Gospels . . . what one might call a supernatural physics of the human soul."[27] As in any science, only credible and verifiable evidence is permissible in such a supernatural physics; the strangeness of the data requires that the reporter be exceptionally trustworthy.

Here verification takes the form of the march towards perfection, and consequently one has to accept the word of those who have accomplished it. But we readily accept the word of the scientists, without the least check, concerning what takes place in their laboratories, although we don't know at all whether they love truth. It would be more reasonable to accept the word of the saints, at least of all the genuine ones, for it is certain they have a whole-hearted love of truth.[28]

Miracles thus "enter naturally into the scientific conception of the world,"[29] and the gap between religion and science begins to close.

Miracles are remarkable primarily because they exhibit exceptionally rare physical phenomena. Suppose for a moment that reports of such phenomena are factually correct—what might be the cause of such events? Weil suggests that the unusual physical event is objective evidence of an equally unusual spiritual state.

It is in no way contrary to the laws of nature that a total abandonment of the soul to either good or evil should be accompanied by physical phenomena which are only produced in such a case . . . For every attitude of the human soul is accompanied by a certain particular physical state . . . If the mystical ecstasy corresponds to something real in the soul, it must be accompanied in the body by phenomena which are not observable when the soul is in a different state. The connection between mystical ecstasy and these phenomena is formed by a mechanism similar to that which connects tears with sorrow. We know nothing about the first mechanism. But we don't know any more about the second one.[30]

Accordingly, "miracle" requires a redefinition that will place such phenomena squarely within the realm of the laws of nature. Weil suggests that "a miracle is a physical phenomenon necessitating as one of its prerequisites a total abandonment of the soul either to good or to evil;"[31] in her notebooks, she provides a similar definition:

A miracle is a natural phenomenon which only happens with a man who finds himself in this, that or the other particular state. States likely to produce such phenomena are: sainthood, hysteria, self-mastery brought about by asceticism, and others besides perhaps.[32]

Miracles are to be carefully considered, not because of their unusual physical manifestations, but because of what they reveal concerning the accompanying state of the soul.

To illustrate, consider briefly one of the most familiar miracles reported in the Gospels, Jesus's walking on water. Here is St Matthew's version of the story:

But the boat was now in the middle of the sea, tossed by the waves, for the wind was contrary. Now in the fourth watch of the night Jesus went to them, walking on the sea. And when the disciples saw Him walking on the sea, they were troubled, saying, "It is a ghost!" And they cried out for fear. But immediately Jesus spoke to them, saying, "Be of good cheer! It is I; do not be afraid." And Peter answered Him and said, "Lord, if it is You, command me to come to You on the water." So He said, "Come." And when Peter had come down out of the boat, he walked on the water to go to Jesus. But when he saw that the wind was boisterous, he was afraid; and beginning to sink he cried out, saying,

"Lord, save me!" And immediately Jesus stretched out His hand and caught him, and said to him, "Oh ye of little faith, why did you doubt?"[33]

Suppose, for the sake of argument, that this story is true. Using the traditional definition of miracle, Jesus and Peter have both violated the laws of nature. A believer might say that Jesus did so because He is God and can suspend the laws of nature at will. Peter is able to walk on the water because Jesus temporarily suspended the laws of nature for him; when that temporary suspension ceased, the laws of nature took over and Peter began to sink.

Consider the same story interpreted according to Weil's entirely different definition of a miracle. Now the actions of both Jesus and Peter are entirely within the laws of nature, but laws largely unknown because they are only revealed under highly unusual circumstances. The unusual circumstances are much the same for Jesus and Peter—each finds himself in a heightened spiritual state (which we might call faith, the absence of fear, or, for the sake of simplicity, State X) uniquely joined to a specific physical state (walking on water). Jesus, on the one hand, who is "outside the ordinary run of humanity,"[34] is in State X (or some similarly unusual spiritual state) regularly, frequently producing unusual physical manifestations, such as walking on water. Peter, on the other hand, is presumably squarely within "the ordinary run of humanity"; hence, this may very well be the first time he has ever been in State X. In that state, he is also capable of the accompanying physical act, walking on water. The cause of his being in State X (faith, a heightened recognition of the beauty and goodness of Jesus, or simply an intense emotional reaction to the storm and the apparition on the water) is fleeting. When Peter is no longer in State X, he can no longer walk on water. Jesus's response to Peter's near-drowning is instructive: "Oh ye of little faith, why did you doubt?" Nothing about either State X or walking on water is outside the natural realm; only the fear and doubt that accompany the ordinary existence of ordinary human beings make walking on water appear to be a violation of the laws of nature.

In Weil's estimation, then, penetrating the sharp barrier between science and religion, between fact and value, begins with a deliberate rejection of scientific hubris. In a world in which natural laws govern both the physical and spiritual realm, fact and value are no longer distinctly separate. The problem of miracles, however, is not entirely solved by the establishment of a healthy scientific humility. Weil recognizes that traditional religious interpretations of miracles are equally fraught with problems that contribute to the apparent incommensurability between science and religion.

Miracles and Divine Providence

One of Simone Weil's many important contributions to discussions of both science and theology is her intense focus on the inexorable necessity of the world, the obedience of matter to fixed natural laws, productive of natural beauty and reflective of the divine itself. In *The Need for Roots*, she draws our attention to this conception of God's relationship to the world in the Gospels.

> The conception of an impersonal Providence, and one in a sense almost analogous to a mechanism, is also to be found there [in the Gospels] . . . "He maketh his sun to rise on the evil and on the good, and sendeth rain on the just and on the unjust" (Matthew 5.45) . . . It is that which is held up as a model of perfection to the human soul.[35]

Many of Jesus' parables emphasize this impersonal aspect of divine Providence. In the parable of the sower,[36] for instance, the seed is scattered with seemingly little regard for where it falls. The failure or success of the seed is a function of neither the sower nor the seed; rather, it is a function of the ground upon which the seed falls. "Grace descends from God upon all beings; what becomes of it depends on what they are . . . The non-intervention of God in the operation of grace is expressed as clearly as it possibly can be."[37] If the ground is good, the seed will flourish according to an entirely natural mechanism. The same is true of the spiritual fruit of the seed of divine grace:

> Supernatural mechanisms are at least as dependable as are the laws of gravity; but natural mechanisms are the conditions necessary for producing events as such, without regard being had for any consideration of value; whereas supernatural mechanisms are the conditions necessary for producing pure good as such.[38]

Weil argues that, for a number of reasons, the impersonal aspect of divine Providence has ceased to have any central place in contemporary religious conceptions of God. Now divine Providence is understood only as what Weil calls a "personal Providence":

[This] conception of Providence . . . is that of a personal intervention in the world on the part of God in order to adjust certain means in view of certain ends . . . God violates the natural order of the world so as to bring about therein, not what he wishes to produce, but causes which will produce what he wishes to produce by way of a result.[39]

According to this conception of a personal Providence, the world works according to natural, mechanical laws except on those occasions when God chooses to produce certain effects that would not have been produced within the natural flow of events. A miracle then becomes "the effect of a particular act of volition on the part of God,"[40] a conception "no less absurd," in Weil's estimation, than the definition analyzed in the previous section that a miracle is a violation of the laws of nature.

Why might God occasionally impose causes that violate the laws of nature? One reason might be for their epistemological impact. If God is seeking to convince unbelievers to believe, or to strengthen the belief of uncertain believers, what better vehicle than a spectacularly unusual event caused by divine intervention in the natural workings of the universe? Weil spends little time dismissing this suggestion. It is clear that even Jesus did not intend miracles to serve such a purpose. He frequently refused to perform miracles "on command," and often told his disciples and others not to spread reports of miracles indiscriminately. Seemingly, Jesus did not seek to "seduce" unbelievers into belief through miracles.

For Weil, Jesus's miracles are evidence of the state of his soul, a state that regularly produced physical manifestations that were out of the ordinary. The purpose of such acts is not to cause persons to believe; rather, "the exceptional character of the acts had no other object than to draw attention. Once the attention has been drawn, there can be no other form of proof than beauty, purity, perfection."[41] Any number of things can attract such attention, from the beauty of the world to our fellow human beings (even those who are "of the ordinary run"). In short, the epistemological value of miracles is minimal. They are signposts, but they carry no special value other than as evidence of states of being that can serve as pathways to beauty. "From the religious point of view the miracles are of secondary importance."[42]

To define a miracle as "the effect of a particular act of volition on the part of God" is to err in the same manner as those who define miracles as "a fact contrary to the laws of nature." Just as we do not know with complete certainty what the laws of nature are, and therefore have no way of knowing which facts violate such laws, so we have no basis upon which to select certain events, as opposed to others, as special results of God's volition.

Amidst all the events which take place, we have no right to maintain that certain of them rather than others are the result of God's will. All we know, in a general way, is that everything which happens, without any exception, is in accordance with the will of God considered as Creator.[43]

As Weil writes elsewhere, "the particular designs that are attributed to God are cuttings made by us from out of the more than infinite complexity of causal connections."[44]

Most challenging in Weil's analysis here is the claim that "everything which happens, *without any exception*, is in accordance with the will of God." We know from experience that the harm and suffering that are frequently the result of natural events happen to all persons regardless of their moral and spiritual status. An impersonal Providence, embodied in the events of the natural world, apparently obliterates the moral distinction between the just and the unjust. What are we to make of "that relentless regularity characterizing the order of the world, completely indifferent to men's individual quality, and because of this so frequently accused of injustice"?[45] It is this aspect of the natural world that most frequently causes human beings to question the nature and intentions of the Creator.

The bitterest reproach that men make of this necessity is its absolute indifference to moral values. Righteous men and criminals receive an equal share of the benefits of the sun and of the rain; the righteous and the criminals equally suffer sunstroke, and drowning in floods.[46]

Why do the good suffer? Why do the evil prosper? Should we not expect God to disrupt the natural order in a special way (through a miracle) in order to protect those most deserving from the harm and affliction that frequently accompany the natural order?

One of Weil's favorite examples of the natural complaints arising from the indifference of the order of the world is the story of Job. Job, characterized by all (including God) as a righteous man, suffers a seemingly endless succession of disasters, mostly caused by natural events. The question, of course, is "Why?" The response of Job's wife and friends is that he must have committed some secret sin or sins to incur God's wrath, since (obviously) God would protect a truly righteous person from the natural disasters that have befallen Job. Job, however, steadfastly denies that any such secret transgressions occurred.

Weil argues that the response of Job's "comforters" is rooted in "the ridiculous conception of Providence as being a personal and particular intervention on the part of God for certain particular ends."[47] This conception presumes that while the necessity revealed in the order of the world is indeed reflective of God's general will, those who are righteous or specially favored will in some way be miraculously protected from the blind forces of necessity that frequently afflict others. The absence of such protection is then evidence of the lack of special favor. Weil insists instead that the correct conception of divine Providence is that of "an eternal and universal dispensation constituting the foundation of an invariable order in the world."[48] By understanding that the inexorable order of the world is *itself* reflective of divine Providence, we can begin to bring the scientific and theological conceptions of the order of the world into line. The impartiality of the natural order is, in a real and profound sense, divine Providence itself.

Divine Providence is not a disturbing influence, an anomaly in the ordering of the world: it is itself the order of the world; or rather it is the regulating principle of this universe. It is eternal Wisdom, unique, spread across the whole universe in a sovereign network of relations.[49]

The necessary order of the world, expressed through mathematical regularity, is itself the will of God. "The sum of the particular intentions of God is the universe itself."[50]

Weil's understanding of Divine Providence arises from her understanding of the divine creative act, an act generated from love rather than an expression of power. God's supreme act of love, the creation of the world, literally requires God's absence from the world, since if God did not withdraw from creation, "there would be nothing but himself."[51] Hence, "the absence of God is the most marvelous testimony of perfect love, and that is why pure necessity, necessity which is manifestly different from good, is beautiful."[52] This necessity, embodied in the inexorable physical laws of the universe, often produces events that appear to be evil to our human sensibilities. They are, however, manifestations of divine love.

Relentless necessity, wretchedness, distress, the crushing burden of poverty and of labor which wears us out, cruelty, torture, violent death, constraint, disease—all these constitute divine love. It is God who in love withdraws from us so that we can love him . . . Necessity is the screen set between God and us so that we can be.[53]

Weil uses miracles to illustrate how our contemporary conceptions of the natural order, both from scientific and religious perspectives, must be significantly changed if science and religion are to be unified. In her estimation, both science and religion misunderstand miracles because they fail to grasp that the natural order is a prime expression, perhaps *the* prime expression, of divine presence. In conclusion, I return to Weil's most developed expression in *The Need for Roots* of the contemporary disconnect between science and faith.

The ridiculous conception of Providence as being a personal and particular intervention on the part of God for certain particular ends is incompatible with true faith . . . Christians who, under the influence of education and surroundings, carry within them this conception of Providence, also carry within them the scientific conception of the world, and that divides their minds into two water-tight compartments . . . This makes it impossible for them really to think either the one or the other . . . Unbelievers, not being inhibited by any motives of reverence, detect easily enough the ridiculous aspect of this personal and particular form of Providence, and religious faith itself is, on account of it, made to seem ridiculous in their eyes.[54]

The walls of the "water-tight" compartments of science and faith can begin to break down from the religious side when divine Providence is understood as having its primary expression in the natural order, not in the intervening and intentional violation of natural laws. From the scientific side, the walls break down when we see that while our conviction that nature is law-governed is correct, our belief that we know (in totality) what those laws are is entirely false. Apparent violations of the laws of nature are expressive of the greatest miracle of all: a universe created by, and expressive of, divine love. Understood in this way, science and religion are companions, open-ended investigations of that love united by the belief that "Providence is the proper subject for science,"[55] since "the world is God's language to us. The universe is the word of God, the *Verbum.*"[56]

Notes

1 NR, 235.
2 NR, 244.
3 NR, 258.
4 Stephen Jay Gould, *Rocks of Ages* (New York: Library of Contemporary Thought, 1999), 8.
5 Ibid., 3.
6 Ibid., 5.
7 Ibid.
8 Ibid.
9 Ibid., 9.
10 Ibid., 6.
11 Ibid., 9–10.
12 Ibid., 55.
13 Ibid., 56.
14 NR, 259.
15 NR, 258.
16 NR, 251.
17 SN, 62.
18 SN, 62.
19 SN, 63–4.
20 NB, 243.
21 NB, 243.
22 NR, 263.
23 David Hume, *An Enquiry Concerning Human Understanding* (Indianapolis: Hackett Publishing Co., 1977), 76.
24 Gould, *Rocks of Ages*, 85.
25 NR, 263.
26 Thomas Nagel, *The View From Nowhere* (Oxford: Oxford University Press, 1986), 9–10.
27 NR, 262.
28 NR, 262–3.
29 NR, 266.
30 NR, 264.
31 NR, 263.
32 NB, 243.
33 Matthew 14.24–31, New King James Version.
34 NR, 265.
35 NR, 260.
36 Matthew 13.3–8.
37 NR, 260.
38 NR, 261.
39 NR, 276.
40 NR, 263.
41 NR, 266.
42 NR, 266.

[43] NR, 263.
[44] NR, 279.
[45] NR, 260.
[46] IC, 184.
[47] NR, 279.
[48] NR, 268.
[49] NR, 281.
[50] NR, 280.
[51] GG, 33.
[52] GG, 96.
[53] GG, 28.
[54] NR, 279.
[55] NB, 263.
[56] NB, 480.

Chapter 8

Simone Weil's Analysis of Modern Science as the Basis of Her Critique of the Technological Society

Lawrence E. Schmidt

Arthur C. Clarke, the well-known science-fiction author, once wrote: "Any sufficiently advanced technology is indistinguishable from magic."[1] The truth of this comment is confirmed in our everyday experience. We write on our word processors, we are entertained by our DVDs, and we communicate by e-mail on our Blackberries; we stand in awe of what technology enables us to do. Although most of us have only a superficial understanding of the scientific principles operative in these devices, they magically enable us to be more efficient, creative or competent. Clarke's comment was not a criticism; it was used with approbation, and without irony.

Technology is self-evidently good in our society; it is after all the source of our productivity, and it accounts for our affluence and enhances our freedom. It is generally argued that any given technique may be used for evil purposes, but it is the purposes which are unethical, not the technique itself. A car may be used for transportation, for fornication or for murder. It may be more or less efficient for any of these purposes but, according to the commonly held view, the purpose will determine whether our use of the car is good. It is also admitted that the cumulative effects of a range of techniques may be negative (for example, environmental degradation), but the conclusion drawn is not that there is anything fundamentally wrong with the technological system, but that individual techniques should be perfected and the negative effects eliminated or minimized.

Nevertheless, as the problems which accompany the emergence of a full-blown technological society became more apparent and more menacing in the twentieth century, writers like Jacques Ellul[2] in France,

Langdon Winner[3] in the United States, E. F. Schumacher[4] in England, and George Grant[5] and Ursula Franklin[6] in Canada, called this common understanding and evaluation of technology into question.[7] Simone Weil anticipated their critique in her social and political writings of the Depression era. It is not the purpose of this chapter to elaborate the full depth of Weil's social critique. My purpose is rather to examine Weil's analysis of modern science. She argued that it was the source of our social problems, and was in need of radical reform before any positive social change could be effected.

Weil based her criticism of modern science and technology on its "magical" quality. In the early thirties, before she undertook her work in Paris factories, she wrote:

The more scientific progress accumulates ready-made combinations of signs, the more the mind is weighed down, made powerless to draw up an inventory of the ideas which it handles. Of course, the connection between the formulas thus worked out and the practical applications of them is often itself, too, completely impenetrable to the mind, with the result that it appears as fortuitous as the efficacy of a magic formula. In such a case work finds itself automatic, as it were, to the second power; it is not simply the execution, it is also the elaboration of the method which takes place outside the control of mind.[8]

She therefore contended that modern science was laying the groundwork for political tyranny because, paradoxically, it was creating a more and more unintelligible (and therefore irrational) social world. In such a world, human beings would find it increasingly difficult to act in a reasonable or ethical way. The essential relationship between action (or labor) and thought in human life was being destroyed by modern science. In the process, so was human liberty.

For Weil, as James Calder has explained,[9] labor or work is the foundation of human culture. "The secret of the human condition," she wrote in her *First Notebook*, "is that equilibrium between man and the surrounding forces of nature which 'infinitely surpass him' cannot be achieved by inaction; it is only achieved in the action by which man recreates his own life: that is to say, by work."[10] In order to continue to live within nature we must make or bring forth things which will guarantee our survival: food, clothing, shelter. But nature is in a constant process of change or becoming. Human language functions to fix, determine and define nature so that human beings can relate to and manage it.

Language is both indispensable and inadequate to the representation and the understanding of our experience of nature. For Simone Weil, reality or truth is attained not in language alone, nor in labor or human activity, but it arises out of a particular relation of the two, which gives rise to thought. Language provides that essential support for human memory that gives us things *in time* and allows us to relate the seen to the unseen. Labor, or human activity, gives us things *in space*. Thought arises in the conjunction of language and labor, and enables us to limit chance in our actions.

In Weil's account, a thought is an image of relation that is revealed in the mind suddenly and from an indiscernible point of origin[11] during this act of attention to language. The revelation of thought through attention is purely a function private and unique to the individual. Through expression, however, thought enters into the public or collective domain of language. In her description, this social aspect of language is of an essentially *material* character. Through expression, thought is expropriated from the individual and embodied in things— in texts, techniques, machines, skills, habits, customs, artifacts of all kinds and, finally, in the very organization of society itself. By its very nature, human language is such that expressions of thought can serve as the basis of activity without the need, or even the opportunity, to be re-thought and thus assimilated by the individual. We can say more than we know. We can act on the basis of what we say. In this way, the signs of language threaten to interpose themselves between thought and activity in the lives of each of us.

In Weil's understanding, mathematics is the quintessential form of human language.[12] It images the most basic of all relations: that of function (or number). A functional relation holds between two quantities that vary proportionately by virtue of a fixed relation. The *constant* (or fixed relation) determines a particular range or set of *variables*. It is, precisely, through linguistic images of functional (or necessary) relation that thought combines the fixity of language with the fluid character of our experience of a phenomenal world constituted by being in the process of unfolding.

For Weil, labor or work is the center and pivotal point within our existence at which thought may enter into contact with each essential realm of our experience, nature and history. It is labor or work which enables us to visualize the relationship between human beings and the world in terms of necessity rather than caprice and magic. In addition, work enables human beings to move "from necessity endured to necessity methodically handled"[13] if that work is informed by thought: "The attention is directed exclusively to the combinations formed by the movements of inert matter, and the idea of necessity appears in its purity, without any admixture of magic."[14] Then the attentive laborer is free.

Weil did not understand human freedom as the ability to obtain what is pleasurable without effort, nor did she, like modern liberals (Marx included), advocate the emancipation of the passions as the means of human fulfillment. For her, "true liberty is not defined by a relationship between desire and its satisfaction, but by a relationship between thought and action."[15] This is why she could state that "the absolutely free man would be he whose every action proceeded from a preliminary judgment concerning the end which he set himself and the sequence of means suitable for attaining this end."[16]

However, a problem emerges at this point, a problem which is related to the development of modern science and has led to a range of crises in our technological society. The problem has two aspects. Firstly,

he who applies method has no need to conceive it in his mind at the moment he is applying it. Indeed, if it is a question of something complicated, he is unable to, even should he have elaborated it himself; for the attention, always forced to concentrate itself on the actual moment of execution, cannot embrace at the same time the series of relationships on which execution as a whole depends. Hence, what is carried out is not a conception but an abstract diagram indicating a sequence of movements, and as little penetrable by the mind, at the moment of execution, as is some formula resulting from mere routine or some magic rite.[17]

Secondly, any method, once developed, can be applied without ever being understood by the person who applies it. This analysis formed the basis of Weil's critique of the modern industrial system that, in her view, dedicated itself to the maximization of the productivity of the worker, whether manual or intellectual, rather than to the expansion of the worker's freedom.

Modern and Postmodern Science: Classical Science and After

The modern industrial system is a function of the development of modern science. Simone Weil argued that the dissociation of thought and action was first effected in that realm. She describes the devolution in this way:

> Classical science, the science which was revived by the Renaissance and perished around 1900, tried to represent all phenomena occurring in the universe by imagining, between two successive states confirmed in a system by observation, intermediate stages analogous to those traversed by a man executing a simple manual labor. It conceived the universe on the model of the relation between any human action and the necessities which obstruct it by imposing conditions.[18]

Weil went on to point out the impenetrable obscurity in the fundamental notions of physics: they must succeed in imagining "work with no worker" or "an obstacle that opposes nothing."[19] Nonetheless, in spite of this obscurity, classical science "was able to subsume the study of every natural phenomenon under the simple notion of energy, which was directly derived from that of work."[20] Energy, like work, was defined in terms of distance and weight.

But this view was complicated in the nineteenth century when classical science added the idea of entropy, which applies "to energy that necessity which, together with work, weighs most heavily upon human life."[21] Weil is referring to time, which, unlike space, is unidirectional. One cannot go back to the future. Thus, "it is assumed that every phenomenon involves a transformation of energy such that, once the phenomenon is accomplished, it is impossible by any means or in any condition to restore the initial state exactly as it was throughout the system."[22] Classical science expressed this notion of entropy "in an algebraic formula, in the language of mathematics applied to physics."[23]

It is beyond the purview of this chapter to summarize in detail Weil's description of the history of the four centuries of "classical science," the substantial material accomplishments of which she does not deny. I want rather to focus on her understanding of its limitations. First, she states, classical science is monotonous. "Once the principle has been grasped, that is to say the analogy between the events of the world and the simplest form of human work, it has nothing new to offer, no matter how long it goes on making discoveries."[24] Secondly, classical science offers only a partial account of the universe. "The universe it describes is a slave's universe and man, including slaves, is not wholly a slave."[25] Classical science excludes the entire question of the good; it excludes those types of knowledge which can only be achieved by participation in, or attention to, the good. "It finds no place for the good even by way of contrast, as an opposing term."[26]

Weil explains that every civilization or culture develops a paradigm of knowledge, that is, an understanding of "the relation between an aspiration of human thought and the effective conditions for its realization."[27] Classical science employs a paradigm of knowledge which seeks only "objectivity." Positive knowledge is attained, as Bacon indicated, by summoning some phenomenon "before a subject and putting it to the question so that it gives us the reasons for being the way it is an object."[28] Classical science can in these terms be contrasted with ancient Greek science, which had a different aim: "the desire to contemplate in sensible phenomena an image of the good."[29]

Up until the end of the nineteenth century, classical science, in spite of its monotony and the limitation of its paradigm of knowledge, still had some relationship to common sense and to other types of human thought. Weil argued that in the twentieth century, it lost this. With the development of quantum theory by Planck, it abandoned the "analogy between the laws of nature and the conditions of work, that is to say, its very principle."[30] Science replaced the notion of necessity with probability, and the notion of continuity with discontinuity. Planck, on the basis of his experiments with black-body radiation, reconceptualized "energy, or rather action, the product of energy and time, as a quantity which varies discontinuously, in successive jumps, and these jumps are what is known as quanta."[31]

According to Weil, quantum theory gave rise to numerous contradictions. The net effect was that physics was disrupted by

the introduction of the discontinuous, and the improvement of measuring instruments . . . Chemistry was born when the balance was able to register simple and fixed numerical ratios between separate substances which enter into combination; and this weight-measurement already implied that discontinuity and number would again become of the first importance in the science of nature. Further, it became possible, by means of apparatus, to observe phenomena of extreme smallness, by human standards, such as Brownian movement. Discontinuity, number, and smallness are enough to give rise to the atom, and the atom has returned to us, accompanied as always by chance and probability.[32]

What this meant was that scientists used the idea of probability "as a bridge between the world as it is given to us and the hypothetical and purely mechanical world of atoms; the consequences of the quantum theory, which derived from the study of probability, led them to introduce probability among the atoms themselves."[33] The atomic world, the world of microphysics, was to be understood in terms of probability, while the world of mechanics was to be understood in terms of necessity; and the two different worlds were left unrelated.

With the emergence of atomic physics came the replacement of the fundamental notion of continuity with discontinuity, the replacement of the notion of necessity with probability, and the replacement of ordinary language with algebra. This latter substitution was particularly ominous in Weil's view because "ordinary language and algebraic language are not subject to the same logical requirements; relations between ideas are not fully represented by relations between letters; and, in particular, incompatible assertions may have equational equivalents which are by no means incompatible."[34]

Weil concluded that classical and twentieth-century science emancipated the study of nature, originally understood on the analogy of work (that is, in terms of energy), from the idea of the good and the idea of necessity. The results have been devastating: there is "practically nothing left to control the workings of [scientists'] thought. There is hardly anything except algebra, which controls only in the sense that one has to adapt to any simple instrument in order to handle it; and algebra is a very flexible instrument."[35] Though flexible, it is totally inadequate in Weil's view. Scientific research, "like all other efforts, [must] be oriented towards something; all human effort is oriented and when man is not going in any direction he is motionless. He cannot do without values. For all theoretical study the name of value is truth."[36]

The fundamental problem, Weil wrote in 1941, is that "present-day scientists have nothing in their minds, however vague, remote, arbitrary or improbable, which they can turn towards and call it truth."[37] In the absence of any conception of truth, opportunism and pragmatism dominate the scientific community:

So soon as truth disappears, utility at once takes its place, because man always directs his effort towards some good or other. Thus utility becomes something which the intelligence is no longer entitled to define or to judge, but only to serve. From being the arbiter, the intelligence becomes the servant, and it gets its orders from the desires. And, further, public opinion then replaces conscience as sovereign mistress of thoughts because man always submits his thoughts to some higher control, which is superior either in value or else in power.[38]

The Manhattan Project: Necessity and Probability

In the same year that Simone Weil was engaged in the previously discussed analysis of classical and contemporary science, Robert Oppenheimer, a brilliant American physicist, was hired by the United States
Army to head up the celebrated Manhattan Project which was carried
out in Los Alamos, New Mexico. Over four years, the project brought
together some 150,000 workers, military personnel and scientists. Less
than 100 of them knew exactly what their purpose was: the splitting of
the atom and the development of the first nuclear weapon. In many ways
the Manhattan Project illustrates the crisis of science described above.
Research and development fell into the lap of utility, and it turned out to
be the Allied military machine, which not only paid the pipers and called
the tune, but even supplied the instruments and the auditorium.

Oppenheimer himself described the beginnings of contemporary
physics in a manner quite different from Weil: "Our understanding of
atomic physics or what we call the quantum theory of atomic systems had
its origins at the turn of the century and its great synthesis and resolu-
tions in the nineteen- twenties. It was a heroic time . . . For those who
participated it was a time of creation. There was a terror as well as exalta-
tion in their new insight."[39]

One of the reasons for the terror was the premonition of global
disaster. In the nineteen-thirties, "Leo Szilard and George Gamow began
serious analysis of whether a nuclear chain reaction could accidentally
set off an endless sequence."[40] The question that emerged was this:
"Would conditions be created in the interior of a nuclear explosion
which might fuse under great heat and pressure, hydrogen, helium and
nitrogen, and thereby ignite the world's atmosphere?"[41] This anxiety
became a real preoccupation once serious research and development
began in New Mexico. In fact it gave rise to the only quasi-ethical concern which was allowed to surface and to slow down the scientific
research. F. M. Szasz relates that

in July of 1942, a group of scientists began discussion of the issue in
Le Conte Hall on the campus of the University of California. Edward
Teller made some of the initial calculations and his figures indicated
that the bombs would indeed create enough heat to ignite the earth's
atmosphere. Oppenheimer immediately called a halt to the meetings
and sought out Arthur Compton, head of the metallurgical laboratory
of the University of Chicago . . . The scientists met frequently to analyze

the issue. In a 1959 interview with author Pearl Buck, Compton recalled that he took the initiative in the early days of the discussion. If the calculations showed that the chances of igniting the atmosphere were more than approximately three in one million, he said he would not proceed with the Manhattan project. Nothing, not even the horrifying possibility of a Nazi victory, was worth this. Revised calculations showed figures slightly under that and so the project continued.[42]

No indication is given as to where the figure "approximately three in one million"[43] came from. We do know that the revised calculations were done by Edward Teller and Hans Bethe, who later assured the American public: "We were sure on theoretical grounds that we would not set the atmosphere on fire."[44] In light of the fact that by the time actual plans were being made to test the atom bomb, by the end of 1944, it was clear to American intelligence that German physicists had taken a wrong turn in their atomic research, and were in no position to develop an atomic weapon, we must assume that Bethe's account is to be trusted. In view of Weil's analysis of twentieth-century science, we should note the contradiction between the language of probability used by Compton (which framed the ethical question about whether to proceed with the first atomic explosion in terms of a certain upper limit to the risk scientists should take with the future of the planet), and Teller's and Bethe's language (which speaks in terms of theoretical impossibility or necessity, and denies the risk). If the language of probability was accurately and truthfully used, how was it determined that a three-in-one-million probability was a reasonable cut-off point? If the language of necessity was accurately and truthfully used, how was it concluded that a probability under three in one million represented a theoretical impossibility?

These are hypothetical questions raised to illustrate the practical significance of Weil's reflections on quantum theory. In 1942 she wrote that "probability can only be defined as a rigorous necessity, of whose conditions some are known and some are unknown; the conception of probability, divorced from necessity, is meaningless."[45] The problem seems to be that some conditions are always unknown, so that prior to an experiment the results are merely probable. Where the consequences of an experiment are not potentially destructive, the possibility of error is unimportant. However, when experiments move to the atomic level and the experiments may have lethal consequences in the real world, the possibility of error becomes the possibility of catastrophe. After the experiment, necessity can be asserted, but prior to the experiment probability reigns. And as Weil pointed out: "Divorced from necessity, probability is no more than a résumé of statistics, and the only justification of statistics is practical utility."[46]

Statistics were used to justify practical utility. Nevertheless, on the morning of 16 July 1945, anxiety remained about the possibility of a runaway explosion. As the first atomic bomb lit up the New Mexico desert, a senior officer shouted: "Good God! I believe that the long-haired boys have lost control."[47] In fact, they had not. Or at least they had not in the way the officer feared. Oppenheimer, though he is more famous for his quotation from the *Bhagavad Gita* ("I am become death, the shatterer of worlds") remarked that his "faith in the human mind had been somewhat restored"[48] by the success of the blast.

Weil would have sided with the senior officer. The long-haired boys had lost control. They had nothing in their minds which they could turn to and call the truth. Utility had taken its place. The Manhattan Project illustrated what Weil expressed in her pre-war letter to Jean Posternak: "science is entering a period of crisis graver than that of the fifth century [BCE], which is accompanied, as then, by a moral crisis and a subservience to purely political values, in other words to power."[49] Modern science is essentially, not accidentally, a collective enterprise which relies on specialization for its advancement. That specialization combined with the complexity of its research allows for, when it does not demand, great secrecy and centralized control, whether such control is in the hands of a military, industrial or educational bureaucracy. Such specialization means that no single mind can grasp even a sub-discipline. Researchers take over not only the results but the methods developed by their predecessors, without understanding them or their relation to the whole. Formulaic knowledge, usually expressed in algebraic equations, is generally appropriated without verification. "Every theory in physics is a synthesis whose elements are facts which are conceived as being analogous to one another. And since the facts accumulate with each passing generation of scientists, while the capacity of the human mind remains the same, the quantity of facts to be embraced comes to exceed by far the range of any mind; hence the scientist no longer has facts in his mind, but the syntheses evolved from the facts by other minds, syntheses which he in turn synthesizes, without having revised them."[50]

Modern science, then, creates syntheses without simplification or integration. "It is a science essentially incapable of being popularized because it replaces simplicity by generality. hence [sic] the subordination, no longer of the complex to the simple but, on the contrary, of the simple to the complex."[51] Weil concluded that in the modern world the "scientist is crushed by science"[52] in much the same way that the worker is crushed by his work: "the overturning of values is the same in science as in labour: the scientist is made to exist for the sake of science (to add to it), instead of science for the scientist (to make him wise)."[53] Moreover, the scientist participates in a process the ethical implications of which she cannot know even if she understands comprehensively the particular research she is engaged in. Thousands of the most brilliant scientists of their generation were holed up in a desert camp for years and had no clear idea that they were developing atomic weapons. They could perforce have had no intimation that the products of their genius might be dropped on the civilian populations of Hiroshima and Nagasaki.

But some of them might have understood what Weil had written in 1934:

> A science like ours, essentially closed to the layman, and therefore to scientists themselves, because each of them is a layman outside his narrow specialism, is the proper theology of an ever increasingly bureaucratic society. 'It is secrecy, mystery, that is everywhere the soul of bureaucracy,' wrote Marx in his youth; and mystery is founded upon specialization. Mystery is the condition of all privilege and consequently of all oppression; and it is in science itself, the breaker of idols, the destroyer of mystery, that mystery has found its last refuge.[54]

Science, Algebra, and Technology: The Destruction of a Human Scale

If the scientist is made to exist for science, what does contemporary science exist for? Weil answered the question in this way:

> There are as many forms of knowledge of the world as there are relations . . . conceivable by man [between an aspiration of human thought and the effective conditions for its realization]; and the value of each form of knowledge is neither more nor less than the value of the relation that serves him as principle. Further, some of these forms are mutually exclusive while others are not. But, as for contemporary science, what is one to think? What is the relation that serves it as principle and determines its value? The question is difficult to answer, not because there is any obscurity but because it is embarrassing to reply.

The philosophic significance, the profound thought at its centre, are like the Emperor's clothes in the story; to say they do not exist is to be branded a fool and ignoramus, so it is more prudent to call them inexpressible. Nevertheless, the relation which is the principle of this science is simply the relationship between algebraic formulae void of meaning, on the one hand, and technology on the other.[55]

Technology is, then, what contemporary science exists for. Technology is the issue of a method for blindly exploiting the possibilities of action intrinsic to the language of science, a language which no longer puts us into contact with necessity. In committing itself to technology, our society has exchanged thought and freedom for action into nature. We have thus exposed ourselves to the play of chance. Technologies like the computer represent the synthesis of scientific research. This means that no single human being can comprehend them. And yet their use can be popularized. Whether we have any theoretical grasp of them or not, as long as we can make them work, they magically enhance our efficiency. But that simply means that we are able to act more often and more potently without knowing the implications of our acts.

This need not be the case, in Weil's view.[56] "One can conceive of a science whose ultimate aim would be the perfecting of technique not by rendering it more powerful, but simply more conscious and more methodical . . . Such a science would be, in effect, a method for mastering nature, or a catalogue of concepts indispensable for attaining to such mastery, arranged according to an order that would make them palpably clear to the mind."[57] Science itself could be reoriented so that the link between theory and practice could be grasped by the average man: "On the day when it became impossible to understand scientific notions, even the most abstract, without clearly perceiving at the same time their connection with possible applications, and equally impossible to apply such notions even indirectly without thoroughly knowing and understanding them—on that day science would have become concrete and labor would have become conscious."[58]

Such a science would be based on images of equilibrium on a human scale. If science is to remain on a human scale it must subordinate complexity to simplicity, and eschew the accumulation of experimental facts beyond the point where they can be grasped by a single mind; and it must eschew research into those areas which are too small or too large for the human being to discern. This classical science and contemporary science had not done.

Science, Weil argued, is limited. "It is well that it should remain limited because it is not an end to which many men ought to devote themselves; it is a means for every man. What is needed now is not to try to extend it further, but to bring thought to bear upon it."[59] The destructive social effects of science's failure to respect limits were clear to Weil over 70 years ago; the very notion of human scale had been destroyed.

We are living in a world in which nothing is made to man's measure; there exists a monstrous discrepancy between man's body, man's mind and the things which at the present time constitute the elements of human existence . . . From the concrete point of view certain units of measurement have hitherto remained invariable such as the human body, human life, the year, the day, the average quickness of human thought. Present-day life is not organized on the scale of all these things; it has been transported into an altogether different order of magnitude, as though man were trying to raise it to the level of the forces of outside nature while neglecting to take his own nature into account.[60]

But human scale cannot be restored to human society without the radical transformation of science itself. This means that most contemporary scientific research and technological development can only exacerbate the problem.

With the transformation of science could come the transformation of labor, society and social ideals. "One can . . . widen bit by bit the sphere of conscious work, and perhaps indefinitely so. To achieve this end it would be enough if man were no longer to aim at extending his knowledge and power indefinitely, but rather at establishing, both in his research and his work, a certain balance between the mind and the object to which it is being applied."[61]

To achieve this balance in the work place, technique would have to be such as to make continual use of methodical thought; the analogy between the techniques employed in various tasks would have to be sufficiently close, and technical education sufficiently widespread, to enable each worker to form a clear idea of all the specialized procedures; co-ordination would have to be arranged in sufficiently simple a manner to enable each one continually to have a precise knowledge of it, as concerns both co-operation between workers and exchange of products; collectivities would never be sufficiently vast to pass outside the range of a human mind.[62]

As she lived through the Depression, Simone Weil was not optimistic that science would be reformed, or that the role of technology would be limited, or that we would regain a sense of human scale in our social organization. In 1934, she wrote: "In a civilization based on competition, on struggle, on war . . . there is no means of stopping the blind trend of the social machine towards an increasing centralization, until the machine itself suddenly jams and flies into pieces . . . The present system will go on existing to the extreme limit of possibility."[63] But this did not lead her to counsel despair or passivity. Rather, she proposed that the history of the sciences be written, and that technique be studied "from an entirely new point of view, which would no longer be that of output, but that of the relation between the worker and his work."[64] This would enable us "to escape the contagion of folly and collective frenzy by reaffirming . . . over the head of the social idol, the original pact between the mind and the universe."[65] If that pact were reaffirmed, the most advanced technologies would put us in contact with necessity, as well as with the order and beauty of the world.

Notes

[1] Editors' note: Clarke's "third law." See Arthur C. Clarke, *Profiles of the Future* (New York: Harper & Row, 1973), 21.
[2] See Jacques Ellul, *The Technological Bluff* (Grand Rapids, MI: Wm. B. Eerdmans Publishing Co., 1990).
[3] See Langdon Winner, *The Whale and the Reactor: A Search for Limits in an Age of High Technology* (Chicago: University of Chicago Press, 1986).
[4] See E. F. Schumacher, *Small is Beautiful: A Study of Economics As If People Mattered* (London: Sphere Books, 1974).
[5] See George Grant, *Technology and Empire* (Toronto: House of Anansi Press, 1969) and *Technology and Justice* (Toronto: House of Anansi Press, 1986).
[6] See Ursula Franklin, *The Real World of Technology* (Toronto: House of Anansi Press, 1999).
[7] See Lawrence E. Schmidt with Scott Marratto, *The End of Ethics in A Technological Society* (Montreal: McGill Queen's University Press, 2008).
[8] OL, 94.
[9] See James Calder, "Labour and thought in the philosophy of Simone Weil: Preface to a philosophy of education (Ph.D. thesis, Dalhousie University, 1985).
[10] FLN, 18.
[11] For crucial texts of Weil concerning the nature of thought, see "The Pythagorean doctrine," in IC, 178ff.
[12] IC, 161–3.
[13] FLN, 22.

[14] OL, 91.

[15] OL, 85.

[16] OL, 85.

[17] OL, 92.

[18] SN, 6.

[19] SN, 7.

[20] SN, 7.

[21] SN, 8.

[22] SN, 9.

[23] SN, 9.

[24] SN, 10.

[25] SN, 11.

[26] SN, 12.

[27] SN, 21.

[28] Grant, *Technology and Justice*, 21.

[29] SN, 21.

[30] SN, 22.

[31] SN, 50.

[32] SN, 24.

[33] SN, 61.

[34] SN, 54.

[35] SN, 62.

[36] SN, 62.

[37] SN, 62.

[38] SN, 63– 4.

[39] Robert Jungk, *Brighter Than A Thousand Suns* (New York: Harcourt Brace and Company, 1958), 8–9.

[40] Ronald W. Clark, *The Scientific Breakthrough* (New York: G. P. Putnam's Sons, 1974), as quoted in Ferenc Morton Szasz, *The Day The Sun Rose Twice* (Albuquerque: University of New Mexico Press, 1984), 56.

[41] Szasz, *The Day The Sun Rose Twice*, 56.

[42] Ibid., 56–7.

[43] For one explanation of "three in one million," see Daniel M. Kammen, Alexander I. Shlyakhter and Richard Wilson, "What is the risk of the impossible?" in *Technology: Journal of the Franklin Institute*, Vol. 33, 1 A (1994), 97–116; http://people.csail.mit.edu/ilya_shl/alex/riskOfTheImpossible.pdf (accessed 10 January 2009).

[44] Szasz, *The Day The Sun Rose Twice*, 58.

[45] SN, 61.

[46] SN, 61.

[47] Szasz, *The Day The Sun Rose Twice*, 60. See also Jungk, *Brighter Than A Thousand Suns*, 200.

[48] Szasz, *The Day The Sun Rose Twice*, 89.

[49] SL, 90.

[50] SN, 11.

[51] FLN, 24–5.

[52] FLN, 28.

[53] FLN, 29.
[54] OEL, 264, as quoted in SN, 87.
[55] SN, 21–2.
[56] See Joseph K. Cosgrove, "Simone Weil's spiritual critique of modern science: An historical critical assessment," *Zygon* Vol. 43, No. 2 (June 2008). http://digitalcommons.providence.edu/cgi/viewcontent.cgi?article=1006&context=philosophy_fac (accessed 10 January 2009). I agree with Cosgrove that Weil is "too optimistic about modern science because she underestimates how much would be required to reorient science towards the mystical" though, unlike Cosgrove, I am inclined to think that the reason for this is that "the symbolic form of representation [is] intrinsic to mathematical science, as opposed to a merely convenient shorthand for quantitative relations that could, and ideally should, be conceived non- symbolically" (355). I am grateful for Cosgrove's personal communication on this topic. I fear that we may disagree both with Simone Weil and with each other about the prospects for the reform of contemporary science.
[57] OL, 99.
[58] OL, 99.
[59] SN, 80.
[60] OL, 102.
[61] OL, 90.
[62] OL, 93.
[63] OL, 113–4.
[64] OL, 117.
[65] OL, 117.

Chapter 9

The 'War' on Error? Violent Metaphor and Words with Capital Letters

A. Rebecca Rozelle-Stone and Lucian Stone

Words of reason drop into the void.

—*Simone Weil*[1]

Introduction

Susan Jacoby, in her book *The Age of American Unreason*, writes that "the current American relationship to reading and writing . . . is best described not as illiterate but as a-literate."[2] She cites a survey conducted by the National Endowment for the Arts in 2002 that indicates that "fewer than half of adult Americans had read any work of fiction or poetry in [2001]" and "only 57 percent had read a nonfiction book"[3] that year. Her wholly justified worry is that, given such an atmosphere of a-literacy, not only is the enjoyment of reading at risk, but the public's ability to think critically is also endangered. These worries are further substantiated by an "info-tainment" culture and "the videoization of everything" that serve to

foster the illusion that the ability to retrieve words and numbers with the click of a mouse also confers the capacity to judge whether those words and numbers represent truth, lies, or something in between. This illusion is not confined to America, but its effects are especially deleterious in a culture . . . with an endemic predilection for techno-logical answers to nontechnological questions. . .[4]

Of course, these "technological answers" are always easily obtained, eas-ily assimilated into prejudices, neatly conformed and accommodated to any need for any case (e.g., one can find "evidence" for any claim via the Internet). Hence, they are not genuine answers in the sense that they do not fully correspond to external reality or truth; as a result of being partial, abbreviated, rushed and decontextualized, these "answers" are erroneous. Naturally, however, these answers appeal and contribute to a culture that does not want to bother with reading but is engrossed with efficiency, specialization, and the production of capital.

That is, such "technological answers" are undoubtedly the result of technological thinking, and just as we are right to question whether these answers *are* answers in any real sense, we must also wonder whether technological thinking is actual *thinking*. What is the precise nature of our contemporary relationship to concepts and language, especially given our predilection for the technological? Does this relationship with language—whatever it may be—portend a certain orientation towards other people, as well as a certain view of ourselves? In other words, is there an ethical-political component, beyond any pragmatic or "technical" concerns, to technological thinking and answering? Without qualification, we respond affirmatively to this last question, and offer as an argument certain insights proffered by Simone Weil. Although Weil lived and recorded her thoughts more than half a century ago, her grasp of the crucial linguistic (and thereby ethical-political) mistakes that humanity commits transcends any particular era. In this chapter, we will (1) give attention to Weil's diagnosis of our diseased relationship with language, and to the resulting violence; (2) weigh further effects of this sort of language, including the endangerment of dialogue, and the enhancement of sophistry; and (3) consider a new model for language and our relationship to it, finally reflecting upon the readiness of the "technological culture" for a radical reorientation towards language.

Dissociations, Caricatures and Abstractions

Weil was especially prophetic in diagnosing and explaining what we have been calling "technological thinking." In particular, when we look at her writings, we find Weil's recognition of three primary and interrelated characteristics of this sort of thinking, all of which are in her view fundamental errors. First, she identifies "the technique of error" as "setting aside" (*mettre à part*).[5] "Setting aside" indicates the neglect of relationships between things, especially between our desires and actions, and between suffering and evil. We cannot bear to recognize our intimate associations with evil and the ways in which we cause pain, so we obscure these con-nections in our minds. This sort of neglect is not always conscious or intentional, however. As Weil tells us, "We set things aside without know-ing we are doing so; that is precisely where the danger lies."[6] Frequently, though, the neglect *is* intentional, or at least it is accomplished by "an act of the will that is furtive in relation to ourselves."[7] Because we do not want to know or believe that we have made the dissociation, we reach the point where we cannot know it and cannot see ourselves.

An example may clarify this characteristic of technological thinking which Weil, making a Platonic allusion, calls "the ring of Gyges." Hannah Arendt, after having observed the Nazi war criminal Adolph Eichmann at his trial in Jerusalem, later reported his "banality"—his shallowness, his lack of thought, originality or creativity, and his accompanying adher-ence to standardized codes of expression, clichés and stock phrases—as a sufficient cause for even the magnitude of evil which he committed. It was apparent from his behavior and language during the trial that he had set things aside. Arendt describes:

[Eichmann] knew that what he had once considered his duty was now called a crime, and he accepted this new code of judgment as though it were nothing but another language rule. To his rather limited supply of stock phrases he had added a few new ones, and he was utterly help-less only when he was confronted with a situation to which none of them would apply, as in the most grotesque instance when he had to make a speech under the gallows and was forced to rely on clichés used in funeral oratory which were inapplicable in his case because he was not the survivor. Considering what his last words should be in case of a death sentence, which he had expected all along, this simple fact had not occurred to him, just as inconsistencies and flagrant contra-dictions in examination and cross-examinations during the trial had not bothered him.[8]

For Arendt, this "setting aside" is none other than a suppression of con-science—conscience understood as that partner to oneself that, returning to the etymology, is a "knowing with and by myself." For Weil, suppres-sion of that internal partner is precisely what the ring of Gyges allows, except that her emphasis is on the invisibility to self, as opposed to the traditional emphasis in the myth on invisibility to others. Not surpris-ingly, Weil warns, "The faculty of setting things aside opens the door to every sort of crime . . . It provides a key to absolute license. That is what makes it possible for men to behave in such an incoherent fashion."[9] Weil's comment here is entirely congruous with Arendt's depiction of Eichmann: the one who "sets aside" is not perturbed by his/her own inconsistencies because they are not recognized.

Thus, technological thinking is first characterized by such disconnection and occasionalism in thought. Again, as Weil explains it, the problem with the ring of Gyges is not so much that we become invisible to others and thereby immune to social justice, but that we become invisible to ourselves. The "ring" consists in Gyges saying, "I have become king, and the other king has been assassinated," without any connection being made between these two events. Or, in another example Weil provides, when the owner of a factory thinks, "I enjoy this and that expensive luxury and my workmen are miserably poor," and despite feeling pity for his workers, he nevertheless does not form the connection between his lifestyle and their condition.[10]

The second characteristic of technological thinking evident in Weil's writings is an extension of the practice of "setting aside." When a person does not make the necessary connections between events and conditions, caricatures of ourselves and others are created, and these distortions/errors too often evolve into pernicious stereotypes. Typically, we exaggerate the perceived negative qualities of others while indulging in uncritical self-aggrandizements. In this way, our expectations of others are frequently unjust, especially considering the impunity we always extend to ourselves. To put this into Arendtian terms, we rebel against the very concept of the "banality of evil," for it implicates *us*; we are forced to recognize that the difference between Eichmann and ourselves is only a difference of degree (of thoughtlessness) and circumstance, not a difference in kind. The caricature is much more accommodating to our desires, and of course is not seen as such: By definition, we are *the good* and they are *the others* (i.e., *the bad*).[11]

Chris Hedges provides concrete evidence of this tendency to caricature, in his book *War is a Force that Gives Us Meaning*. Describing the intoxication of war that occurs only when we have carried out certain dissociations and created various illusions, he writes:

> Once we sign on for war's crusade, once we see ourselves on the side of the angels, once we embrace a theological or ideological belief system that defines itself as the embodiment of goodness and light, it is only a matter of how we will carry out murder . . . Patriotism, often a thinly veiled form of collective self-worship, celebrates our goodness,

our ideals, our mercy and bemoans the perfidiousness of those who hate us . . . We define ourselves. All other definitions do not count.[12]

The effects of the distortion are not always on the scale of war, of course. But any instance of forgetfulness of human interdependency and connectedness constitutes an act of violence, even if the amnesia does not manifest physically. To return to Weil's earlier example, if I am a factory owner increasing my profits every year, and thus having increased access to healthy foods, quality education, clean neighborhoods and recreational areas, it is natural that I begin to think of myself as making "smart choices," as opposed to those made by the pitiful people who work for me. I may reflect, "If only they were more industrious, more resourceful, more intelligent, then they would not find themselves socially and economically paralyzed." Perhaps I eventually think, "The poor are quite lazy!" I have, in this process, left my own role out of their condition, and have imposed harsh demands and judgments on them. Weil tells us that we must forgive others the debts created by our imaginations, and "accept the fact that they are other than the creatures of our imagination[s]." Significantly, she continues, "I also am other than what I imagine myself to be,"[13] which usually means that we are not the self-sufficient, independent creatures that we think we are. If the first characteristic of technological thinking is brought on by neglect or setting aside, the second characteristic (caricaturing) is triggered by the imagination.

The third characteristic of such thinking follows naturally from the second, for it is only the crystallization of the caricatures into idolatrous concepts and words. Once our images and expectations of others and ourselves have become detached from reality, we begin to speak and write in analogous ways that shape the world according to these illusions; we begin the process of fabrication in the world of humans, a sort of reification.[14] There are several points to take note of regarding this crystallization. For one, the resultant abstracted language—what Weil calls "words with capital letters" in her essay "The power of words"[15]—reinforces the first two characteristics of technological thinking. A vicious cycle is established, wherein reductionist language derives from the processes of disconnected thought and imaginative projections, but in turn, it produces and disseminates more of the same kind of "thought." George Orwell once wrote, "If thought corrupts language, language can also corrupt thought. A bad usage can spread by tradition and imitation, even among people who should and do know better."[16] Quickly then, thought and language descend into a downward spiral of meaninglessness and abstraction from what is real. We have lost "the very elements of intelligence" by neglecting ideas of "limit, measure, degree, proportion, relations, comparison, contingency, interdependence," etc.[17] Instead, we speak in absolutes but with words that are empty. It is for this reason that Weil writes, "In this so-called age of technicians, the only battles we know how to fight are battles against windmills."[18] Words like "democracy," "freedom" and "terrorism" have been recently employed in this isolated, abstracted and absolute way so that they can mean whatever we would like them to, at any given point in time, even if our disparate meanings end up in contradiction, and even if our enemies and heroes are imagined.[19]

Therefore, this reductionist language consists of words and phrases denuded of rational content or definition and stripped of their nuance, but "all swollen with blood and tears"[20] (i.e., emotional content resulting from the caricatures). They are, at one and the same time, stripped bare and blown up large. These words and phrases naturally become slogans or clichés because they provide the energy and satisfaction echoing the collective which speaks them, while not demanding anything of them in the way of ethical or intellectual responsibility. They are, as Orwell describes them, "a continuous temptation, a packet of aspirins always at one's elbow."[21] In this sense, such language easily becomes a wall of defense, protecting us from reality, including a clear vision of ourselves. Here again, in describing Eichmann's banal language, Arendt affirms this product of technological thinking:

> Clichés, stock phrases, adherence to conventional, standardized codes of expression and conduct have the socially recognized function of protecting us against reality, that is, against the claim on our thinking attention which all events and facts arouse by virtue of their existence. If we were responsive to this claim all the time, we would soon be exhausted; the difference in Eichmann was only that he clearly knew of no such claim at all.[22]

Weil may depart from Arendt insofar as, for Weil, it is imperative that we always be attentive and fully responsive to the claims presented by real facts and events; exhaustion cannot legitimize such a-voidance.[23] These "words with capital letters" do function as insulation, as we are well aware in the case of euphemisms (which, being quite literally "happy phrases," are precisely the sort of words that are abstract representations of complex and problematic situations). As Orwell soberly notes, "Political language has to consist largely of euphemism, question-begging and sheer cloudy vagueness."[24]

In Book VIII of Plato's *Republic*, we find the degradation of language and the rise of euphemism accompanying the destruction of the psyche. In particular, the "democratic" soul—already many stages inferior to the best or "aristocratic" soul, and on its way to becoming the worst or "tyrannical" soul—gives a prominent place to the desires, and is "empty of knowledge, fine ways of living, and words of truth."[25] These "words of truth" had previously served as "guardians of the thoughts" of virtuous men, but in their absence "false and boastful words . . . rush up and occupy [the psyche]."[26] Later, these "boastful words" serve to "close the gates of the royal wall within him"[27] to prevent the soul's true allies from coming near. In a process we might think of as rationalization (the attempt to eliminate the *sense* of inconsistency), these new guardians assign new names to the allies and their associated virtues: "won't they call reverence foolishness and moderation cowardice," and "won't they persuade the young man that measured and orderly expenditure is boorish and mean?"[28] Conversely, the vices must be spoken of euphemistically, calling "insolence good breeding, anarchy freedom, extravagance magnificence, and shamelessness courage."[29] In all these ways of speaking, protection is afforded to the soul which gives priority to its desires and subordinates reason; "words with capital letters" function as anaesthesia to our own destructive tendencies. In light of this fact, the irony that "true crime cannot be felt"[30] by the criminal, but only by the innocent victim, becomes apparent.

This reified language, therefore, not only serves as a defense mechanism, but by virtue of that, it also becomes a tool of violence. This sort of reduced but swollen language can only be used in the service of what Weil calls "gravity," that all-too-natural pull toward moral and spiritual baseness. The entire existence of reified language is predicated upon an initial caricature (illusion), and an ongoing desire for self-protection or even self-advancement. When one becomes anaesthetized to sufferings in the world, one is certainly in a better position to inflict suffering, for it cannot be felt/known. Beyond that, always and everywhere, the mere assertion of such swollen words precipitates violence. First, as a reification of and detachment from phenomena that are much more complicated and in process, this language manifests a necrophilia. Paulo Freire writes that it is a tendency of "the oppressor consciousness to 'in-animate' everything and everyone it encounters."[31] Words divorced from genuine meaning are sadistic, for in themselves they indicate the speaker's penchant for that which is "cut off from the roots." As Freire notes, "Sadistic love is a perverted love—love of death [necrophilia], not of life."[32]

Second, the de-rooted words in question dictate certain postures and actions which are always the antithesis of humility and genuine love. Consider the phrase "national security." Weil writes, "What is called national security is an imaginary state of affairs in which one would retain the capacity to make war while depriving all other countries of it."[33] Why does "national security" represent an illusion? Whenever the term is used by political leaders, it is spoken of absolutely. But what would absolute national security entail except the absolute domination, or rather annihilation, of all others?[34] To remove all threat is to remove all contingency, which is to remove all that is living, free and unpredictable, i.e. human. Unless this is the intended goal, "national security" in its current usage is a fiction. Nevertheless, we initiate and wage wars, give up our civil liberties, and justify acts of racial/ethnic profiling for its sake.[35]

These "battles against the windmills" may evidence misdirected or groundless wars, but they are wars nonetheless, and there is nothing imaginary about the human lives that are lost. Weil reminds us:

> Words with content and meaning are not murderous . . . But when empty words are given capital letters, then, on the slightest pretext, men will begin shedding blood for them and piling up ruin in their name, without effectively grasping anything to which they refer, since what they refer to can never have any reality, for the simple reason that they mean nothing . . . It is true, of course, that not all of these words are intrinsically meaningless; some of them do have meaning if one takes the trouble to define them properly.[36]

Unfortunately, personalities who seek some sort of advantage—in social prestige or in military conquest, for example—will gravitate towards inflated language and symbolism, knowing its rhetorical power and usefulness in the manipulation of the masses. All of the great propagandists have understood this, from Joseph Goebbels to Karl Rove.[37] In addition, when support is rallied for a war built around an empty concept (but of course not recognized as such), it is not necessarily the case that support weakens as the deaths of one's soldiers accumulate. People are all too prone to be misled by the 'sunk-cost fallacy,' wherein conclusions are drawn on the basis of not wanting to recognize irretrievable losses, of wanting to make loss meaningful, even when it is the result of real error. Thus, we still hear in the United States, as deaths due to our invasion of Iraq continue to mount, that these troops are "fighting for our freedom."

It would be unbearable to admit the possibility that these thousands of deaths have been in vain.

Dialogue's Demotion, Sophistry's Promotion

The three stages of technological thinking—"setting aside," caricature, and abstracted language—imply a politics of self-anaesthetization and violence. The only content of such thinking and language on a national level is, as Weil says, "millions of corpses, and orphans, and disabled men, and tears and despair."[38] However, there are other effects of technological thinking that we encounter on a daily basis and that contribute to the overall climate which grants "words with capital letters" their efficacy and force. Two effects, or rather, two sides to the same effect, are worth mentioning and analyzing in this context. On one hand, we observe a denigration of genuine dialogue, and on the other, a growing support for and promotion of modern sophistry. Understanding these phenomena will lend us more insight into the violent potential of uprooted language.

To discuss the value of dialogue in our time, it is important to underscore what is meant by this word. The presence of dialogue indicates mutual interest in and desire for finding the truth of a matter. It supposes, therefore, sincerity on the part of all interlocutors, an earnest quest for understanding and wisdom. It is best epitomized by the figure of Socrates, whose recognized lack of complete knowledge about the *being* of concepts like "justice" and "piety" served as the fount of his dialogues with others, who often asserted their possession of such knowledge. The (Socratic) dialogue, then, is the embodiment of the *reach* toward fulfillment/knowledge. As the reach out of nothingness towards being, out of lack towards satisfaction, the dialogue represents a form of love: *eros*, desire.[39] But this is a desire unlike that which reigns over the tyrannical soul, for the latter seeks to possess particular objects while the former—dialogue as desire—is void of object, since what is sought is by definition *unknown*, and thus un-objectified.

Anne Carson, who has written about Simone Weil and the ancient Greeks among other subjects, explains the experience of the sort of desire that constitutes dialogue:

As you perceive the edge of yourself at the moment of desire, as you perceive the edges of words from moment to moment in reading (or writing), you are stirred to reach beyond perceptible edges—toward something else, something not yet grasped. The un-plucked apple, the beloved just out of touch, the meaning not quite attained, are desirable objects of knowledge. It is the enterprise of eros to keep them so. The unknown must remain unknown or the novel ends. As all paradoxes are, in some way, paradoxes *about* paradox, so all eros is, to some degree, desire *for* desire.[40]

It is important to understand dialogue as this sort of desire-without-an-object, even though there is an orientation towards truth; this is because what is real, beautiful and good resists reduction and possession. Without latching onto any final object, then, we can (and should) nevertheless latch onto the voided desire. In Weil's words: "To lose someone: We suffer because the departed, the absent, has become something imaginary and unreal. But our desire for him is not imaginary. We have to go down into ourselves to the abode of desire which is not imaginary. Hunger: We imagine kinds of food, but the hunger itself is real; we have to fasten onto the hunger."[41] The point here is that a person (or society) that values dialogue is invested in an erotic project, but *eros* must be understood as something which demands self-renunciation in the perpetual experience of falling short of consummation. The love is never fully requited, for "love no longer knows how to contemplate, it wants to possess."[42] We must come to appreciate that tension produced from the dialectic reach, that ever-present void of which we are increasingly reminded the more we come to understand.

In short, the value of dialogue indicates the appreciation and embodiment of humility. Technological thinking, however, drives towards objectness, reification, and the cessation of the experience of hunger and desire. It seeks immediate gratification/consummation through easy caricatures and denuded words. It is no surprise, then, that technological thinking has also given rise to the perversion of dialogue, for the idea of "fasten[ing] onto hunger" is beyond the narrow limits of that paradigm. Therefore, rather than dialogue being understood as eros and necessitating humility, it is framed in the only language that resonates with the technological thinker: words suggesting conquest, domination and submission, i.e. violent metaphor. George Lakoff and Mark Johnson have commented on this tendency. In *Metaphors We Live By*, they demonstrate our seeming vision of philosophical argument as "war" by reference to a variety of expressions in our everyday language:

Your claims are *indefensible*.
He *attacked every weak point* in my argument.

His criticisms were *right on target.*
I *demolished* his argument.
I've never *won* an argument with him.
You disagree? Okay, *shoot!*
If you use that *strategy,* he'll *wipe you out.*
He *shot down* all of my arguments.[43]

Lakoff and Johnson point out that what is significant is not just that we *talk* about dialogue and argument in terms of war-language, but that in doing so, we create a hostile atmosphere: "We can actually win or lose arguments. We see the person we are arguing with as an opponent. We attack his positions and defend our own," and so on.[44] Although there is no physical battle in such a scenario, there is a verbal battle, and thus the frame of competition and mastery is a constant. It is precisely this framework, moreover, that is the problem, for the desire to conquer implies a love of death. Weil understood this imitation and perversion of dialogue, and what it portended: "We read, but also *we are read by* others. Interpenetrations in these readings. Forcing someone to read himself as we read him (slavery). Forcing others to read us as we read ourselves (conquest). A mechanical process. More often than not, a dialogue between deaf people."[45]

Realizing that Weil's metaphorical use of the word "deaf" means a refusal to listen, we understand, of course, that such a dialogue is no dialogue at all, but this "mechanical process" is precisely what goes on at many meetings that bill themselves as "philosophy conferences," and in classrooms that emphasize "triumphant" logic, and sometimes in informal disputes, not to mention in international "peace talks" and negotiations that seek concession rather than understanding the roots of problems. Where the drive to dominate takes precedence in an argument, truth falls by the wayside, and interlocutors become more concerned with avoiding shame, embarrassment—and, in Weil's terms, "slavery." This preoccupation can hardly be avoided when a framework of domination is established from the beginning. The results of such pseudo-dialogues can only be utter humiliation (on one side) and inflation of ego (on the other). An objective of seeking truth and the embrace of that search would humble both parties and preclude a violent relationship.

As mentioned, the flip side of the denigration of dialogue is the emboldening of sophists. In the ancient Greek context, the sophists were the paid travelling educators who promised to teach the sons of the newly emergent class of aristocrats how to win arguments and win over the masses, so as to attain political power.[46] Winning did not (and does not) necessitate a desire for truth or the learning of virtue; in fact, the triumph of persuasion is often hindered by attention to truth and virtue, for the latter are frequently uncomfortable, inconvenient and, as we have noted, elusive. For this reason, the sophist is the master of technological thinking; this is thinking that guarantees "success." The phrases he employs are easy on the mind, and they have the air of nobility which listeners automatically identify with themselves. The audiences are carried away, but such sophistic speech is no poetry, for poetry is not easy or reduced or dissociated from complexities and the multitude of contexts. Instead, this sort of speech is actually mechanical—like the speaker himself, in Orwell's depiction:

> A speaker who uses that kind of [sophistic] phraseology has gone some distance towards turning himself into a machine. The appropriate noises are coming out of his larynx, but his brain is not involved as it would be if he were choosing his words for himself. If the speech he is making is one that he is accustomed to make over and over again, he may be almost unconscious of what he is saying, as one is when one utters the responses in church. And this reduced state of consciousness, if not indispensable, is at any rate favorable to political conformity.[47]

Orwell is right to characterize the sophist as one who is nearly "unconscious," not really choosing his own words. To say this is not to deny the sophist's responsibility, for there was at least an initial consent to the orientation of domination rather than to genuine *eros*. But the unconsciousness *does* tell us something about the gravitational pull and restriction of freedom that accompanies the prioritization of conquest.

Plato, as we know, charged the sophists with studying the "great beast," the collection of convictions expressed by the masses when they are gathered together.[48] The metaphor is apt because the opinions of the majority are not rooted in anything real but are capricious, arbitrary, and generally shaped by what is immediately pleasing. While the beast is a force to be reckoned with, as a *beast*, the sophist studies it so as to subdue and manipulate it. Of course, it is the nature of the beast that it does not recognize itself as such, and it is the nature of the sophist to be blind to the fact that his "success" is predicated on obedience and submission to the moods of the beast. Hence, he is not genuinely free, and his words are not his own. But to protect himself from this recognition, he employs euphemism, in this case calling the knack for manipulation of the beast "wisdom." What he actually possesses is relative, not absolute, knowledge because, as Plato reminds us, "In truth, [the sophist] knows nothing about which of these convictions is fine or shameful, good or bad, just or unjust, but he applies all these names in accordance with how the beast reacts."[49] So whatever the masses enjoy is "good," and what displeases them is "bad;" and whatever the sophist is "compelled to do" in their service is "just."[50]

For Weil, the "great beast" is "the object of all idolatry" and "the only object of idolatry."[51] The danger lies in the fact that the collective, unlike an individual human, can really create a sense of consummation and satisfaction when someone associates with it. The "great beast" lends prestige, for "it is the social which throws the color of the absolute over the relative;"[52] it thereby negates the experience of void and hunger and puts an end to desiring-without-an-object (since an object has been found). The reverence of the great beast puts an end to dialogue, as any worship of object-ness would.[53] In its place spring up a variety of poor substitutes: the initiation of meaningless word games (construed as "argument," but with championship rather than the sincere search for truth in mind[54]); the exchange of trivia (i.e., that which is trivial); the bandying of euphemisms and "words with capital letters," divorced from all relationships; and, perhaps most dreadfully, the creation of myths and monsters out of latent fears and prejudices, the latter of which are in turn bolstered by their own fictive creations. The irony here is that, like Gyges, we have become invisible to ourselves, not recognizing our own monstrosity.[55]

Possibilities for Radical Language

Given these observations, it is apparent to us that a mere reformation of our exploitative relationship to language would be insufficient to bring about the radical changes that are needed in an a-literate society with a penchant for technological thinking. In Weil's words, "There is nothing more desirable than to get rid of [the ring of Gyges]. It should be thrown to the bottom of a well whence it can never again be recovered."[56] By casting away this ring, she means that we would stop "setting things aside," and we would start making the connections that can, of themselves, prevent violence. Such an action would constitute, not a reformation of values, but a revolution, in the quite literal sense: a "turning of the whole soul."[57] What follows from this reorientation? Let us first consider the potential for "radical language," before turning to the question of our preparedness to embrace it.

Language, indeed, when it is meaningful, is radical; in the etymological sense of that word, it is *rooted*. But the roots of meaningful language are "in the sky,"[58] so that we need not presume that meanings are fixed or words are static. On the contrary, we must understand that words are like signposts pointing to truths which are beyond our reach. When we forget this and begin to think that language can capture the absolute, our minds become enclosed in language, as in a prison. "If a captive mind is unaware of being in prison, it is living in error,"[59] and it is this error which is a great temptation, especially for those who are intelligent and can deftly wield words, though they do not engage in genuine dialogue. For this reason, Weil claims: "A village idiot in the literal sense of the word, if he really loves truth, is infinitely superior to Aristotle in his thought, even though he never utters anything but inarticulate murmurs."[60] It is because the village idiot has a real hunger for truth and would really value the erotic dialogue, if he were capable of engaging in it, that he surpasses the mere intelligence of one like Aristotle.

Not only must we remember the limitations of language in general, but we must also be discriminate, as we have seen, about the abilities, potentials, and uses of language in orienting us towards (or away from) truth. Certainly, words like "democracy," "fascism" and "freedom" are prone to losing their roots and becoming inflated.[61] But even in an atmosphere of technological thinking, sophistry, and the idolatrous reverence of the collective towards its language, Weil suggests that beauty may be dimly perceived, and it is crucial that we are attentive to its presence. "It sometimes happens," she writes, "that a fragment of inexpressible truth is reflected in words which, although they cannot hold the truth that inspired them, have nevertheless so perfect a formal correspondence with it that every mind seeking that truth finds support in them. Whenever this happens a gleam of beauty illumines the words."[62] This glimmer of beauty, then, is necessary to inspire language to be a reliable signpost to ultimate truths. While beauty itself "says nothing," and is not reducible to words, it "cries out and points to truth and justice who are dumb, like a dog who barks to bring people to his master lying unconscious in the snow."[63]

The beauty of good poetry has this potential to move us to throw away the ring of Gyges. Inspired words reorient us towards truth, and thereby commit us to genuine and sincere dialogue. *These* words, unlike their violent counterparts, will be humbled, in the sense that connections will be re-established and abstractions will be resisted, but these words will not be impoverished. On the contrary, language imbued with meaning will be rich in real associations, multiple interpretations, and varied contextual definitions. Such language will be nuanced and complex and will not be suitable for banners, emblems, slogans, clichés, or collective chants. Such words will be sufficiently concrete and defined, however, so that we are held accountable to our own terms and disturbed by inconsistency. If, for instance, we give a broad definition to the word "terror" in order to gain great flexibility in identifying enemies under that heading, we need to be prepared to recognize that our own actions may situate ourselves within that expansive definition. On the other hand, if we give a narrow definition to "torture" in order to have license to employ "intensive interrogation techniques" (for we, by definition, do not "torture,") then we need to be prepared to accept other parties' adoption of a similar definition in relation to us. In clarifying the meanings of words, we will necessarily be reminded of our interdependence with others, and will see ourselves *in relation.*

Yes, the beauty of good poetry has the potential to save lives by awakening desire for truth and replacing the spirit of dominance with the spirit of humility. Yet "the beautiful poem is the one which is composed while the attention is kept directed toward inexpressible inspiration, in so far as it is inexpressible."[64] In a distracted culture filled with every sort of technological device designed to further reduce and impoverish language, what are the chances of artistic attention? And if beautiful poems are crafted, what are the chances that *they* will be attended to? In these matters, Weil was pessimistic. She wrote, "We hate the people who try to make us form the connections we do not want to form."[65] The artists who, being inspired by beauty, make a revolution of language (and hence, politics) possible, are like the educators returned to the Platonic cave who may facilitate the reorientation of the prisoners' souls. The technological thinking that rules the minds of the prisoners may dictate that the artist-educator and her words be *targeted, shot down, demolished.* Certainly, this has happened and continues to happen, to Simone Weil and those like her, and to their writings. But by bearing the brunt of this violent framework, continuing to speak radical language, and going on loving in the void, they may, without knowing it, reveal the emptiness of some of our idols, and thus detonate some of our readied bombs.[66]

Notes

1   SWA, 179.
2   Susan Jacoby, *The Age of American Unreason* (New York: Pantheon Books, 2008), xviii.
3   Ibid.
4   Ibid.
5   GG¹, 191.
6   GG¹, 191.
7   GG¹, 191–2.
8   Hannah Arendt, *Responsibility and Judgment* (New York: Schocken Books, 2003), 159–60.
9   GG¹, 192.
10 GG¹, 193.
11 Cf. Richard Kearney, *Strangers, Gods and Monsters: Interpreting Otherness* (New York: Routledge, 2003), especially Chapters 1, 3 and 4.
12 Chris Hedges, *War Is a Force that Gives Us Meaning* (New York: Anchor Books, 2002), 9, 10.
13 GG¹, 54.
14 Hannah Arendt distinguishes "fabrication" from "action" by noting that the latter "is never possible in isolation; to be isolated is to be deprived of the capacity to act." On the other hand, "the popular belief in a 'strong man' who, isolated against others, owes his strength to his being alone is either sheer superstition, based on the delusion that we can 'make' something in the realm of human affairs—'make' institutions or laws, for instance, as we make tables and chairs, or make men 'better' or 'worse'—or it is conscious despair of all action, political and non-political, coupled with the utopian hope that it may be possible to treat men as one treats other 'material.'" Hence fabrication, for Arendt, is reification, in that it involves taking material from a natural location/process and thus arresting it. Therefore, the "element of violation and violence is present in all fabrication." Hannah Arendt, *The Human Condition* (Chicago: University of Chicago Press, 1998), 188, 139.
15 SWA, 221.
16 George Orwell, "Politics and the English language," in *A Collection of Essays* (San Diego: Harvest Books, 1981), 167.
17 SWA, 222.
18 SWA, 223.
19 Notice, for example, the implicit appeal to tradition in the fallacious association fabricated in terms such as "Islamo-fascism." This association seemed, of course, natural to an audience who were informed, at best, by Orientalist academic discourse, and at worst by the mass media's representation of Islam only in sensationalist terms. See: Edward Said, *Orientalism* (New York: Vintage Books, 1979); and Edward Said, "Islam as news," in *The Edward Said Reader*, ed. Moustafa Bayoumi and Andrew Rubin (New York: Vintage Books, 2000).
20 SWA, 221.
21 Orwell, "Politics and the English language," 168.
22 Arendt, *Responsibility and Judgment*, 160.

23 In A. Rebecca Rozelle-Stone's unpublished dissertation, "Voiding distraction: Simone Weil and the religio-ethics of attention" (Southern Illinois University Carbondale, 2008), she used the term "a-voidance" to refer to Weil's idea of negating the void by filling it with consolations, imaginative projections, materials, distractions, idols—in short, anything that suffices to close/fill the emptied-openness that comprises attention. Hence, when we are being inattentive, we a-void. Editors' note: See also Chapter 2.

24 Orwell, "Politics and the English language," 166.

25 Plato, *Republic*, trans. G. M. A. Grube (Indianapolis: Hackett Publishing Co., 1992), 560b.

26 Ibid., 560c.

27 Ibid.

28 Ibid., 560d.

29 Ibid., 560e.

30 GG¹, 122.

31 Paulo Freire, *The Pedagogy of the Oppressed*, trans. Myra Bergman Ramos (New York: Continuum, 2003), 59.

32 Ibid.

33 SWA, 224–5.

34 Recall President Dwight D. Eisenhower's "Farewell address to the nation," delivered 17 January 1961, in which he warned the nation about the dangers of the "military-industrial complex." "Only an alert and knowledgeable citizenry," he noted, "could prevent this menace from undermining "our liberties or democratic processes." http://www.vlib.us/amdocs/texts/ddefarew.html (accessed on 10 March 2009).

35 Richard Kearney notes that "recurring phenomena [such as] witch-hunting, xenophobia, racism, anti-Semitism," which occur "often in the name of 'national security' . . . operate on the fantasy that it is the evil adversary outside/inside the *Volk* who is poisoning the wells, contaminating the body politic, corrupting the unsuspecting youth, eroding the economy, sabotaging peace and destroying the general moral fabric of society. Moreover, the popular media in modern societies often play a pivotal role in ostracizing some commonly identified 'alien' (individual or group)." Kearney, *Strangers, Gods and Monsters*, 38.

36 SWA, 221–2.

37 Cf. Jacques Ellul, *Propaganda: The Formation of Men's Attitudes*, trans. Konrad Kellen and Jean Lerner (New York: Vintage Books, 1973).

38 SWA, 225.

39 Plato, *Symposium*, trans. Alexander Nehamas and Paul Woodruff (Indianapolis: Hackett Publishing Co., 1989) 203c. Eros ("love") was conceived by the intercourse of Poros ("resource") and Penia ("poverty"), as Diotima informed Socrates. Not only was Eros between wealth and poverty, and between immortality and mortality, but he was "between wisdom and ignorance as well" (204a).

40 Anne Carson, *Eros: The Bittersweet* (USA: Dalkey Archive Press, 2000), 109.

41 GG¹, 68. Editors' note: See also Chapter 2.

42 GG¹, 116.

43 George Lakoff and Mark Johnson, *Metaphors We Live By* (Chicago: University of Chicago Press, 2003), 4.

44 Ibid. Conversely we employ colloquialisms such as "war games," turning the use of violent force into mere play. More perniciously, Hamid Dabashi has observed that the recent rise in terrorist attacks "has once again raised the fear of Islam as the principal nemesis of 'the Western civilization,' . . . asserting categorically that there is something inherently violent about their religion and culture . . . Under these frightful circumstances, terms and phrases have assumed iconic power of their own, with no or merely vacuous connections to reality. If a desperate teenager in Palestine blows himself and everything around him up into smithereens that is a 'terrorist *attack*'; but if the IDF (Israeli Defense Force) razes an entire Palestinian village or refugee camp to the ground, or else carpet bombs from air, sea, and land from one end of Lebanon to the other, it is a '*defensive* act.' If Iraqi people of varied political persuasions defend their country against a foreign invasion, they merit the term 'terrorists,' but if the deadliest military machinery in history is brought in to 'shock and awe' them into submission it is called 'liberation' through something called 'Operation Iraqi Freedom.' In the midst of such linguistic obscenities, foreclosing the violent spiral of fear and fury, 'Islam and the West,' projected as two eternal arch nemeses, are once again posited as the principal coded categories of this global confrontation between irreconcilable adversaries—two cosmic forces of good and evil." Hamid Dabashi, *Islamic Liberation Theology: Resisting the Empire* (New York: Routledge, 2008), 33. We would do well to recall former President George W. Bush's State of the Union Address (January 2002), during which he proclaimed the so-called "Axis of Evil" (Iraq, Iran and North Korea).

45 GG¹, 188–9.

46 Cf. Ellul, *Propaganda.*

47 Orwell, "Politics and the English language," 166.

48 Plato, *Republic*, 493b.

49 Ibid., 493c.

50 "[P]ropaganda must not concern itself with what is best for man—the highest goals humanity sets for itself, its noblest and most precious feelings. Propaganda does not aim to elevate man, but to make him *serve*. It must therefore utilize the most common feelings, the most widespread ideas, the crudest patterns, and in so doing place itself on a very low level with regard to what it wants to do and to what end. Hate, hunger, and pride make better levers of propaganda than do love or impartiality" (Ellul, *Propaganda*, 38).

51 GG¹, 216.

52 GG¹, 217.

53 Ellul writes: "Propaganda cannot be satisfied with partial successes, for it does not tolerate discussion; by its very nature, it excludes contradiction and discussion. As long as a noticeable or expressed tension or a conflict of action remains, propaganda cannot be said to have accomplished its aim. It must produce quasi-unanimity, and the opposing faction must become negligible, or in any case cease to be vocal" (*Propaganda*, 11).

54 George Orwell wrote, "The great enemy of clear language is insincerity" ("Politics and the English language," 167).

55 Dabashi lists the blatant lies and deception committed under the banner of "Operation Enduring Freedom" (the US invasion of Afghanistan) and the seemingly unending "War on Terror" propagated by US government officials in the build-up to the invasion of Iraq (March 2003). "Every single member of the Bush administration, beginning with the President himself, down to Secretary of State Colin Powell and Secretary of Defense Donald Rumsfeld . . . [were] aided, abetted, and endorsed by CNN, *The New York Times*, Fox News and the rest of the US propaganda machinery, systematically [lying] and [deceiving] Americans, and with them the rest of the world." And even when the truth finally saw the light of day, and these deceptions were revealed, "No one was fired, no one was impeached." Dabashi, *Islamic Liberation Theology*, 4–5.

56 GG¹, 192.

57 Plato, *Republic*, 518d.

58 SWA, 66. Weil writes, "It is the light falling continually from heaven which alone gives a tree the energy to send powerful roots deep into the earth. The tree is really rooted in the sky."

59 SWA, 69.

60 SWA, 67.

61 See Orwell's discussion of these words, "Politics and the English language," 162.

62 SWA, 72–3.

63 SWA, 73.

64 GG¹, 150.

65 GG¹, 193.

66 One such recent poet who loved in the void and whose poems point to inexpressible truths is the late Leonardo Alishan. Consider his poem "Tired Thoughts," which inspired the conclusion to this chapter:

> They have buried ten million mines
> in Afghanistan, one land mine
> for every two or three Afghans,
> regardless of age or ethnic background.

> They have planted death in the womb
> of the mother. Prosthetic limbs are airdropped
> with food. They have planted a mine
> under God's pillow and his dreams of doves.

> Every night a new dark dream spreads
> its wings in my sleep. This morning I woke
> with a throbbing headache. I woke tired.
> I had defused or detonated mines all night.

> A dream so real, I checked my limbs.
> They were still mine. A dream so dark

I checked my heart. God was still there.
But also still mine and also still there

was the problem of ten million mines,
ten million limbs, ten million lives, ten million
dreams, blown apart in the heart of a God
who plows with the farmers and lives in my heart.

Winner of the "People Before Profits Poetry Prize" (Burning Bush Publications, 2003), http://www.bbbooks.com/winner2003.html (accessed on 10 March 2009).

Chapter 10

Despair is the Handmaiden of War[1]

E. Jane Doering

Once Simone Weil acknowledged that pacifism was not a viable option for blocking a determined aggressor, she had to make hard decisions concerning the parameters for exerting force. After accepting the use of force in extreme cases both on a national scale and an individual level, her major preoccupation was to convince her readers that violence contaminated both perpetrator and victim. Contamination meant that both parties became activators in the spiral of force and that they risked losing the most essential part of their being: their soul. Given this terrible reality, she wanted to find ways to limit the contagion of violence, so that anyone engaged in a justified use of force would be wary of its infectious quality.

She believed in her heart that non-contaminating options existed for stopping an adversary bent on havoc, among them an unwavering respect for justice and a reliance on supernatural grace. Her quest uncovered guidelines for confronting force and for sharpening a people's alertness to agendas hidden behind their leaders' demands to exact a pound of flesh for a perceived wrong. Weil proposed a new attitude towards withstanding the worst effects of force by solidifying a nation's reliance on integrity, humility, impartial justice, and confidence in humankind's natural love of liberty. We will trace her reflections concerning the need, particularly in times of violence, to maintain a firm respect for the human person, and we will examine its pertinence both to the twenty-first century "War on Terror" paradigm and to the Second Gulf War.

Rejection of Pacifism

Until Hitler violated the Munich Accords by invading Prague, Simone Weil had adhered to a pacifist doctrine. She had not yet grasped the full extent of Hitler's megalomania, but after 1939 she painfully assumed responsibility for her misjudgment of his drive to conquer. At this point, she rejected pacifism as no longer serving in the current circumstances, yet she never forswore her personal liability for having encouraged conciliation. Her sense of guilt for having promoted the pacifist "ideology" was unassuageable. Her position had, however, been based on a profound respect for human dignity, which needed social order founded on justice in order to flourish. This concept of respect remained a cornerstone of all her actions.

Just Uses of Force

Prior to her recognition of the obligation to exert violent action in strictly defined circumstances, Weil had started to set down basic principles about war, pinpointing the futility of embarking on an aggression without having carefully analyzed both the ultimate goal and the means to attain it. At this point in her thinking, she did not believe that any conditions, rationally assessed, would warrant using violence against others, but philosophically she wanted to lay the groundwork for her readers to be able to apply stringent self-critical criteria, according to the particular historical, political and technological context. Her methodological approach included asking whether the cause was definable and just, the final aim achievable, the means proportionate to the goal, the gains greater than the losses, and whether alternative means might better serve while causing less harm. She had already warned that the capacity of modern weapons for massive destruction belied the assurances that civilians would be protected.[2] In her 1933 "Reflections on war,"[3] written while the drumbeats of international aggression were intensifying, she explored these basic questions, which echoed long-standing precepts of just war theory: just cause (*jus ad bellum*), probability of success, comparative justice (*jus in bello*), proportionality, and last resort.

Simone Weil's technique was to work out all the elements of the problem rationally, using personal observation, history and literature to corroborate what she discerned as the truth. In her fundamental exploration of war, one finds no mention of either Augustine's or Aquinas's opinions on just war theory, or anyone else's. She seldom referenced her thoughts, for she believed that a trained mind could arrive at the truth by reflection, observation, assessment of the facts, and above all an ardent desire to know the truth. She addressed her articles to specific audiences, presenting the philosophical principles that formed the basis for her argument. Her style lent timelessness to her thoughts.

Weil's conviction that force, once it received an initial spark, flamed out of control until its energies were spent, led her to stress the effort needed to avoid the initial onslaught of violence. Untethered violence obscured any final objective because passions overwhelmed the ability to reason and allowed the base desire for vengeance and power to gain the upper hand, leaving despair in its wake. This despair drained the motivation to seek escape from an impossibly painful situation, so the fighting continued. In an early notebook, she wrote: "The dreaded handmaiden of war has always been despair. Constrained to adapt to a situation in which all its aspirations are purely and simply denied, the soul works violence on itself . . . The objectives for the war are forgotten, it is necessary to deny any goals at all. They endure [nevertheless] despite their absurdity, but precisely because they are absurd."[4]

Her mystical experience added depth to this aspect of her belief by illuminating the efficacy of grace for activating a counterforce that could temper whirling violence. Great sacrifice, however, was unavoidable. Her call to arms was rooted in a moral appeal to enforce a concept of justice that guaranteed each person's freedom to put down roots in a culture with its own language, environment and traditions. Supernatural experience had sharpened her conviction that this rooting comprised each person's bridge to what she called the "reality outside the world, that is, outside space and time, outside man's mental universe, outside any sphere that human faculties could attain."[5]

Reflections on War

Weil argued in her 1933 essay, addressed to workers, that their hopes of achieving the goals of dignity, liberty and power by ceding to the siren call of war were illusory, as was the fantasy that past successes could be relived. She warned them that language often veiled private intentions of leaders seeking greater control over the people. They should be wary of public figures evoking past victories with rhetorical flourishes, or inflaming their emotions with national hymns like the *Marseillaise*. Historically, the claims of liberty following the French Revolution were manipulative, for the Reign of Terror had brought tighter domestic control, which was heightened during Napoleon's imperial rule. Above all, giving primacy to the objective rather than to the means was a defective method of assessing the need to go to war.

Modern combat, with its advanced technological weaponry, required an increasing centralization of power, which reduced the people's individual freedoms in the name of something supposedly more glorious. She maintained that, as a minimum, any justification for using force to obtain a goal required a prior objective study of war's mechanism and its effect on a people's social and economic relationships. She wrote: "One cannot resolve nor even pose a problem relative to war without having first dismantled the mechanism of the military struggle, i.e., having analyzed the societal relationships entailed in the given technological, economic, and social conditions."[6]

Weil observed that technological innovations necessitated a fresh evaluation of war, for they had created radical breaks from former conflicts. One major change increased the subordination of men to technology, as the modern instruments of warfare became progressively more oppressive. Men subjected to industrial demands had the freedom to seek other work, whereas military personnel were ordered to expose their very lives for a cause decided by authorities far from the battlefield. She claimed, "In our times, war is characterized by the subordination of the combatants to the instruments of combat; and armaments, the real heroes of modern wars, are, just like the men devoted to their service, directed by those who do not do the fighting."[7] No vulnerable social stratum in society should ever lightly take on war as an easy means to gain freedom from oppression.

War and Domestic Politics

Another major difference from former times, in Weil's calculation, was modern war's projection of economic competition into the arena of international diplomacy. Each country, needing to appear more powerful than its neighbors, had to dedicate its economy to creating the impression of strength. Thus, arms production served to advance a nation's supremacy, while its goods, produced at a profit for the industrialists and financiers, served as the preparation for future wars. Weil's prophetic warning found an echo in Dwight D. Eisenhower's later identification of the military-industrial complex. Weil attributed this dangerous interdependence to a permanent quest for hegemony which, since it was illusory and unstable, initiated an unending cycle of violence. The great mistake of most war studies, she insisted, was to consider war as an episode of foreign politics when, on the contrary, it constituted a cruel reality of domestic politics.[8] Domestic political relationships determine foreign political relationships. In any case, whether the government called itself fascist, democratic or a dictatorship of the workers, Weil asserted, "Arms wielded by the apparatus of a powerful State can bring liberty to no one."[9]

Her imperative message was that war constitutes, in each epoch, a well-determined type of violence, whose mechanism must be studied before making any judgment whatsoever. To illustrate this point, she cited the revolutionaries Saint-Just and Robespierre, who had participated in the rising protest against the *ancien régime* as advocates for democratic equality. However, having gained absolute power, they became tyrannical despots during the Reign of Terror and oppressed the very people they had planned to liberate. Saint-Just admitted ruefully on the eve of being guillotined: "Only those who are in the battles win them, while only the powerful profit from them."[10] Robespierre too, facing his approaching death, denounced those who profit from war: "War is good for military officers, the ambitious, the speculators . . . [and] for those with executive power."[11] Weil repeated that the legendary image depicting the Revolution of 1789 as a glorious victory of the weak over the strong contradicted historical reality and could not serve anyone's just cause. Exploited patriotic myths lure gullible followers into a form of despotism that diminishes their freedom as individuals.

Weil saw violence as an inherent part of social interaction, so she wanted her readers to be attentive to the mechanism of every political system that tended to swallow up the weaker members of society. To endure honorably in this struggle and to maintain the mental stability to think rationally, one must remain faithful to human values and never participate in trampling them underfoot, no matter what sacrifice the social institutions might deem necessary. Weil saw society as an immense machine with no one at the controls, ceaselessly snapping up individuals. Those who sacrificed themselves for social morality resembled people who grabbed onto the gears and belts of the transmission in an attempt to stop the machine. They were crushed in their turn. Nevertheless, the essential rule for survival with integrity, given the relentlessness of the struggle, was never to subject one's moral compass to a state, or a military or economic organization, that undermined human values.

"Reflections in View of an Assessment"

Six years later, observing the intensifying fear encumbering her countrymen's spirits as they watched the Third Reich grow more menacing, Weil made another attempt to remind her fellow Frenchmen of the "obligation to evaluate clearly the overall situation."[12] With pacifism off the table, she identified self-defense for one's endangered homeland as a justification for using force. France's existence was at risk. She and a group of fellow intellectuals put their minds to imagining a wider range of means to confront aggressive nations by presenting postures of strength without relying on trickery, violence or hypocrisy.

In her 1939 contribution, "Reflections in view of an assessment,"[13] Weil stepped back from the immediate conflict to probe innovative techniques that might be fruitfully employed before violence broke loose. She explored the paradoxes in traditional attitudes towards diplomacy and in military build-ups for self-defense. She gave primacy to a nation's ethical conduct. Her major intent was to incorporate into international relations a critical pause for reflection and an objective assessment of all contending factors prior to any decision that set off self-generating violence.

Established procedures between negotiating nations had an unfortunate ambiguity: concessions were perceived as weakness, and gains as strength. Such interpretations could provoke an aggressive nation to grow overconfident in its ability to dominate. The second quandary in traditional methods was that as each nation developed its arsenal of weapons for self-defense, other nations felt compelled to follow suit. Paradoxically, a nation preparing for eventual military protection put its own survival in peril by spurring a competitive arms race with states that felt targeted. This created an endless cycle of recurrent wars interspersed with brief periods of calm. It was, however, in the tenuous interim between conflicts that Weil saw creative possibilities for extending the period of peace.

Fault Lines in Despotic States

Weil perceived in the stages between intervals of all-out war the potential for allowing other crucial elements to affect the outcome. She wanted domestic tension, resulting from thwarting the desire for liberty, to be treated as a component in her proposition for an alternative statecraft. The fragile transitional moment existed only as long as a trouble-making state did not have full confidence in its ability to win. Her proposal for astute diplomatic give-and-take bargaining encouraged the virtue of patience: waiting and watching for an iron-fisted regime's tight control to fragment. Experience has shown that interior fault- lines of despotic regimes diminished the long-term grip of totalitarian leaders. Given time, those inner points of friction loosened a state's stranglehold. Weil's prime example of a warlike nation crumbling from within because of domestic tensions was the overbearing government in Russia that gained the upper hand after the 1917 revolution and civil war. She pointed out that the panic among the established European authorities, who felt threatened by this "workers' state," had subsided by 1932, without any nations having to go to war. A later example, equally valid, though one she never lived to see, was the corrosive Stalinist tyranny in the Soviet Union during the Cold War. That too ended by implosion due to economic stagnation, massive military spending, and its failed promise to the Russian people of freedom from oppression. Weil died before this second checkmate, but it also demonstrated her principle of keeping a holding pattern until the regime collapsed under the weight of its own inner flaws applied. This kind of calm attentive watching and waiting regretably lacks the flamboyant appeal of a call to arms.

Ethical Behavior as a Moral Force

The capacity of brute force to obliterate spiritual values, thus increasing the difficulty of courageously withstanding oppressive conditions, preoccupied Weil. Her belief that we must love the world here below led her to intuit the existence of an alternative galvanizing drive that could counter destructive force. Nations and individuals could spread and increase this beneficial motivation by strictly adhering to a code of moral behavior. National virtues such as probity, justice, generosity, and respect for liberty, offered paradigms and courage to freedom-loving individuals all over the world, and enabled them to recognize and stand against encroaching evil actions. A military regimen, by contrast, with all its constraints and limitations on freedom, frittered away those values by severely limiting their ability to radiate inspiration. In Weil's philosophy, a behavior based on an eternal criterion of the "Good" and reinforced by an overtly respectful reliance on freely assumed moral values became in itself a formidable negotiating technique.

In her "Assessment," Weil explored ways that a positive moral stance could add credibility to a country's diplomacy in times of peace, staving off the unleashing of ruthless force by opening valuable space for an objective evaluation of the situation and for the elements of goodness to cohere. The idea that nations could curb the amount of violence in the world by banking on their reputation for ethical behavior indicated a new direction in her thought. She proposed that sustaining a state's peaceful stance required that actions be solidly grounded in a core of ethical conduct. Within limits, nations and individuals monitored the impression they gave to the rest of the world, which played an important psychological role in international relations.

The idea of judging nations by the humane quality of their actions gained momentum after the toll of physical and mental damage done to combatants and non-combatants in World War Two. In 1948, 48 members of the General Assembly of the United Nations adopted the Universal Declaration of Human Rights, which opened with these words:

> Recognition of the inherent dignity and of the equal and inalienable rights of all members of the human family is the foundation of freedom, justice and peace in the world.
>
> Disregard and contempt for human rights have resulted in barbarous acts that have outraged the conscience of humanity.

One year later the Third and Fourth Geneva Conventions, relating to the treatment of prisoners of war and to the protection of civilians, were signed. Humankind took an enormous step forward with these covenants, which set standards for civil, political, economic and social rights on an international scale.

Weil would have appreciated their potential to safeguard the dignity of human beings, recognizing that the power of these documents resided in the global commitment to high standards of morality. Consequently, when a respected democracy violates any articles of these agreements, their transgressions influence predatory leaders elsewhere, who leap on the example to justify their own mistreatment of dissenters. Lamentably, the climate of fear and uncertainty created by the 11 September 2001 attacks on the World Trade Center set the stage for numerous violations of human rights perpetrated by the very liberal democracies that had formerly been avid promoters and protectors of human rights.

Stalwart dependence on probity as a guide for action in difficult times requires confidence in one's moral compass. Weil understood that both nations and individuals could be pressured by expediency, but she insisted that nothing merited the dismissal of human values. Periodic recurrences of power clashes diminish a people's self-assurance and tempt them to bypass long-standing ethical codes when the situation appears desperate. Weil's keen interest in bolstering the spirits of people overwhelmed by intimidating obstacles led her to evoke survivors of past despair-inducing events in order to share human compassion across the ages. She cited a Persian's observation to Herodotus: "The most unbearable human suffering by far is to understand a great deal and be able to do nothing."[14] In other words, people engulfed by disheartening circumstances were not alone; in the face of inexpressible suffering, they could endure, particularly by remembering that humankind's unquenchable love of freedom necessarily made conflict part and parcel of the human condition.

The Twenty-first Century in Light of Weil's Philosophy

Weil was not alone in recognizing that global relationships benefit when powerful democracies ensure respect for human rights and base all their actions on the rule of law. Adversely, liberal democracies that violate human rights and circumvent the legal framework let loose a torrent of disorder and misery. In 2009, a panel of "eminent jurists", as an independent branch of the International Commission of Jurists, released the results of their three-year study of the responses to the events of 9/11.[15] They found that the cumulative impact of the free-ranging counterterrorism policies adopted since that attack has imperiled the international legal structure that safeguards human rights, so assiduously assembled over six decades.

The jurists identified the "War on terror" paradigm initiated by the US administration, with its flawed application of the laws of war to a criminal act, as the origin of a callous indifference to humanitarian laws. According to their interviews, this conflation of criminal acts with acts of war had weakened hard-earned respect for human rights and led to illicit practices such as extraordinary rendition, secret detentions, enforced disappearances, and torture.[16] By officially sanctioning illtreatment of suspected "terrorists", the United States Government had undermined its moral standing, allowing other states that routinely violated human rights to justify their own wrongdoing by comparisons with the US.[17] Concerned that "the international legal order based on respect for human rights was in jeopardy,"[18] the panel urged the global community to repeal all policies inconsistent with the obligations implied in humanitarian law. They insisted that the prohibition against torture is a non-negotiable safeguard. "Torture violates the principle of human dignity that lies at the heart of the broader international human rights framework, and as such is never acceptable."[19] The present world situation illustrates Weil's claims about the ability of brute force to contaminate and to self-generate beyond original intentions.

An application of Weil's ideas to the intangible value of ethical behavior as a way to minimize the increase of violence within and between countries could benefit the United States, which has always prided itself on being a positive example of respect for human dignity. A reliance on force has manifold disadvantages, while an extension of the negotiating process, as Weil recommended, could facilitate more patient and shrewd diplomacy when dealing with saber-rattling states. Very importantly, consistent respect for human dignity, and honest humility for a nation's past failings and present transgressions—one's own and those of others—radiates positive inspiration to countries tempted to waver on core values.

There is sufficient evidence that Weil's advocacy of an innovative style of diplomacy should have merited serious consideration when the United States dealt with Saddam Hussein in 2002–2003. Offering more non-military assistance to improve the Iraqis' living conditions and reduce their oppression would have better served the goal of winning hearts and minds. Whichever of Weil's criteria for justifying the use of force one chooses—a definable just cause (i.e., the elimination of Saddam Hussein and his "weapons of mass destruction"); an attainable end (i.e., a viable democracy); proportionate means (i.e., destruction kept to a minimum); gains exceeding losses (i.e., survivors anticipating a better future); and alternative routes weighed (i.e., continued United Nations weapons inspections)—the cascade of violence in Iraq fails to reach a single standard of justice.

Just Cause

The misleading linkage of Iraq to the 2001 World Trade Center attacks intentionally obfuscated the American people's ability to think through the mission clearly.[20] Leaders intent on putting their war policy into action insisted that there was no time to ponder over the validity of the cause, intimating that a second terrible threat to the United States hung in the air. But rushing into a violent onslaught with full-blown advanced lethal technology, against a country that had not even attacked the United States, has proven to be unwise and unjust. There were no weapons of mass destruction. Saddam Hussein's dictatorship had created many domestic points of friction that, with external pressures coordinated through the United Nations, showed signs of eroding his regime from within. The unleashed violence, however, has crippled the country's social support system with dire consequences for all, especially women and children.[21] Weil had warned: "Where thought has no place, neither do justice nor prudence have a place. That is why armed men act so harshly and madly."[22]

Illusion of Gain

The Second Gulf War, euphemistically called Operation Iraqi Freedom, has inflicted an incalculable amount of suffering summed up in the grim statistics of car bombs, corpses, wounded bodies, cholera, refugees,[23] and the malfunctioning of the energy, food and water supplies. There is little evidence that any increased measure of "freedom" was brought to the people, despite valiant efforts to safeguard various elections. Nevertheless, no one seems to be able to specify an exit strategy, and so the violence spirals on with a poignant loss of lives and wellbeing. The reality of so many US troops having given their lives for this undefined cause paradoxically feeds the enduring American desire for "victory." War continues because the thought that beloved friends and family members might have died for no valid reason causes deep anguish and despair. Weil noted that giving one's life in a futile effort is unbearable,[24] and so the violence persists even against oneself. United States Army officials have confirmed that suicides among US soldiers in 2008 rose for the fourth consecutive year.[25]

Proportionate Means

The decision to unleash staggering force through the strategic bombing of Iraq with precision-guided Cruise missiles, Predator drones and other "smart bombs" that demolished lives, communities and huge swathes of Iraqi land immeasurably, has increased the potential for violence worldwide. The massive air-strikes in the first 48 hours of the "Shock and Awe" campaign over hundreds of targets were designed "to produce the non-nuclear equivalent of the impact that the atomic weapons dropped on Hiroshima and Nagasaki had on the Japanese."[26] One is hard-pressed to consider the means deployed as meeting an ethical criteria.

Weil warned against the immorality of destroying the natural resources needed to sustain human lives. She wrote, "One owes respect to a field of wheat, not for itself, but because it nourishes human beings. Analogously, one owes respect to a collectivity, be it country, family, or all others—, not for itself, but as nourishment for a certain number of human souls."[27] The obligation to honor the basic human needs of the Iraqi people was not respected, as shown by the number of bombing forays that have continued to fly daily over Iraq since 20 March 2003. Any humanitarian objectives were lost in the rubble. The Iraqi people's desire to live in a free and dignified fashion after the death of Saddam Hussein remains unfulfilled. Weil's main principle obtains: "Arms wielded by the apparatus of a powerful State can bring liberty to no one."[28]

Force Generates Force

Weil's parry-and-thrust diplomacy might have been effective in avoiding the terrible upheaval, but it was not allowed to happen. In Iraq, waging war was tried one more time and found wanting in its ability to assure anyone's well-being. On the contrary, the loss of precious lives from many countries, and of an ancient cultural heritage, is irreplaceable. Saddam Hussein and his henchmen could hardly have wreaked more ruin on the country than was inflicted by the recent years of virulent chaos. Weil insisted that if politics was an art, far more artful ways to fend off potential international bullies existed than just opposing them with rampant force. She believed that an active, consistent and honest support of liberty could slow and even halt a forceful march towards domination by the unscrupulous.

Love of Neighbor

Far too many Good Samaritans, who tried to halt the juggernaut of violence, have perished in this plague visited upon Iraq, which has indiscriminately annihilated terrorists and advocates for peace. One such humanitarian was the multilingual Brazilian Sergio Vieira de Melo, who as a United Nations Ambassador volunteered in 2003 for the dangerous task of helping with the UN Assistance Mission in newly bombed Baghdad. A truck bomb blew him up, along with 21 members of his staff, shortly after their arrival. His death was an acute loss to humanity. Weil's belief in the radiance of love of neighbor shown by acts of goodness towards others finds its verification in the courageous dedication of the many non-governmental organization workers striving—in dangerous circumstances—to bring assistance to suffering people all over the world. They are guideposts enabling others to realize the beneficial effects of truly loving actions for humankind.

A Wavering Beacon of Hope

Simone Weil had wanted France to be a beacon of hope: a country that merited its long-standing reputation for behaving ethically, for safeguarding freedom, and for inspiring liberty-loving people all over the world. In her declaration that no one who loved liberty should have any reason to hate France, she was alluding to the 50 million subjects in the French colonies—many living in abject conditions—who deserved equal dignity with French citizens. A nation that claimed to honor human dignity must root out hypocrisy, she believed, and make its actions and words correspond. The exploitation of the colonial population tormented Weil, and she rightly foresaw catastrophic repercussions if France delayed granting them independence.

Weil died before the 16 blood-soaked years of revolt began, first in Indo-China and then in Algeria, and before France undermined its respect for the "rights of man" and the Geneva Conventions by condoning torture as an instrument of state policy during the Algerian revolution. This turn of events would have disheartened Weil to the extreme. Scholarly support exists for the idea that France's belief in her mission to bring civilization to the "uncivilized" (her ideology of a *mission civilisatrice*) enabled France, in a tortuous way, to feel justified in resorting to the inhumane treatment of prisoners. Dr. Rita Maran argues that too many French felt confident they were bringing noble gifts to the Algerians, and as donors thought they had the right, if not the obligation, to use whatever means necessary to achieve that esteemed goal.[29]

An unfortunate echo of France's high-minded assumption of being the bearer of a civilizing mission resonates in the presumption of America undertaking the mission to spread democracy to other countries, regardless of the means. The oft-used biblical allusion to America as a "city on the hill" with a mission from God implies a moral superiority that dispenses with accountability.[30] The flaunted slogan: "God bless America" reinforces the same notion, with its self-laudatory aura devoid of any hint of humbly petitioning for forgiveness.

During "Operation Iraqi Freedom," which claimed to be bringing democracy to the Persian Gulf, the US government also rejected its noble past as an ardent defender of human rights by condoning, in violation of the Fourth Geneva Convention, inhumane treatment of prisoners. Just as French administrators concealed their official approval of torture until their hand was forced, so the United States adamantly denied its authorization of torture until President George W. Bush announced candidly, some years after the fact, that he and his top national security advisors had indeed known about and approved "enhanced interrogation" of detainees, including "waterboarding" or simulated drowning.[31]

Souls in Contact with Force

Simone Weil found the merciless imposition of force by the strong on the defenseless heinous because the perpetrator became blinded to the horror of his acts, and the victims, who had been human, turned, in her words, into "stone."[32] She described the latter as "these unhappy beings who, without dying, become things for all their lives, another type of human, a compromise between man and a cadaver . . . Their death stretches out a whole lifetime; a life that death froze a long time before suppressing it."[33] While this description applies to a victim transformed by torture, the torturer too becomes less human, losing his ability to feel compassion. She wrote: "The one who possesses force walks in a non-resistant environment, in which nothing in the human material around him is of a nature to impel, between the impulse and the act, that brief interval in which thought lodges."[34] Weil elicited here the effects on the conqueror, whether he was part of an armed troop raging against an enemy or whether he had one person under his total control whom he could abuse with impunity. Where strength holds sway over weakness, the menaced life loses all importance, and both dominator and dominated lose part of their humanity.

Weil wanted her co-citizens to think about force and its lasting effects on themselves and their foes: "As mercilessly as force crushes, just as mercilessly it intoxicates whoever possesses it, or believes he possesses it."[35] She added: "The sole art of war is to provoke such transformations . . . The very soul of the combatants is the true object of war. No matter the situation, the property of double petrifaction is essential to force. A soul placed in contact with force only escapes by a type of miracle. Such miracles are rare and brief."[36]

Weil's preoccupation with the dangers of overwhelming force has relevance to America and Americans in the twenty-first century. The United States has allocated 44.4 per cent of its 2009 tax revenue to military expenditures; in 2008, military spending by the US was almost half of the entire global military budget.[37] The disastrous results of fifteen years in Vietnam and now six years in Iraq—and still counting—have shown that bludgeoning force does not serve positive goals, either for individuals or for nations. But having the capacity to destroy entices a country to overstep its limits, because it is easy to forget that victory is transitory and will pass in time to others. Mary Robinson, president of the Eminent Jurists Panel, former UN High Commissioner for Human Rights, and former President of Ireland, has called on the United States to resume its leadership role in promoting and upholding human rights by conducting "a transparent and comprehensive investigation into serious human rights and/or humanitarian law violations committed in the course of the 'War on Terror.'"[38] Conceding this request would be entirely in keeping with Simone Weil's regard for human dignity and her belief in the radiance of good acts.

Pertinent to Weil's insistence on the essential value of national humility was the Nobel Laureate Archbishop Desmond Tutu's 19 February 2009 statement to BBC News: "It would be wonderful if the US president could apologize for the US-led invasion of Iraq on behalf of the American people." The use of excessive force in recent years has not benefited America, but rather has aroused bitter feelings. Simone Weil's conclusion in her 1939 *The* Iliad, *A Poem of Force*, offers valuable standards to the United States: "It is only possible to love and to be just if one knows the empire of force and if one knows how not to honor it."[39] By embracing Weil's advice, a powerful nation, asking pardon in true humility for transgressions against humanity, could inspire a global reorientation of attitudes towards watchful cooperation.

Notes

[1] OC VI.1, 79. All translations are the author's.
[2] OC II.1, 85–6.
[3] OC II.1, 288–9. (FW, 237–8.)
[4] OC VI.1, 79.
[5] EL, 74.
[6] OC II.1, 292.
[7] OC II.1, 293.

8   OC II.1, 293.
9   OC II.1, 294.
10 OC II.1, 294.
11 OC II.1, 295.
12 Oe, 512.
13 Oe, 511–26. (SE, 177–94.)
14 Oe, 515–6.
15 Report of the Eminent Jurists Panel on Terrorism, Counter-terrorism and Human Rights, *Assessing Damage, Urging Action*, Executive Summary, Geneva, Switzerland, (2009).
16 Ibid., 11.
17 Ibid., 9.
18 Ibid., 9–10.
19 Ibid., 12.
20 The Center for Public Integrity identified 935 false statements in the two years after 9/11 by key administration officials, who stated unequivocally that Iraq had weapons of mass destruction (or was trying to produce or obtain them) and/or links to Al Qaeda. See Charles Lewis and Mark Reading-Smith, *False Pretenses*, 23 January 2008, http://projects.publicintegrity.org/WarCard/ (accessed on 8 March 2009).
21 Among Iraqi women aged 15 to 80, 1 in 11 are estimated to be widows. A United Nations report estimated that during the height of sectarian violence in 2006, 90 to 100 women were widowed each day, while only one in six received any state aid. Fatherless children abound. See Anwar J. Ali and Suada al-Salhy, "Need dire and aid scant, Iraq war widows suffer," *New York Times*, 24 February 2009, pp. 1, 6.
22 Oe, 537.
23 In early 2009, the official US military death toll topped 4,300; the Iraq body count of documented civilian deaths is 90,608–98,911. The count of the wounded has been harder to calculate. See: http://www.iraqbodycount.org/ (accessed on 8 March 2009).
24 OC VI.1, 237.
25 Lizette Alvarez, "Sucides of soldiers reach high of nearly 3 decades," The *New York Times*, 29 January 2009. See: *http://www.nytimes.com/2009/01/30/us/ 30suicide.html* (accessed on 8 March 2009).
26 See Harlan K. Ullmann and James P. Wade, *Shock and Awe: Achieving Rapid Dominance* (Washington, D. C: National Defense University, 1996), xxiv.
27 Oe, 1030.
28 OC II.1, 294.
29 See Rita Maran, *Torture: the Role of Ideology in the French-Algerian War* (New York: Praeger, 1989).
30 John Winthrop's first allusion in 1930, referring to the Puritans' covenant with God, was echoed by John F. Kennedy, Ronald Regan, and several political figures in the 2008 presidential campaign.
31 The President made his statement in a public interview with ABC-TV on 11 April 2008.
32 Oe, 530.

[33] Oe 532–3.

[34] Oe, 537.

[35] Oe, 535.

[36] Oe, 546.

[37] Travis Sharp, Center for Arms Control and Non-proliferation (2009), as cited by Anup Shah, *World Military Spending*, http://www.globalissues.org/article/75/world-military-spending (accessed on 16 March 2009).

[38] Report of the Eminent Jurists Panel, 18.

[39] Oe, 551.

Chapter 11

Power, Subjectivity, and Resistance in the Thought of Simone Weil and Michel Foucault

Krista E. Duttenhaver and Coy D. Jones

In spite of the steady growth in recent decades of scholarly interest in Simone Weil and her philosophy, there remains a surprising lack of investigation into the relevance of her thought to current trends in French philosophy. Although several individual studies have explored Weil's personal and intellectual relationships to contemporaries who are influential on post-war French philosophical developments—thinkers such as Emmanuel Levinas, Albert Camus and George Bataille[1]—less attention has been paid to important conceptual affinities which exist between Weil's thought and that of the later generation of leftist thinkers whose constellation of political interests and critical methodologies dominated the French intellectual world of the 1960s and beyond under the label of "poststructuralism." Of course, scholars of Weil have often noted the aspects of her work which appear proleptically postmodern in light of certain concerns held in common with poststructuralist philosophers on issues such as subjectivity, alterity, and the nature and function of institutional power structures; however, it has been difficult to find specific points of engagement between her ideas and those of leading figures of the poststructuralist movement. Part of this difficulty is due, no doubt, to the singularity of Weil's own philosophical idiom, but it is certainly also the case that the metaphysical and religious nature of her thought has further prevented it from finding its proper place among the largely atheistic, deconstructionist tendencies of the contemporary French Left. And while new intellectual trends in Weil's home country have allowed for a more receptive attitude to the religious metaphysics in which her postmodern insights are embedded,[2] assimilation of her ideas by the philosophies of recent decades has often come at the price of sacrificing the peculiar leftist politics integral to her own brand of radical mysticism. Ultimately, if there is anything to be gained from comparing Weil's striking spiritual formulae to a poststructuralist atheology (as opposed to a phenomenological theology), it is the recognition that metaphysics itself—even a transformed *Platonist* metaphysics—is capable of generating a political spirituality equally radical in its love for the world "here below."

In that respect, the work of Michel Foucault is especially appealing in its potential for dialogue with Weil's thought. On the positive side, a comparison between the two thinkers reveals an important set of shared thematic interests. Indeed, these two enigmatic philosophers are fundamentally united by their common experience of social existence as a place of imprisonment and incarceration. More negatively, though, a comparison between Weil and Foucault serves as a kind of "test" of the continuing ability of Weil's writings to engage those beyond the circles of her more familiar interlocutors. Certainly, Foucault's thought is predisposed to be less sympathetic to Weil's philosophical style than would be other figures among the poststructuralists. Unlike a Deleuze, whose fondness for metaphysics might permit a connection to Weil's own philosophical idiom, or a Derrida, whose attraction to negative theology might allow for comparative interpretation against a common background of religious tradition, Foucault's thought is much more resistant both to metaphysical elaborations and to mystical readings. Because Foucault's approach to philosophy is so alien to Weil's own philosophical tendencies, however, the significance of any genuine common ground between them can only be heightened.

For Foucault, philosophical concepts are fundamentally instruments of war, crafted specifically to elude the kind of reconciling gestures inherent in the rhetoric of metaphysics and mysticism. In fact, where Foucault's ideas do retain traces of these tendencies, the residual negative theology whose outlines emerge in his work seems to be more akin to Bataille's atheistic mysticism of transgression and the "limit experience" than anything resembling Weil's own eccentric brand of Christian Neo-Platonism.[3] Certainly, in the case of Bataille—with whom Weil was personally acquainted briefly from 1933 to 1934 when the two worked together as contributors to the journal *La Critique sociale*—her dismissal of his political philosophy and spirituality is unequivocal in its forcefulness. Furthermore, in summarizing the stark differences between herself and Bataille, Weil's words might easily be imagined also to have Foucault as their target, had she lived to assess his works. She writes: "The revolution is for him [Bataille] the triumph of the irrational, for me of the rational; for him a catastrophe, for me a methodical action in which one must strive to limit the damage; for him the liberation of the instincts, and notably those that are generally considered pathological, for me a superior morality. What is there in common?"[4]

Indeed, many scholars of Weil, as well as those of Bataille and Foucault, are no doubt inclined to ask precisely this question. Foucault's philosophical rhetoric, formed under the deep influence of the French *avant garde*, must seem to a thinker steeped in Weilienne thought to be too contaminated not only by the existentialist's heroic ethic of self-alienation and self-liberation, but also by the irrationalist celebration in *lebensphilosophie* of creativity and imagination. No doubt such a philosopher might even detect in Foucault's writings a nihilist's mockery of the love of truth and of revolutionary hope. Foucauldians, for their part, would no doubt have reservations concerning a Weilienne ethic marked so decisively by the themes of Christian asceticism. Certainly, they would distrust a philosophical language seemingly infused with pastoral theologies of self-decipherment and self-renunciation, and with disciplinary technologies of bodily obedience and methodical action. In a great many ways, Weil's Platonist metaphysics and Foucault's Nietzschean perspectivalism inhabit two different intellectual worlds. It is reasonable to inquire whether there can be any communication between these two worlds.

Prudence, of course, requires that one should not ask for too much from a comparison of such dissimilar thinkers, and that one should be prepared to find at most mutual resonances instead of exact correspondences in Weil's and Foucault's ideas. Nevertheless, it is also important to recognize that difficulties of comparison between Weil and Foucault are exacerbated by the fact that both are victims of uncomprehending caricatures by friends and foes alike. Indeed, the fundamentally conflicting intellectual commitments which the two thinkers are alleged to represent in their respective philosophies are in fact more the product of appropriation of their thought by others than of positions they themselves assume in the course of their philosophical polemics. In Weil's case, a proper appreciation of her thought has suffered not only from hagiographical treatment by spiritual writers overzealous in their efforts to assimilate her works to more classical modes of Christian mysticism, but also from attacks by her secular and religious critics against what they perceive to be her psychopathology and doctrinal heterodoxy.[5]

By the same token, an accurate understanding of Foucault's work has been obscured by hasty categorizations of his ideas on the part of his liberal and traditionalist opponents, as well as by the sensationalism manufactured by his admirers, who, through the exaggeration of his writings' mystical implications, have attempted to fashion out of his life a kind of "secular hagiography."[6] In particular, James Miller's influential biography of Foucault, *The Passion of Michel Foucault*,[7] reflects and reinforces Foucault's popularity with the American counter-culture by amplifying transgressive themes in Foucault's work and by imbuing his thought with a mystical and occult interpretation which virtually fuses Foucault's own views with those of *avant garde* writers like Bataille. In mingling Foucault and Bataille uncritically, Miller imagines Foucault to be participating with Bataille in the same drug-induced pursuit of mystical "limit experiences," waging the same war against oppressive Christian ascetic practices, flirting with the same cult of death, and exhibiting the same fascination with the spiritual potency of sacrifice—and ignoring all the while the many differences in viewpoint and temperament that exist between the two men. At the very least, "Foucault's texts are reconstituted by Miller in terms of Bataille's account of mystical experience and eroticism and show no appreciation of the shifts in direction and changes of emphasis that take place in Foucault's own reflections."[8]

Interestingly, such shifts prove in fact to be conceptual movements that push Foucault's thought closer to Weil and further away from Bataille; these significant reorientations include, most notably, an increasingly positive appreciation for Western practices of asceticism, a growing sympathy for the Apollonian no less than the Dionysian elements of Greek philosophy and spirituality, as well as a rising opposition to economic structures predicated on sacrifice. Whether Foucault registers this opposition to such sacrificial structures as a warning against the genocidal impulses of modern "biopolitics,"[9] or as a critique of the ascetic techniques of self-renunciation that undergird modern "technologies of the self,"[10] his political spirituality distinguishes itself from Bataille's by its "aspiration to life and not to death, to effective action and not to sacrifice."[11] For these reasons, it is unlikely that any insight will be uncovered by efforts to find intellectual analogues of Foucault's thought among Weil's own contemporaries.

Nor does one learn much about Foucault's affinities to Weil by substituting immediately in her place a Plato or a Descartes. The laziest of postmodern interpreters, trained to detect any trace of metaphysical language and to dismiss its authors out of hand, would certainly have an easy time with Weil. In the first place, her praise of the most rigorous, mathematical science[12] seems naïve and almost anachronistic in its apparent reification of scientific truth. Furthermore, her recourse to categories of the "supernatural" and the "transcendent" appears to perpetuate a misguided quest for universality and for eternal certainties upon which to ground one's knowledge of the world and to draw consolation in the face of historical contingency. Yet even if these accusations might have some merit in connection with those philosophical traditions from which Weil draws so much inspiration, they nevertheless completely miss the respects in which Weil is able to transform the language of the metaphysicians and the mystics in order to open up arenas of thought foreign to the purposes of those traditions, and often antithetical to them as well.

For instance, it is tempting to read Weil's Platonic meditations on mathematical certainty as evidence of a continuation of a theoretical orientation to truth—a habit long established in Western metaphysics as a relation to truth predicated on detachment and control—an orientation described by Heidegger as the "theoretical attitude"[13] and one which is repeatedly criticized by Foucault as a "will to knowledge."[14] However, rather than taking up a relation to truth reminiscent of Cartesian science, Weil is in fact activating a more archaic and defamiliarized language of science in order to undermine this very same orientation to knowledge against which Foucault is himself struggling. Of course, Weil's emphasis on the objectivity of science does indeed aim at a kind of detachment, but one whose mode is less *theoretical* (in which detachment refers to the distance postulated between the subject of knowledge and its object) than it is *ethical*: a science that, for Weil, includes a handful of rigorous spiritual exercises by which one can detach oneself from one's own subjectivity.

Far from constituting a discursive practice according to which the subject exercises power and reinforces itself in its own being, Weilienne science is a contemplation of the mathematical "beauty of the world," and its aim is simply to allow a release from oneself and from the evils inherent in the perspective of the individual ego. As such, it is a science whose attitude is that of impartial attention rather than calculative grasping. Even if the fundamental comportment of Weil's notion of science remains a "beholding," one should note carefully that its mood is aligned with the receptive obedience of the student rather than the commanding gaze of the master. In this respect, Weilienne science has much in common with the relation to truth that Foucault himself attempts to put into practice: a non-strategic, non-instrumental will to truth which he understands simply in terms of *curiosity*. "Not the curiosity that seeks to assimilate what is proper for one to know," he writes, "but that which enables one to get free of oneself."[15] If Weil's conception of science differs so profoundly from the theoretical attitude whose nascent form exposes itself already in the metaphysics of Plato—and even more so in Aristotle—then would it not be the case that, from such a radically dissimilar metaphysical method, one would also expect to find equally drastic departures in the metaphysical conclusions that follow from such a method?

Indeed, in the case of Weil's work, close readers will discover that much of her metaphysical philosophy—developed under significant influence from arch-metaphysicians such as Plato, Descartes and Kant—is in fact emptied of both its old content as well as its old pretensions. For the Foucauldian attuned to the intimate connection between the will to knowledge and the will to power, it is quite easy to see how traditional metaphysics serves as a fantasy of control for those committed to its universal principles. The eternal truths of metaphysics, in their most innocent form, serve as comforting fictions for thinking, allowing thought to rise above the fray of historical contingency and to survey the tumult in imagined insulation from the cruel and unpredictable force of events to which thought is itself also subject. Yet when these comforting fictions are consolidated into an overarching complex of power-knowledge, the consequent vision of reality constrains the perceptions and actions of all those within its structure, producing discursive practices which serve mostly to further the interests of those who shape the discourse itself, while also maintaining the inequalities of power which depend upon that discourse. However, is it the case that Weil's philosophy also partakes of these metaphysical illusions of power? Does it draw strength from the consolations that these illusions offer? It could be argued that only the most limited reading of Weil's texts could answer these questions affirmatively without noticing the ways in which she redeploys metaphysical language in a striking new manner in order to turn it to different purposes, to reverse the ideological course of its doctrines, and even occasionally to make it testify against itself.

Weil's reconfiguration of metaphysics is less a deconstruction of metaphysics than a wholesale transformation of it; after all, she endeavors not merely to expose what is false in metaphysics but also to preserve in it what remains true. Moreover, the metaphysical verities which she deduces ultimately conform in their consequences to the intentions which likewise inform her conception of science; as with the aims of scientific understanding, her metaphysical investigations yield as their specific fruits an effacement of the self and the removal of those categories of subjectivity which prevent the self from viewing the world in its stark reality. Indeed, in comparison to the classical metaphysician, Weil is radical in her desire to withhold metaphysical consolation and to uproot the self from its transcendental hiding-places. Although she is apparently traditional in her affirmation that the world participates in a universal order, this order, which she calls "necessity," is not one in which it is possible for any soul to find rest or to take solace.

To the extent that terms like "supernatural" or "transcendent" have meaning for Weil, they are meanings that must be found within the confines of the order of necessity itself. But these aspects of reality are certainly not islands within the crushing network of necessity, since necessity thwarts all purposes, starves all desires, and erodes all bulwarks against the meanderings of time. Consequently, instead of appealing to the supernatural in order to issue metaphysical guarantees which might compensate for necessity's ravages, Weil counsels only a purposiveness without purpose, a desire without object, and a time that renews itself cyclically. For all of these reasons, the metaphysics of necessity turns out to be something else entirely than a metaphysical fantasy. After all, what classical metaphysician would want it, except perhaps to redeem it?

Too broken to suit a mechanic wishing for a machine, too lifeless to please a naturalist longing for an organism, and too anarchic to satisfy a governor hoping for a cosmopolis, the concept of necessity is a far cry from the dream of an orderly universe for which the metaphysician is perpetually in search. It is certainly not the perfect set of forceps by which one can take hold of reality or get a grip on it in its totality. Necessity's universality in fact lies only in its inescapability; its objectivity, only in its indifference. In this respect, necessity functions for Weil almost precisely as history functions for Foucault. Necessity is a stage for purposeless drift, chance occurrence and dramatic reversals of fortune. It is a network of pure means, but entirely bereft of ultimate ends. In her words, "[t]his world, the realm of necessity, offers us absolutely nothing except means. Our will is for ever sent from one means to another like a billiard ball."[16] Consequently, the roiling movement of necessity also constitutes that torrential flow which powers the endless mill of discourse: discourse which professes to speak of necessity, but whose teleological and essentialist veils only hide its true nature. For Weil, then, to give the order of the world any meaning other than that which may be drawn from its blind yet relentless operation, is to succumb to the falsehoods of discourse, or to put the point in more Foucauldian terms, to transmute a will to truth into a mere will to knowledge.[17]

Clearly, Foucault's "analytics of power" bears a strong resemblance to Weil's concept of "necessity." Indeed, both thinkers' discussions of power are tied closely to their examinations of what Foucault calls the "power/knowledge" relation. Whereas Foucault follows a straightforward Nietzschean course in his analysis of discourse as a power effect and as a strategy of power, Weil explores the power/knowledge relation in a more Platonic idiom, all the while yielding analogous results. Like Foucault, she posits a profound connection between necessity and the collective formation of social structures and individual identities. According to Weil, the intellectual edifice generated and sustained by the power/knowledge relation is an idolatrous and illusory system of social abstractions: the "Great Beast."

Of course, these two analyses of the power/knowledge relation do not exhaust the points of genuine commonality between Weil and Foucault. On the contrary, there are a number of other resonances to be identified in their ideas. For instance, both thinkers share a distrust of humanism in all of its guises: Personalist, Marxist, or Existentialist. Weil and Foucault are also connected by a common interest in disciplinary techniques, especially techniques designed specifically to govern labor, or in which the body itself serves as a strategic site of domination and resistance. Finally, it is possible to detect in the ethical and political works of both thinkers a mutual skepticism regarding juridical models of power; for the most part, their respective analyses of ethical discourses invoking "natural rights" are in each case aimed primarily at discrediting moral strategies which depend upon the construal of power as a right of sovereignty. Although it is impossible here to discuss in any convincing detail all of the various linkages which exist among the ideas of Weil and Foucault, as diverse as they are, it is possible to gesture at least towards the parallel structures still waiting to be uncovered by closer comparison of their works.

Aside from the structural similarities to be found between Weil and Foucault, there is a more basic set of shared thematic interests directing both philosophers in their thinking. Arguably, what fundamentally unites these two enigmatic thinkers is their deep and abiding experience of human life as a place of imprisonment. In Foucault's case, "[t]he single experience which was always at the source of his thought was the reality of imprisonment, the incarceration of human beings within modern systems of thought and practice which had become so intimately a part of them that they no longer experienced these systems as a series of confinements but embraced them as the very structure of being human."[18] His treatment of discourses on madness and sexuality, of the practices of penal institutions, of techniques of government and of the hermeneutics of the self are all directed, in one way or another, to delineating this reality of imprisonment and discovering the various lines of flight still open to those who refuse to be ensnared by it completely. And in the case of Weil, imprisonment also surfaces as one of the major underlying themes of her work. Her many reflections on the irresistibility of gravity, the enclosure of Creation in the realm of necessity, and the illusory autonomy of the ego, all reflect different dimensions of this overwhelming experience of the essential captivity of human life.

Although Weil is perhaps more traditional in her philosophy than Foucault in assigning the cause for humanity's captive condition to the materiality of existence, she does not remain content with an easy Platonism that sees the body only as a prison for the soul. Indeed, the entire person is a prison for Weil, and one of the most important projects for her philosophy,[19] and also for Foucault's, is to learn to free oneself of oneself, to find a technique for rescuing the self in some way from its own subjectivity. But unlike the solutions of Gnosticism—with which both thinkers' philosophies have been charged[20]—neither Weil nor Foucault offers the hope of a complete *liberation* from this prison of subjectivity or a metaphysical transport to an "outside." On the contrary, they offer only the possibility of a *communication* with this outside: an orientation that allows the outside limited entrance into the self's prison by turning the constraining forces of the soul's captivity to new purposes. In Weil's words, "[t]his world is the closed door. It is a barrier. And at the same time it is the way through. Two prisoners whose cells adjoin communicate with each other by knocking on the wall. The wall is the thing which separates them but it is also their means of communication. It is the same with us and God. Every separation is a link."[21] Instead of hating power or abominating matter, the prisoner must learn to love what at first seems base so as to purify it, wielding these mechanisms of nature in order to produce out of them supernatural effects. For Weil and Foucault alike, the clues to this rigorous method emerge first and in clearest form among the ancient Greeks.

Thus, for each of these two philosophers, an authentic political spirituality begins out of a return to the Greeks. Indeed, Greek civilization serves for them as a decisive inspiration and an original point of departure in their independent efforts to forge new spiritual practices for the present. Yet whereas Weil's reflections on these Greek "intimations of Christianity" frequently take the form of short, enigmatic commentaries on equally short and enigmatic Pre-socratic fragments, Foucault generates volumes of detailed archival work, analyzing material from across the ancient world that ranges from Platonic dialogues to early Christian ascetic manuals. However, Foucault's rich genealogical research, in spite of its differences in style from Weil's writing, actually shares much in common with Weil's own mystical meditations. What clearly announces itself in Weil's work is her effort to retrieve a pristine Greek Christianity, untainted by those foreign elements which she condemns as the contamination of Hebrew tribalism and Roman imperialism. She writes that "the Greeks had such strength of soul as preserved them from self-deception. For this they were recompensed by knowing in all things how to attain the highest lucidity, of purity and of simplicity. But the spirit which is transmitted from the *Iliad* to the Gospels, passed on by the philosophers and tragic poets, has hardly gone beyond the limits of Greek civilization."[22] Yet while Foucault's historicism would certainly lead him to deny the possibility of the return to primordial origins suggested in Weil's language, his own spiritual quest nevertheless assumes a surprisingly similar form to Weil's. He seeks to rediscover exercises of *askesis* in their earliest development among the Greeks, before the accretion of monotheistic pastoral techniques and their eventual confusion with juridical forms of imperial sovereignty. These exercises would be capable of unlocking possibilities not only for a reconstitution of the self, but also of a genuine *parrhesia*, a frank speech able to critique the lies and self-deceptions of power.

Weil sees the first outlines of this political spirituality arising as early as the time of the Homeric epics. In her famous essay on the *Iliad*, Weil already detects in the poem a nascent awareness of the real nature of necessity, conceived as *might*. She observes that the "true hero, the real subject, the core of the *Iliad*, is might."[23] Indeed, according to Weil, might (or force) is the real subject of all human history; it is that which both constitutes and structures reality. Force represents for Weil a dynamic, diffuse network of relations comprised of power or energy. It is neither static nor substantial, and it cannot be appropriated or employed by a subject acting upon an object. Rather, force is something that operates in and through subjects who are in some sense channels for it, acting under the illusion that they control it and wield it, when in fact they are at least partly constituted by it, and are almost wholly subject to its capricious and relentless movements.

Weil's commentary on the *Iliad* is a probing and subtle analysis of the operations of force and power, and the ways in which they form and destroy individuals and the social orders in which human beings are rooted. Like Weil, Foucault attempts to analyze and understand the workings of power; indeed, just as necessity is for Weil one of the concepts to which she continually returns and which serves as a hub for many of her most significant ideas and themes, so also is the concept of power an important organizing principle for Foucault, and one of the most significant and perduring elements of his thought. Foucault's description of power has much in common with Weil's view of necessity and force which resides there:

> Power must . . . be analyzed as something that circulates, or rather as something that functions only when it is part of a chain. It is never localized here or there, it is never in the hands of some, and it is never appropriated in the way that wealth or a commodity can be appropriated. Power functions. Power is exercised through networks. And individuals do not simply circulate in these networks; they are in a position to both submit to and exercise this power . . . They are always its relays. In other words, power passes through individuals.[24]

Power, according to Foucault, is not something deployed by an autonomous subject who uses it at will, or who becomes the object of that power when it is used by another. For both Weil and Foucault, necessity/ power is both everywhere and nowhere. It is characterized by an impersonal, dislocated, and disindividualized omnipresence that most humans experience as a "force which governs the world and makes every man obey,"[25] or as "an arrangement whose internal mechanisms produce the relation in which individuals are caught up."[26]

For Weil, necessity functions on two levels: that of the natural, and that of the social. While they are not, for Weil, two entirely distinct versions of necessity, they are nevertheless distinguishable. Regarding the former, she writes of "[t]he absolute domination throughout the whole universe of a mechanical, mathematical, absolutely deaf and blind necessity,"[27] which, despite its apparent mechanism, appears to human beings as something arbitrary and often destructive and evil. Necessity of this sort serves as Weil's shorthand for the networks of power that make up the cosmos; human beings are embedded in these networks and are channels for the energy that flows through and structures the universe. Ultimately, one has no choice but to consent to this embeddedness, since there is no getting outside of these power relations any more than one can escape gravity. *Social* necessity, however, belongs to the realm of what Weil calls the imaginary or the illusory. She observes that the social element is intensely powerful and compelling: "Agreement between several men brings with it a feeling of reality. It brings with it also a sense of duty.

Divergence, where this agreement is concerned, appears as a sin . . . The state of conformity is an imitation of grace."[28] Each human being cherishes the illusion that they are an independent agent who chooses their actions and elects to participate in the social order on their own terms. But Weil problematizes such a view, claiming instead that the network of social relations in which all human beings are enmeshed in fact *constitutes* human subjectivity, and that what passes for reality or truth is in fact an effect of social necessity. Because "all power is unstable,"[29] it constantly reproduces and reconfigures itself in the structures of necessity that form the social organism. Despite this inherent dynamism, however, the power relations that comprise social necessity at any given moment serve to fix identities, sanction truths, codify laws, and construct hierarchies, all of which generally offer humans false and facile consolation.

This Weilienne understanding of social necessity has much in common with Foucault's description of power relations. Foucault, while largely ignoring the sorts of phenomena interpreted by Weil as the working of natural necessity, nevertheless sees power in the realm of the social, not as "something that is acquired, seized, or shared, something that one holds on to or allows to slip away; [rather] power is exercised from numerous points, in the interplay of nonegalitarian and mobile relations."[30] According to Foucault, chief among the effects of this decentralized set of power relations is the individual subject: "[O]ne of the first effects of power is that it allows bodies, gestures, discourses, and desires to be identified and constituted as something individual . . . The individual is in fact a power-effect."[31] Compare this to Weil, who writes,

There is never anything in human thought but relationships. Even where the objects of the senses are concerned, it becomes clear, as soon as one analyzes the perception of them in a fairly strict manner, that what one calls objects are simply groups of relationships which impose themselves upon the mind by the intervention of the senses . . . We have in us and about us only relationships. In the semi-darkness in which we are plunged, all is relation for us. . .[32]

For both Foucault and Weil, then, relations of power are in some sense primary, and it is by means of these relations that subjects can be said to exist and act. Both thinkers understand subjectivity as something that neither transcends nor pre-exists necessity/power; and both also develop on the basis of their schemas of social relations an understanding of autonomous subjectivity as an artifice of some kind—illusory, or fragmented.

For both Weil and Foucault, wrestling with the implications of this newly discovered role that necessity/power plays in the formation of subjectivity in fact becomes a central task for their respective philosophies. Is the autonomous subject a myth or a construction? How do subjects become?[33] What role does power play in constituting or decreating subjects? Indeed Foucault writes that, while he has focused a great deal on descriptions of power in his work, the underlying goal has in fact "not been to analyze the phenomena of power . . . [but] instead . . . to create a history of the different modes by which, in our culture, human beings are made subjects."[34] Weil, too, spends much of her time working out the meaning and possibility of subjectivity, as well as the problems she associates with subjectivity considered in terms of autonomy, substantiality, and personality. According to both thinkers, one of the results of the way in which power operates is the production of a spurious subjectivity—an "I" which appears to function as a unified, transcendental subject, but which in reality is fragmented, or in some way chimerical. Subjectivity's fragmented or chimerical character derives in no small part from the illusion that it somehow possesses the capacity to get outside of necessity, or to gain a perspective external to the encompassing network of power relations. While both thinkers deny that one can somehow escape to the "outside" of power, they nevertheless retain a kernel of the emancipatory hope that such a desire reflects, insofar as they both offer a form of transcendence situated not beyond but within the immanence of power.[35]

However, if there is to be a space within power open for the supernatural, for justice and for resistance, this space must be established in a manner opposed to the expansive force according to which power usually circulates. Practically speaking, the possibility of ethics requires, in one way or another, a contraction of subjectivity. Yet such a result cannot be achieved by an imaginary collapse or implosion of power, which in fact runs contrary to its nature, a nature which Weil, following Thucydides, considers to be naturally, ineluctably and maximally expansive.[36] So ultimately, if a space is to be vacated within the immanent field of power, this void can only be opened up when the individualizing power behind subjectivity is made to double over against itself in order to undo its own original configuration. Consequently, Weil and Foucault both formulate a largely negative ethic of *askesis*, in which spirituality takes the form of a peculiar self-renunciation and refusal—a folding of power back on to itself in order to disassemble the artificial unity of the self—not for the sake of discovering a true self behind the epiphenomenal subject of power, but for the sake of a self-emptying whose void becomes a node of resistance in the network of power. As Foucault puts it, "[T]he target nowadays is not to discover what we are but to refuse what we are."[37] This process Weil calls the "decreation" of the self, in which the self is submitted to the forces of necessity in a manner that accomplishes not an abolition of power, but rather its transmutation into a power which is supernatural justice. Foucault elaborates, on the other hand, his own version of this *askesis*: a "care of the self" in which modes of subjectification are analyzed and deconstructed in order to harness these regimes for the sake of reconstituting new forms of subjectivity.

By submitting the self to practices whose relations to self and to truth lead to the recognition of oneself as a technology of power, such an *askesis* produces forms of subjectivity which are free ultimately to become new technologies of power. However, these decreated subjectivities are peculiar as technologies of power, insofar as their power lies not in their function as relays within an existing network of power, but in their capacity to resist present configurations of power, disrupting and rechanneling its circulation in order to generate entirely novel social relations. In Weilienne language, such is the nature of the persuasive power that the supernatural good exerts over the coercive power of necessity. And in Foucauldian terms, such is the fruit of the labor of the self's disassembly of itself: to be released, not from all mechanisms of power, but from those particular mechanisms by which it retains its grip on the self. These two accounts not only testify to the impersonality and the omnipresence of power, but also coincide in their contention that a dismantled or evacuated subjectivity yields the only real hope for disrupting the oppressive effects of power.

Notes

[1] On Weil and Levinas, see Gillian Rose, "Angry angels: Simone Weil and Emmanuel Levinas" in *Judaism and Modernity: Philosophical Essays* (Oxford: Blackwell, 1993). On Weil and Camus, see John Randolph LeBlanc, *Ethics and Creativity in the Political Thought of Simone Weil and Albert Camus* (Lewiston, NY: Edwin Mellen Press, 2004). On Weil and Bataille, see Alexander Irwin, *Saints of the Impossible: Bataille, Weil, and the Politics of the Sacred* (Minneapolis, MN: University of Minnesota Press, 2002).

[2] In reference to the alleged "theological turn" in recent French philosophy, see Dominque Janicaud et al., *Phenomenology and "The Theological Turn": The French Debate* (New York: Fordham University Press, 2001).

3 See Alexander Irwin's "Introduction" in *Saints of the Impossible*, where he argues that "Bataille used the language of sacrifice and ritual destruction . . . to frame an original and provocative theory of political revolution. At the end of the decade, sacrifice internalized as spiritual violence became the basis of Bataille's model of mystical experience . . . Bataille's mysticism should be seen not as a rejection of political responsibility, but rather as a provocative effort to model an alternative mode of resistance . . . in a context where notions of duty, virtue, and virile action seemed to Bataille to have been emptied of their content. Bataille never abjured his taste for transgressive violence" (xxvi–xxvii).

4 Simone Pétrement, *La Vie de Simone Weil* Vol. I (Paris: Fayard, 1973), 422, as quoted and translated by Alexander Irwin in his *Saints of the Impossible*, 84. See also Simone Pétrement, *Simone Weil: A Life*, trans. Raymond Rosenthal (New York: Pantheon Books, 1976), 208.

5 Even those who can be considered generally sympathetic readers of Weil resort to her psychology as a kind of "master key" to her thought instead of evaluating it on its own merits. Mary Dietz, *Between the Human and the Divine: the Political Thought of Simone Weil* (Totowa, NJ: Rowman and Littlefield, 1988) offers one such example. Such a hermeneutic, however well-intentioned, often leads to a misreading of Weil, as David Rice observes in his essay, "Misreading Simone Weil: Psychobiography, pathos, and politics" (paper presented at the annual meeting of the American Political Science Association [APSA] 2008 Annual Meeting, Hynes Convention Center, Boston, Massachusetts, 29 August 2008). Readers who are unsympathetic to Weil, and who focus on her perceived psychopathology and/or her religious heterodoxy, are too numerous to mention, but include Thomas Nevin, Charles Moeller, Joyce Carol Oates and Jillian Becker.

6 Alasdair MacIntyre, "Miller's Foucault, Foucault's Foucault," *Salmagundi*, No. 97 (Winter 1993), 42.

7 James Miller, *The Passion of Michel Foucault* (London: Harper Collins, 1993).

8 Jeremy R. Carrette, "Prologue to a confession of the flesh," in Michel Foucault, *Religion and Culture*, ed. Jeremy R. Carrette (New York: Routledge, 1999), 26.

9 See Foucault's final lecture in *"Society Must Be Defended": Lectures at the College de France, 1975–1976*, trans. David Macey (New York: Picador, 1997), 239–63.

10 See Foucault's Howison lectures, "About the beginnings of the hermeneutics of the self," reprinted in Foucault, *Religion and Culture*, 181. He argues: "Maybe our problem now is now to discover that the self is nothing else than the historical correlation of the technology built in our history. Maybe the problem is to change those technologies, or maybe to get rid of those technologies, and then, to get rid of the sacrifice which is linked to those technologies."

11 OC II.1, 300, as quoted and translated by Alexander Irwin in his *Saints of the Impossible*, 85. In this statement, Weil praises the spirit of Rosa Luxemburg while at the same time making a veiled reference to the difference between Luxemburg's revolutionary ideals and Bataille's. The contrast highlighted by Weil is useful as well in describing the basic dissimilarity in outlook that separates Foucault and Bataille.

12 Weil's profound appreciation for and engagement with ancient Greek science and mathematics manifests itself throughout her corpus. See especially Weil's

La source grecque, Intuitions pré-Chrétiennes, and *Sur la science*. For an excellent assessment of the influence of Greek science and mathematics on Weil's thought, see Vance Morgan, *Weaving the World: Simone Weil on Science, Mathematics, and Love* (Notre Dame: University of Notre Dame Press, 2005).

[13] To understand the contrast between Heidegger's analysis of science founded on the "theoretical attitude" and his own alternative "existential conception of science," see his *Being and Time*, trans. John Macquarrie and Edward Robinson (New York: Harper Collins, 1962), 408–15.

[14] Foucault deals extensively with this orientation to truth in the first volume of his three-part history of sexuality. See *The History of Sexuality, Vol. I: The Will to Knowledge*, trans. Robert Hurley (London: Penguin, 1998).

[15] Foucault, *The History of Sexuality, Vol. II: The Use of Pleasure*, trans. Robert Hurley (New York: Vintage Books, 1990), 8.

[16] GG, 133.

[17] Drawing on Foucault's distinction between a *volonté de savoir* and a *volonté de vérité*—a "will to knowledge" versus a "will to truth," the latter of which is appraised much more positively by Foucault—one might say that Weil's thought retains its own powerful will to truth even while remaining vigilant against the lures of a will to knowledge. See Michel Foucault, "The will to knowledge," 12.

[18] James W. Bernauer, "Michel Foucault's ecstatic thinking," in James Bernauer and David Rasmussen, eds., *The Final Foucault* (Cambridge, MA: MIT Press, 1987), 45.

[19] While it is true that Weil's psychology allows for what she calls a "supernatural" part of the soul that possesses a capacity for contact with divine love, this part of the soul is coextensive with our autonomous existence and hence represents for Weil precisely that part of us which must be decreated. Moreover, this part of the human being remains largely inaccessible to us and never serves as a consolation. As Weil observes, "Being and having—Man has no being, he has only having. The being of man is situated behind the curtain, on the supernatural side. What he is able to know about himself is only what is made available to him by circumstances. *I* is hidden in my case (and in that of other people): is on the side of God . . . is in God . . . is God (Atman)" (NB, 127).

[20] For some examples regarding Weil, see Thomas Idinopolus, "Necessity and nihilism in Simone Weil's vision of God," *Mysticism, Nihilism, Feminism: New Critical Essays on the Theology of Simone Weil*, ed. Thomas Idinopolus and Josephine Knopp (Johnson City, TN: Institute of Social Science and Arts, 1984); J. M. Perrin, ed., *Réponses aux questions de Simone Weil* (Paris: Aubier/Éditions Montaigne, 1964). In Foucault's case, a prominent example of this interpretation comes from Miller's biography. Miller states that "Foucault's subterranean link . . . to a Manichaean kind of Gnosticism, forms an unspoken subtext to the interpretation I will offer . . ." (*The Passion of Michel Foucault*, 445).

[21] GG, 132.

[22] SWR, 181.

[23] SWR, 153.

[24] Michel Foucault, *Society Must Be Defended*, 29.

[25] IC, 182.
[26] Michel Foucault, *Discipline and Punish: The Birth of the Prison*, trans. Alan Sheridan (New York: Pantheon, 1977), 202.
[27] IC, 198.
[28] GG, 147.
[29] SWR, 136.
[30] Michel Foucault, *The History of Sexuality: An Introduction, Vol. 1*, trans. Robert Hurley (New York: Vintage, 1990), 94.
[31] Foucault, *Society Must Be Defended*, p. 30.
[32] IC, 197.
[33] Editors' note: See Chapter 12.
[34] Foucault, *Society Must Be Defended*, 208.
[35] While it is true that Weil seeks "not to submit to society outside the domain of natural necessity" (Weil, "God in Plato," IC, 87), it is nevertheless the case that this resistance in no way involves for her a removal from the power networks (natural or social) that constitute the universe. (Editors' note: See Chapter 14.) She views such an understanding of transcendence as illusory and falsely consolatory, arguing that there can be no miraculous passage to a realm of freedom, even for the decreated individual. She writes, for example: "Ideal. 'From the realm of necessity to the realm of freedom'—No, but from necessity endured to necessity methodically handled. And from *capricious* and *unlimited* constraint (oppression) to *limited* necessity" (FLN, 22). Or elsewhere: "Illusory choice. When we think that we have the choice, it is because we are unconscious, compassed about by illusion, and we are then but toys. We cease to be toys when we lift ourselves above illusion right up to Necessity, but then there is no longer any choice; a certain action is imposed by the situation itself, clearly perceived" (NB, Vol. 1, 57).
[36] Cf. "To accept the void," in GG.
[37] Interview with Foucault in Hubert Dreyfus and Paul Rabinow, *Michel Foucault: Beyond Structuralism and Hermeneutics* (Chicago, IL: University of Chicago Press, 1982), 216.

Chapter 12

An Ethical Account of the Self Who Might Be Otherwise: Simone Weil and Judith Butler

Cynthia Gayman

What we owe to others is an ethical question fraught with political and social ramifications, given systemic inequalities in education, opportunity, cultural environment, and access to resources. Why we are accountable for a debt not personally incurred is beside the point, for the reality of the social world implicates us in relations and responsibilities we do not choose or control. Accountability extends to the factors of our own lives over which we have had little or no say. We do not choose the circumstances of our own birth, for example, much less control the genealogical, social or geographical factors leading up to its contingent inevitability, which might give us pause before taking sole credit for accomplishments won thereafter. Who is self-grounding? The conditions of the emergence of the self, subject to the world, and subject to the particular social force of any human configuration, are fractious, multi-layered and many-factored. But if not self-grounding, are we, as selves, any less accountable? At issue here is a question of ground: upon what basis and towards what end is responsibility to be borne? The focus of this chapter is on Simone Weil's concept of the "impersonal," which does not describe a foundation in being but an orientation. As such, the impersonal is the condition for the possibility of ethical responsibility and justice, allowing us to make good on our debts. The impersonal is that towards which the self must be directed. Meanwhile, where does this leave the self?

The question of the self must be clearly answered if an account of ethical responsibility is to be unambiguous. This is Weil's point of departure in her essay "Human personality,"[1] and she begins the essay with a critique of what she considers to be an ill-conceived understanding of the self and the consequently inadequate morality developed on its behalf. But is there any sense in which the self can be definitively pinned down? Can the "I" be understood apart from the social context that conditions moral perception in the first place? This latter question orients the sustained inquiry by Judith Butler in her book, *Giving an Account of Oneself.*[2] Here I consider Weil's schema in light of the challenge Butler's question raises, and my intention is not to pit two views against each other, but rather to examine moral responsibility and the question of the self with respect to what both philosophers agree is an ambiguity of social conditions.

Within every framework of moral theory a definition of the self is assumed if not made explicit, and the unidentified specter is no less accountable for injunctions towards action, whether overtly drawn or covertly assumed, according to duty, good will, respect for rights, recognition, or a certain mode of address. In the main, and very broadly speaking, there seem to be two major philosophical trajectories tracing the subject of moral responsibility. One trajectory locates the site of rectitude in an ahistorical subject in whom an attribute or capacity of being prompts the perception or formulation of the good. Attributes or capacities such as virtue, self-interest, reason and goodwill inform thought and direct action. The self is the source of moral efficacy, but unexamined is the coincidence between the values discerned by the self and the societal context from which they happen to emerge and likely converge.

The other historical trajectory places the self within the context of a pre-existent social world, where communal norms, laws, values and beliefs inform the moral sensibilities of the subject, and not the reverse. The social world is the site of the ethical, and societies are diverse; differing cultural, historical and geographical contexts engender different values, which persons in that society appropriate (or refuse to appropriate, but in order to be refused or questioned, values have to be recognized as societal norms in the first place). Members of a social body may well believe their values to be universal in nature, even as global diversity counters with evidence that values are in nature social. Whether the relativization of values results in the devaluation of values may be difficult to assess if the site for the appropriation of values is also the site of their origination. In the latter case, the question arises whether the self can be morally accountable at all, or if responsibility is borne merely in conformity to social norms.

In *Giving an Account of Oneself,* Butler describes the social world as a matrix of relations and norms, which are "the condition for the emergence of the 'I.'"[3] This condition is constitutive, which means that there is nothing outside it, not that the self is a consequence or construct of social formation. How the "I" emerges from the social world, as a self who can be accountable for itself and others, is Butler's project, which I can only address in broad strokes here, unfortunately. Butler argues that the world to which the subject belongs is not only the site for being and belonging, but as constitutive matrix it is that through which the self is able to perceive and conceive of itself as a self in the first place, and to "tell its story," as it were. But this self is never "on its own," never independent of the site of its emergence, and never free of the relational ties that irremediably bind being to the social world. "The 'I' has no story of its own that is not also the story of a relation—or a set of relations—to a set of norms," Butler states.[4] There is no definitive boundary of the self since subjectivity as such is always "already implicated in a social temporality that exceeds its own capacities for narration."[5] Birth may seem to give us a free pass, a place from which to begin the unique story of our lives, but no one is a blank slate; the emergent self arrives on the scene with social/historical background, never mind physiology and genetics, and not to mention a likely anticipated future that serves to foreground much of life in the ongoing present.

As subjects we are implicated in extenuating circumstances and relations over which we have no say or no control, and these extend beyond the boundaries of our own lives—that is, beyond the "I," for which we are somehow accountable every time we assert it in the form of "I think" or "I can" or "I will." But on what grounds does the ego assert itself? We are to a great extent blind to ourselves. Butler states that "the very terms by which we give an account, by which we make ourselves intelligible to ourselves and to others, are not of our making. They are social in character, and they establish social norms, a domain of unfreedom and substitutability within which our singular stories are told."[6]

Opacity is "built into our formation" as selves because we "are formed in the context of relations that become partially irrecoverable to us."[7] "Truth," then, that is, the truth of who we are, must be contextually revealed to us through the "crucible of social relations, variously established and iterable . . ."[8] Others call us out, in other words. We express ourselves in what we say, how we say it, and others challenge our accounts. "And when we do act and speak," Butler writes, "we not only disclose ourselves but act on the schemes of intelligibility that govern who will be speaking beings, subjecting them to rupture or revision, consolidating their norms, or contesting their hegemony."[9] Critique or contestation of any iteration occurs through the course of interaction, which introduces the possibility of a new narrative account, equally contestable, for the irreducible condition of "relationality" binds us to others in such a way as to make evident in every interaction the limitations of ourselves as selves, that is, our incapacity for giving an adequate account, which interaction with others prompts us to recognize.[10]

But this begs the question: If the conditions for the possibility of being and the parameters of what it means to be a self are social, can persons be held to moral accountability? Butler asks: "Does the postulation of a subject who is not self-grounding, that is, whose conditions of emergence can never fully be accounted for, undermine the possibility of responsibility and, in particular, of giving an account of oneself?"[11]

It is this question that I address in light of Weil's philosophical insights, for Weil's account of the subject also pulls the rug out from under the grounded self-certain "I" whose belief in his or her own efficacy is unmoored by the reality of the world. For life is not and will not be as we imagine, hope, dream, fear, or wish it to be. As Weil puts it, "the substance of our life is almost exclusively composed of fiction. We fictionalize our future . . . we fictionalize our past, refashioning it to our taste . . . If reality administers a hard enough shock to awaken us for an instant . . . we soon relapse into the waking dream peopled by our fictions."[12]

For Weil there is a distinction to be drawn between our "waking dreams" and a reality that is itself "un-peopled"—that is, a reality that exists apart from the emergent revelations of truth in the course of interaction with others. For it is not the truth of the interrelational self that is revealed when it is called to account and dreaming is interrupted; rather, it is the irruption of what is experienced as the "I"—"ego" or personality—that turns attention towards a reality already present. The possibility of experiencing reality, of suddenly recognizing even for a moment that our own account, our grasp of a situation, is fictional, suggests that there are gaps within the self's "primary opacity," to use Butler's phrase.[13] This would only be the case if the reality grasped were not merely constituted within and relative to social context but pointed beyond it, which is what Weil intends; what we might awaken to is the truth of ourselves, the sacred and impersonal level of being: "Impersonality is only reached by the practice of a form of attention which is rare in itself and impossible except in solitude; and not only physical but mental solitude."[14] Thus, it is important to draw "the line in the sand" marking the difference between Butler's view of the self as emergent from and through the matrix of social relations, and this first intimation of Weil's, that the self, in the most fundamental sense, is absent from the socially informed and emergent "I" altogether.

"My 'I' is hidden for me," Weil writes, making opacity an opportunity for being, rather than a condition of our existence; indeed, what is hidden is the pure absence of the socially emergent "I."[15] In "Decreation," Weil describes this in overtly religious terms, that the "I" hidden for the self "(and for others)" is "on the side of God, it is in God, it is God."[16] In "Human personality," this hidden self is "sacred," and it is oriented towards and arising from the impersonal.

If Butler's schema is clearly aligned with the trajectory of thought tracing the subject of moral responsibility in the context of the social world, it cannot be said, even at first glance, that Weil's is clearly aligned with the trajectory making the self the locus of moral efficacy. While the "impersonal" stands in contrast to the "personal," and seems to suggest a universal if not universalizing mode of being, it must be emphasized that the impersonal is no trait of being at all; it is not an attribute of the self, but an implicit orientation of the self towards others and, ultimately, towards the good. And it is within the context of the social world that the orientation of the self towards the impersonal is expressed; likewise, that it is compromised or vitiated. Thus, in an important sense, Weil's schema is also aligned with the trajectory of thought emphasizing the social world as the context for moral accountability and the responsibility of the self. What I want to establish here is that both Weil and Butler understand the social world to be of constitutive influence, although Weil, of course, does not give it the final say. And while she could not have addressed Butler's careful analyses of the socially emergent self, Weil does begin "Human personality" with a rejection of a superficial version of the self in its social instantiation: personality.

In "Human personality," Weil inveighs against "personality" as a way of defining the self because it delimits the self as merely social, as if what it means to be is only that which appears within the context of the social world, which, for Weil, is not the case. Personality is thoroughly social; even making allowances for genetic proclivities with respect to temperament, personality traits shift or are honed in response to feedback and ongoing social interaction. Personality is social in another way, as Weil states: "The full expression of personality depends upon its being inflated by social prestige; it is a social privilege."[17]

Privilege does not give the subject greater accountability in terms of what can be disclosed and expressed; privilege too is part of the "domain of unfreedom," to recall Butler's phrase, but surely some persons are less bound by the need to give an account or justify their positions than are others—precisely due to their position within the social order. And because of this, a contestation of privilege is unlikely to arise within the milieu of its emergence as a self-account. "They"—that is, the privileged—"are not the ones to say that privilege is unworthy to be desired," Weil states.[18] Further, those who are of higher social standing are also those "who have the monopoly of language," which at the very least explains why rich and poor alike are conscripted by collective values, expectations, desires, habits, and shared concern over the rise and fall of the stock market.[19] Weil writes, "In an unstable society the privileged have a bad conscience."[20] Some respond by rationalizing their higher status as more deserved; others give lip service to social equality. Both responses emerge within the context of the collectivity, and Weil sees either response as "encouraging people down the road of evil, away from their true and unique good . . ."[21] Here the social world is the source of evil because it lays claim upon individuals with an account of life, of values, of meaning, of truth generated according to the dominant narratives within that world that serve to oppress those who are not in a position of advantage within the collectivity.

Yet we are social beings. We seek from others recognition, respect and understanding. We might yearn for real connection beyond the superficialities of everyday life, but this desire is sublimated at every turn as we accommodate ourselves according to certain "narrative expectations," whether at work or at the grocery store or at church or alongside the soccer field. We know the language of "business-speak" or academese,[22] and take pride in our ability to navigate different social milieus. "Personality" gets us through, and any vestige of the "hidden self" stays hidden.

But perhaps there is no such hidden self if social negotiation is constitutive of becoming a self; it could be said that it is due to our interactions that we recognize the "self" in hiding. Butler states that "the 'I' has no story of its own that is not also the story of a relation—or a set of relations—to a set of norms."[23] As selves we are at the mercy of others' expectations and demands right from the start; social interchange is the site of ethical responsibility. The "I" is "imposed upon from the start, against one's will, [and this] heightens a sense of responsibility," Butler writes.[24] But this requires that the self relinquish ego and acquiesce to the other, to the point of taking "the very unbearability of exposure as the sign, the reminder of a common vulnerability, a common physicality and risk . . ."[25] The responsibility of the subject who would be accountable requires, it would seem, a degree of personal courage in the willingness to risk disclosure.

Butler describes the self without resorting to an obvious metaphysics; she presumes only the existence of the social world. Weil's schema relies on a two-world theory: the social world and the reality indicated by the impersonal. Both are given within human experience, but cannot exist together. The social world—what Weil refers to as the "collectivity"—is for Weil, no less than Butler, the constitutive matrix for all aspects of being within that world, including, of course, development of personality, and it is that to which individual life is necessarily subordinate. The second world in Weil's schema is reality, to which individuals have access within the world, but not through the collectivity. Reality cannot be subsumed by the collectivity because it is of another order: that of the impersonal. Weil writes, "Men as parts of a collectivity are debarred from even the lower forms of the impersonal."[26] It is only on the level of the impersonal that what is true is not emergent from the social world, but collectively persons cannot arrive at it, even at the most basic level. As if she regularly attended faculty meetings, Weil makes this point: "A group of human beings cannot even add two and two."[27]

The subordination of the self to the collective is not "scandalous," Weil writes, but is a "mechanical fact of the same order as the inferiority of a gram to a kilogram on the scales. The person is in fact always subordinate to the collectivity, even in its so-called free expression," evident in the work of the artists and writers who believe their work to reflect originality, but are only "in bondage to public taste."[28]

Today we have only to think of our own impulses towards self-expression in more mundane matters, represented not only by the clothes we wear or the cars we drive, but even by the ring-tones we download on our cell phones. We are inextricably bound by the world around us, even to the degree we recognize that our "personal" tastes, habits, beliefs, values and everyday concerns, large and small, are not just influenced by but arise within the context of our societal surroundings. Personality itself is the social manifestation of what we think of as our uniqueness. But this is not wholly who we are, according to Weil; the social account leaves out the sacred.

I see a passer-by in the street. He has long arms, blue eyes, and a mind whose thoughts I do not know, but perhaps they are commonplace. It is neither his person, nor the human personality in him, which is sacred to me. It is he. The whole of him. The arms, the eyes, the thoughts, everything. Not without infinite scruple would I touch anything of this.[29]

It is the self in its entirety that is sacred. But "although it is the whole of him that is sacred to me, he is not sacred in all respects and from every point of view."[30] What is sacred is not some element unique to someone's person, but is that which is impersonal—that is, universal, and thus the same for all. "So far from its being his person, what is sacred in a human being is the impersonal in him. Everything which is impersonal in man is sacred, and nothing else."[31] This is a shocking claim, seeming to vitiate the self both with respect to its uniqueness and with regard to the specificities of its experiences and moral claims. But for Weil, this is only the case from the vantage point of the person who bases claims of moral regard on whether his personality is respected, and suitable "rights" accorded it. Recall: "It is neither his person, nor the human personality in him which is sacred to me." No single aspect can stand for the "whole" of the person, to whom attention is oriented. There is no synecdoche here. Weil's schema is directed neither towards a particular aspect, like "blue eyes" or "long arms," nor to an abstract attribute, like "rationality" or "personhood."

Basing a conception of the self on personality brings about an "inadequate notion" of "public morality," according to Weil, whose example of the latter is the framework of "rights," too often used to assert moral claims on the basis of some superficial aspect of identity, even social standing, thus misdirecting the true orientation of responsibility.[32] To put this in a contemporary context, it could be said, for instance, that "the rights of blue-eyed people must be respected; they must be accorded recognition on the basis of their eye color." Like "rights," in the sense used by Weil, ethical responsibility conceived on the basis of identity claims would also seem to be an inadequate account. For which aspect of identity must be accorded respect? Yet surely descriptive traits such as sex/gender, age, size, sexual orientation, religious affiliation, economic status, ethnicity, race, etc., are characteristics of identity that merit claims for recognition and respect, given the history of social marginalization, oppression, and worse. Weil would dismiss the basis for such claims without disregarding particular attributes, for who someone is cannot be defined by blue eyes or black skin; moral regard cannot be given on the basis of particular traits. Weil writes, "To set up as a standard of public morality a notion which can neither be defined nor conceived is to open the door to every kind of tyranny."[33] If ethical obligation were due to some specific attribute like "blue eyes" or "intelligence" then it would be a short step to say that some persons have greater standing because of certain attributes and, conversely, that some in whom such attributes are lacking don't measure up, *as persons.* Lacking or having a wrong qualification has already opened many doors to tyranny.[34]

Butler makes a related point with regard to recognition as the basis for an ethical stance. The moment that recognition is "resolved," as Butler puts it, meaning that we have understood another with respect to his or her defining attribute or personality, the other is "captured" in effect, categorized and dismissed.[35] Because the subject always "falls outside the categories of identity" it is important to "let the question remain open"— that is, the question of "Who are you?"[36] By so doing, "we let the other live," as Butler states, and of course she is not speaking merely metaphorically.[37] But in Butler's schema, the purpose of openness in inquiry is directed by the relationship between persons; ethical accountability is interpersonal. This is a compelling account, but is it an adequate account of a "public morality"? To be fair, this is not Butler's question, but Weil's; still, if the subject is constituted by its accountability, is it then absolved from responsibility for social relations in which no direct interchange takes place? Some persons tell better stories than others, after all, which does not always signify the burden of accountability or translatability, but sometimes points to systemic inequalities within the social world. Who is held to account?

For Butler, moral responsibility begins from an emergent understanding within the social world that the opacity of the self, and the acknowledgment of limits for the possibility of knowing ourselves or others, can "constitute a disposition of humility and generosity alike: I will need to be forgiven for what I cannot have fully known, and I will be under a similar obligation to offer forgiveness to others, who are in partial opacity to themselves."[38] Obligation thus arises from a capacity for self-reflection and empathy revelatory of a profound thoughtfulness, which would seem to be a rarity in the world of real human interaction. But this awareness of the limits of our own self-understanding—humility, in a word—is the catalyst for directing moral attention towards another, who we also understand as limited in the same way.

This limitation, Butler states, is not only "the condition for the subject but [the] predicament of the human community."[39] She adds, "I am not altogether out of the loop of the enlightenment if I say, as I do, that reason's limit is the sign of our humanity. It might be a legacy of Kant to say so. My account of myself breaks down, and surely for a reason. . ."[40] Butler then wants to base moral accountability on the acknowledgement of a universal inadequacy of being: that we cannot speak wholly or even adequately of ourselves. But in her account, it is not on the ground of this fundamental inadequacy that moral responsibility is informed, but on the fact that we can give an account of it.

Weil inverts Butler's account, and traces the self's inadequacy back from its inevitable expression within the social world to an originary expectation of the self, "that good and not evil be done to him."[41] It is this expectation of the good that obligates us to others, and it is that which is in us that is essentially sacred and, as such, is impersonal. Justice exists for all. The expectation Weil describes does not originate from the matrix of social life, but is nevertheless expressed through relationship to others. But this expectation for good is betrayed as well, despite its inviolability. That we are surprised by this betrayal indicates the prior expectation.

It is the violation of the expectation of the good—injustice—that evokes ethical responsibility in the most profound sense, and injustice occurs "every time that there arises from the depths of the human heart the childish cry which Christ himself could not restrain, 'Why am I being hurt?'"[42] This cry should orient moral response, but it will do so only in those who have engaged the level of the impersonal in themselves, in solitude and with focused attention, and live in such a way as to turn towards the good, where "truth and beauty dwell."[43]

Weil traces the impersonal by giving an account of the ways in which it appears in the world, manifests in certain concepts (such as truth, justice, beauty, compassion), shows itself in certain works of art or literature (such as the *Iliad*), or in mathematics, or in what has been elucidated here through the description of the self as sacred in its originating impulse towards the good, bearing each of us towards that which is sacred in another because it is good. It is this that orients ethical responsibility. This orientation is impersonal, and directs us towards reality.

Weil does not make the social world constitutive of the self's accountability. Butler never considers the self in solitude, as if being subject in the world means always and only to be subject to it. She views interrelationality as a "primary and irreducible" fact of being and the "precondition of ethical responsiveness," but what begins with "just we two" can only be extrapolated in theoretical application on a broad scale— this, too, is contingent possibility.[44] It is not just an account of the sacred that Butler lacks, but also a politics—an account of justice that directs moral responsibility towards individuals on the basis of the original expectation of the good. There is a ground for moral responsibility, in other words, that directs attention to something essential, allowing us to participate in the good as we attend to others. Butler's account does not lack heart; rather, it is the case that responsibility for and to others is engendered within the experiential realm of relationships—a very personal morality.

A definition of the self as emergent from the social matrix cannot account for an orientation towards reality, that is, towards the impersonal ideas that "dwell in heaven," as Weil puts it, and manifest in the world as values that are "always and everywhere good": fulfillment of obligation, "truth, beauty, justice, [and] compassion," as Weil describes them.[45] These values are trans-social; they are impersonal, and do not emerge from the collectivity of human persons because the social world has its own order, the force of which subordinates the individual self. The still, small voice is silenced even as the narrative continues.

Notes

[1] Simone Weil, "Human personality," in SWR, 313–9.
[2] Judith Butler, *Giving an Account of Oneself* (New York: Fordham University Press, 2005).
[3] Ibid., 7.
[4] Ibid., 8.
[5] Ibid.
[6] Ibid., 21.
[7] Ibid., 20.
[8] Ibid., 132.
[9] Ibid.
[10] Ibid., 40.
[11] Ibid., 19.
[12] Simone Weil, "Morality and literature," in SWR, 292.
[13] Butler, *Giving an Account of Oneself*, 20.
[14] SWR, 318.
[15] Simone Weil, "Decreation," in SWR, 355.
[16] SWR, 355.
[17] SWR, 326.
[18] SWR, 326.
[19] SWR, 326.
[20] SWR, 326.
[21] SWR, 327.
[22] Editors' note: See Chapter 5.
[23] Butler, *Giving an Account of Oneself*, 8.
[24] Ibid., 99.
[25] Ibid., 100.
[26] SWR, 318.
[27] SWR, 319.
[28] SWR, 319.
[29] SWR, 314.

30 SWR, 314.
31 SWR, 317.
32 SWR, 314.
33 SWR, 314.
34 Anthony Appiah critiques the politics of recognition on this problematic feature of it: making an attribute define an individual's "identity." In his essay, "Identity, authenticity, survival," Appiah responds to Charles Taylor's seminal essay on "The politics of recognition," agreeing with Taylor that the demand for recognition and respect accorded to identity (e.g. gay, black, female, differently-abled, etc.) is politically and morally justified in that it has helped to overturn historical oppression and dehumanization of persons based on attributes or their lack. This is indeed a good, for as Appiah puts it, "If I had to choose between the world of the closet and the world of gay liberation, or between the world of Uncle Tom's Cabin and the world of Black Power, I would, of course, choose in each case the latter" (163). But while granting this, Appiah adds "I would like not to have to choose." His point is precisely that who he is as a self cannot be reduced to his sexual orientation or race, and therefore must not be, for it is not enough, for instance, to "be respected *as a homosexual*" (162). I believe that with respect to defining the self according to an attribute of social identity, Weil is making the same point. Both essays in *Multiculturalism*, ed. Amy Gutman (Princeton, NJ: Princeton University Press, 1994).
35 Butler, *Giving an Account of Oneself*, 43.
36 Ibid., 42–3.
37 Ibid., 43.
38 Ibid., 42.
39 Ibid., 83.
40 Ibid.
41 SWR, 315.
42 SWR, 315.
43 SWR, 318.
44 Butler, *Giving an Account of Oneself*, 8.
45 SWR, 328.

Chapter 13

Mystical Selfhood and Women's Agency: Simone Weil and French Feminist Philosophy

Sarah K. Pinnock

Weil's feminist potential has been largely ignored by scholars, although Weil certainly resisted patriarchy's strictures. She was typically a lone woman in a masculine domain, both as a student of philosophy and as a labor activist. To be taken seriously and treated as equal with men, she directed attention away from her female identity by wearing plain clothing and refusing to make herself pretty. Weil drew admiration as one of the first women admitted to the prestigious École Normale Supérieure in Paris and one of the few female writers among socialist intellectuals. She was also unusual for her intense religious interests, both academic and personal, which integrated Roman Catholicism and Platonism with other pre-Christian sources. As with medieval women mystics, her religious experiences conferred authority on her understanding of God. Since her death she has become a prophetic voice challenging hierarchies in religion and society. In short, her remarkable life evidences feminist attributes because she broke societal limits on women to pursue her intellectual, political and humanitarian goals.

However, Weil's writings do not address women's issues specifically, nor would she likely embrace feminist labeling. Her philosophy explored the human condition, not women's distinctiveness. Consistent with her academic training, Weil uses masculine or neuter pronouns to discuss the self. Although her concern with oppression might have drawn her to women's plight, as it differed among social classes, her focus lay on working-class subordination found in manual labor. Weil is admired for seeking factory and farm employment, where she entered situations removed from her upbringing as a middle-class educated woman. On close examination, her factory journals provide insights into gender discrimination that she faced alongside female assembly line workers, which are not analyzed.[1] Likewise, her mystical thought can contribute to feminist reflections on religious experience although she does not focus on women. My attention in this chapter centers on gender, mysticism and selfhood, which are topics of feminist importance.

Many recent authors have noted a special affinity of women for mystical expression, which offers self-empowerment, paradoxically, by means of devotion and sacrifice. Contemporary historians consider how female medieval mystics gained respect and authority, despite women's subservience in the church and society. Philosophers consider mystical language transgressive of male authority, and theologians propose new approaches to God avoiding masculine assumptions about deity.[2] Altogether, the impact of such scholarship draws attention to the potential of mysticism to assist women's resistance to patriarchal power. Although these endorsements of mysticism post-date Weil, her approach also displays how mysticism may be socially liberating.

Multiple connections could be made linking Weil with feminist authors, but it is particularly relevant to place her alongside twentieth-century French women philosophers who would have been her colleagues. Specifically, this chapter considers Weil in relation to Simone de Beauvoir (1908–1986) and Luce Irigaray (b. 1932), exploring how Weil's philosophical observations about mysticism and selfhood provide rich material for feminist dialogue.

Self and Other: Weil and Simone de Beauvoir

To situate Weil with respect to feminism, it is useful to consider social expectations of women of her time illustrated by her experience and that of fellow student Simone de Beauvoir, who was one year older. This contextualization helps explain why Weil may appear simultaneously feminist and anti-feminist. Evidently, Weil minimized her female identity and avoided associating herself with women's issues because she felt that her ambitions as a philosopher, writer and activist were incompatible with conventional women's place. This chafing at the strictures of conventional womanhood was shared and abetted by her mother, Selma Weil, who encouraged her to develop "not the simpering graces of a little girl but the forthrightness of a boy." In return Weil sometimes referred to herself using male pronouns, and signed letters to her parents from "your respectful son."[3] Weil's androgyny was a way to escape sexism, but it also followed logically from her single-minded dedication to achieving her ambitious intellectual goals rather than seeking approval or love as a woman. Her choices were not intended as a categorically negative judgment on ordinary women generally, or on marriage and family. Beauvoir also found herself defying social conventions for women in order to pursue her intellectual ambitions, but as is well known, her relationship with Sartre perpetuated sexist patterns of subordination.

Weil did not live to see the publication of Beauvoir's extremely influential book, *The Second Sex* (1949), and the development of French feminism.[4] Nevertheless, there are certain commonalities between the two women, born only one year apart. Both grew up in Paris, both studied in the most prestigious institutions of higher learning and managed to overtake their male counterparts, and both sought financial and intellectual independence through teaching. They were among the first handful of female students allowed to sit for the strenuous qualifying exams in philosophy, previously barred to women. From an overview of their writings, Weil shared common philosophical interests with Beauvoir insofar as both were concerned with existential themes such as the achievement of genuine subjectivity in opposition to the alienating forces of modern society.[5] Beauvoir and Weil attended the Sorbonne and the École Normale Supérieure in successive years. Among fellow students, Weil had a more prominent reputation because of her philosophical brilliance, eccentric clothing, and militant socialist ideology.

In her memoirs, Beauvoir recalls finding Weil an intriguing figure. On one occasion, she remembers attempting to converse with Weil at the Sorbonne. The encounter was not a success, however. At the time, Weil was preoccupied with a severe famine occurring in China, and during their conversation she made the unequivocal pronouncement that what the world most urgently needed was a socialist revolution to end hunger and to aid the working class. Disgruntled, Beauvoir recalls replying "no less peremptorily, that the problem was not to make men happy, but to find the reason for their existence."[6] Weil remarked scathingly that it was obvious that Beauvoir had never been hungry. This standoff was the end of relations between them. Beauvoir was offended that Weil dismissed her as a petty bourgeois person, who posed existentialist questions while enjoying the comforts of middle class life. But looking back on the encounter, in light of later political involvements, Beauvoir seems to acknowledge Weil's point. It is safe to conjecture that Weil would have had a similarly negative reaction to Beauvoir's feminist writings for neglecting economic differences and social class privileges that oppress both women and men.

Nevertheless, it is too hasty to conclude that Weil's disagreement with Beauvoir implies her rejection of feminist thought entirely. On the contrary, many feminists would agree with Weil's negative reaction to Beauvoir, and would accept the blindness of mainstream academic feminism to social position.[7] Since the 1970s there has been increasing criticism of liberal feminist authors such as Beauvoir who philosophize in the abstract about women, generalizing and dichotomizing the sexes. Such feminism advances white educated women's interests under the guise of a universal feminist movement. No doubt Weil would agree with recent Marxist feminists who insist that class and labor are causes of oppression more fundamental than oppression due to gender or race.[8] Although contrary to the chronology of "the two Simones," Weil surpasses Beauvoir in feminist terms because she recognizes the importance of material conditions of existence for subjectivity.

While Weil is famous for her emphasis on mysticism, Beauvoir also concerns herself with mysticism and selfhood. In *The Second Sex*, Beauvoir explores how women are forced into the position of Other in society, as foil to the masculine norm. The male self has the prerogative of self-transcendence which enables freedom, creativity and authenticity.[9] As Other, women cannot achieve authentic selfhood and function as the material basis for male transcendence. Women are identified with the body and nature in a position of immanence and passivity.[10] Therefore, mysticism is one avenue for liberation from this sexist framework because the mystic abandons herself to the divine, seeking perfect unity in love, and in this way she becomes a subject for herself.[11] In striving for love, a woman seeks to reach the beloved. Teresa of Avila provides the chief example of erotic mysticism. In Beauvoir's interpretation, mystical love is an extreme on the continuum of erotic love for a man. But the mystical ideal is impossible in one case, due to human limitations on love between man and woman, and in the other case, because God is a projection and not a reality. Yet Beauvoir does not denigrate such mysticism. Viewed historically, she acknowledges that erotic mysticism has given women empowerment, and "can be integrated with a life of activity and independence."[12]

The chapter on "The Mystic" in *The Second Sex* is directly followed by Beauvoir's constructive proposal for liberation of women, which shows its place of importance. Beauvoir concludes that liberation of women requires gainful employment, and active and productive social roles unconstrained by sexism. Given Weil's interest in labor, it is worth noting that Beauvoir does not make any distinction between types of work, and presumes that even assembly-line factory work can provide liberation if a woman is not overburdened by male-imposed domestic labor.[13]

Another difference between Weil and Beauvoir concerns divine relation. Beauvoir's God is a male lover writ large, a personification of erotic desire.[14] So although the female mystic does indeed escape from her passivity as Other, she does not achieve authentic subjectivity through mysticism. Such self-realization requires social involvement, whereas relation to God is unreal. Given Beauvoir's limited acquaintance with the study of mysticism and the divine, it is a remarkable endorsement of mysticism for her to admit that it has any feminist relevance. Her focus only on love mysticism as a form of erotic love makes it impossible for Beauvoir to conceive of mysticism apart from sexist gender roles.

Even so, Beauvoir's assumptions about selfhood and mysticism highlight feminist features of Weil's position. Beauvoir presumes that transcendence and authentic selfhood are in opposition to the feminized body and immanence. In transcendence, the authentic self becomes disembodied and gender differences are erased. She also portrays freedom as conflict with others, leaving the self in relative isolation. Additionally, Beauvoir assumes that all work outside the home is liberating for women, and that domestic roles including motherhood make women unable to exercise free subjectivity. In making these presumptions, she reacts precipitously by limiting women's social options and neglecting class and social position.[15] In contrast, Weil establishes the material roots of selfhood with self-transcendence. She provides an integrated concept of embodiment including meaningful labor, taking into account economic conditions. Moreover, she offers a relational notion of the self, admitting dependence rather than abstract existential freedom. Weil's mysticism does not project a masculine God or involve escape into unreality and detachment, as Beauvoir assumes.

Mysticism and Women's Experience: Weil and Luce Irigaray

Compared to Beauvoir, increased appreciation of mysticism is found in the work of recent French feminists such as Luce Irigaray, Julia Kristeva, Catherine Clément, and Hélène Cixous. Among these authors, Irigaray stands out for intensively developing the importance of mysticism for women's subjectivity in her writings over the course of four decades.[16]

There are particularly striking resonances between the work of Weil and Irigaray in their original thinking about subjectivity and mysticism. They respond to a common intellectual legacy which includes Catholic mystical texts, and Western philosophers such as Plato, Descartes and Marx. Both female philosophers hold that mysticism opens the self to God, nature and other persons, and mystical relation possesses a decisive ethical impetus. Both of them address the dynamics of immanence and transcendence in the subject's encounter with the divine. Like Weil, Irigaray deals centrally with embodiment and the self. I shall consider major statements by Irigaray on the significance of mysticism for women with relevance to Weil's thought.

In her first book, *Speculum of the Other Woman*, Irigaray praises the emancipatory potential of mysticism to resist patriarchy in a central chapter entitled "La Mystérique."[17] She points out that philosophically in the West, man has been the subject in politics, morality and general theory, and religiously, God has been imagined as masculine. Characteristically, a binary opposition is constructed, with man associated with reason and woman with irrational emotion; man with mind and woman with body; man with presence and woman with absence or lack. Woman is the negative mirror image of man. The masculine-paternal God functions to guarantee man's identity, but in medieval Christian mysticism a female subject emerges as previously but no longer oppressed.

Contrary to the ideal of the rational male, feminine discourse emerges in mystical expression characterized by excess, bodily ecstasy, and *jouissance*.[18] Imitating the negativity attributed to women, the mystic's self becomes empty, an abyss swallows up all names and properties, and this self is absorbed by the radiant splendor of divine touch.[19] The mystical soul speaks thus: "A living mirror, this am I to your resemblance as you are mine. We are both singular and plural . . . my body shines with a light of glory that radiates it."[20] The female body becomes fluid and permeable to the divine. In the words of Angela of Foligno, quoted by Irigaray, "The Word was made flesh in order to make me God."[21] Women mystics embark on tasks that Irigaray takes further: countering dominant male subjectivity, and forging a different system of relation with the divine. Weil's originality also manifests how mystical language assists women in articulating theological insights independent of institutional authorities. The enduring influence of Weil's thought, despite her rejection of Roman Catholic baptism, proves the authoritative power of mystical experience which lends credibility to her philosophical insights on selfhood and God.

In distinction from Beauvoir's feminism of equality, where the female self seeks the same autonomy possessed by male selves, Irigaray rejects the framework of abstract selfhood which neglects embodiment, and instead uses metaphors of touch and fluidity to exemplify the possibility of speaking from the body. While Beauvoir considers the mystic's relation to God as feminized and incapable of transcendence, Irigaray thinks that even when enmeshed in masculine discourse, it is possible for mystics of the past to develop new avenues. Responding to the theological doctrine of incarnation, Irigaray takes a positive view, emphasizing the possibility of redeeming physicality, and bridging divine transcendence with the body.[22] Weil too includes corporeality in selfhood, but develops the paradoxical notion of self-annihilation found in relation to God and others.

In Irigaray's philosophy, she advocates the constructive potential of mysticism for overcoming women's oppression. In the essay "Divine women," she asserts that since men have always made God in their image, women need alternative conceptualizations of the divine.[23] For women to be capable of being subjects and not only predicates, to escape from the predicament of women as "Other" in Beauvoir's terms, the answer is simple: women must find a feminine God. Reaching for a new relationship with the divine, Irigaray suggests that women should incarnate God "so that we can be divine for the other, not idols, fetishes, symbols that have already been outlined or determined."[24] Excluded by the masculine Christian Trinity, women should identify instead with the female trinity of mother, daughter and spirit.[25] Weil could agree with Irigaray insofar as she eschews a male omnipotent deity, although we shall see that her philosophical notion of God is largely non-anthropomorphic.

Weil, along with contemporary feminist thinkers like Irigaray, avoids a hierarchical understanding of God's power. In an essay entitled "Love of same, love of other," Irigaray moves in this direction by using the paradoxical term "sensible transcendental" to articulate the bridging of the body and the divine.[26] This understanding of transcendence serves as a foil to classical theism's elevation of God over man, man over woman, and mind over matter. To counter what she considers the typically masculine assumption that the sensible is what is transcended, Irigaray proposes that the sensible itself transcends rather than remains below. Such a shift in mystical thought would herald a new era, she proclaims, overcoming the ills of patriarchal thought and religious exclusion. Citing Heidegger, who approved of the poet Hölderlin's statement that "only a god can save us," Irigaray affirms the need for fresh openness to God discovered in the natural world. Presuming that classical theism sustains oppressive forces, a new vision of deity is needed to resist rapacious technological exploitation.[27] Weil's critique of industrial production and scientific capitalism also points towards non-oppressive social and mystical relations.

Irigaray's constructive suggestions about deity suggest a gender-inclusive mysticism. Namely, she proposes that an antidote to the patriarchal God lies in the four natural elements of pre-Socratic thought—earth, air, fire and water. Her mystical language evokes images of air, the respiration of lovers, a god carried on the breath of the cosmos, as a new vision for the divine. Such a god is not passively awaited, but conjured among and within us "as resurrection and transfiguration of blood, of flesh, through a language and an ethics that is ours."[28] Consciousness of nature, self and divine are mutual, enabling genuine relations between the sexes. This concept of sensible transcendence is amenable to ecotheologians as well as feminists, and Irigaray's position reflects a trend among contemporary theologians who advocate metaphors of air, breath or Spirit to represent God's presence and feminine aspects of the divine.[29]

Irigaray's proposals have drawn criticism for apparent essentialism regarding women. Instead of man projecting his ideal features onto God, she seems to promote women doing the same, effecting a reversal trapped within the same gender dichotomy. It also appears that she reduces women to a unitary subject, overlooking diversity among women and plurality among conceptions of God.[30] Weil would agree with critics who point out neglect of social and economic material conditions, and would certainly reject the exclusivity of a feminine deity in women's mysticism. However, it is a misunderstanding to represent Irigaray as remaining constrained within binary thinking. Irigaray makes clear that she does not advocate a simple replacement of male dominance with female deity, but she attempts to mend the dissociation between human and divine.[31] Nor does she concern herself with women alone, for she also develops natural images of God and considers how sexual difference between men and women manifests the divine.

Particularly in her more recent writings, Irigaray includes men in her framework of transcendence and self-fulfillment. In *I Love To You*, she reflects critically on the mystical notion of ecstasy wherein the self is transported out of itself to reach a divine other.[32] Although medieval women mystics made bold advances on patriarchal limits, new conditions are necessary to establish subjectivity for women and positive relations with men. As an alternative to ecstasy, Irigaray coins the term "enstasy" to explore the notion of sensible transcendence.[33] While ecstasy connotes standing outside the self, enstasy moves between and among subjects. In the phrase "I love 'to' you" (*j'aime à toi*), she creates an abnormal grammatical construction to indicate a type of loving that is not appropriative.

It means that I love "towards" you in a relation that does not annihilate the alterity of the other. In love, the self moves towards the other while at the same time standing in itself (en-stasy). This horizontal form of transcendence allows recognition of sexual difference.[34] Moreover, it involves loss of self. With no fixed boundary between self and other, the self is destabilized and made permeable. At the same time, the self is embodied and sensible. Irigaray's thinking on subjectivity and transcendence sheds feminist light on Weil's conception of mystical selfhood, both in areas where their concerns overlap and where their conclusions diverge.

Mystical Self-Annihilation and Feminist Reflection

For Irigaray, mystical language and relation to the other in terms of the "sensible transcendental" disrupts masculine discourses, affirms women's participation, and conceptually entails a permeable notion of self. These proposals serve feminist aims of dislocating patriarchal authority, and proposing forms of non-coercive agency and non-hierarchical relation. Surely, Irigaray may seem radical in advocating women's unique language and even a feminine deity, proposed heuristically as a response to patriarchal reality. Yet, as the title of this collection of essays indicates, Weil is also radical. It is my aim here to display the implicit feminist potential of her proposal for mystical selfhood unconstrained by patriarchy or social roles.

Weil's notion of mystical self-annihilation is both pivotal to her constructive religious thought, and highly controversial from a feminist viewpoint. She takes an apophatic, imageless approach to God, found in medieval mystics such as John of the Cross, whom Weil admired.[35] What does she mean in asserting that the "I" must be negated in the process of "decreation"? Does the mystical self become a pawn under God's control, in which case the problem of subordination is reinstantiated? Does the female mystic cease activity in the world, in which case freedom from gender oppression entails social abdication? For feminist philosophers Beauvoir and Irigaray, who are protective of women's agency, Weil's mysticism may be judged as destructive or even masochistic. Hence, it is imperative to assess these presumed negative connotations in order to reflect on the feminist dimensions of Weil's thinking.

To explain why mystical relation requires self-annihilation, the point of departure is Weil's analysis of power or force and its harmfulness. She asserts that normally—in everyday life, the workplace, business, politics and war—power is exerted to dominate, conquer, subordinate, exploit and control. Weil illustrates the operation of such force in manifold ways, including her analysis of modern European nationalism, politics, work and war, and in her essay entitled *The* Iliad *or the Poem of Force.* Force in human affairs is also attributed to God. The belief that God possesses commanding and controlling power in the extreme, known as divine omnipotence, takes collective force to the highest level. Weil rejects both this false divinity and this dehumanizing force in society. Her conclusions are widely shared by contemporary feminist and liberation theologians.[36] As a matter of fact, both Beauvoir and Irigaray enumerate similar objections to patriarchal society and religion. These two authors' ideas diverge most markedly, however, with Weil's constructive proposal, which emphasizes human suffering, divine withdrawal, and mystical decreation.

Weil's "Spiritual autobiography" is important in showing how her materialist and mystical insights coalesce. From her participation in factory work and farm labor, she developed extreme sensitivity to those who suffer. Her earlier writings explore oppressive suffering using Marxist tools of social analysis, without excursions into mysticism. Her pivotal mystical experience occurred soon after her time as a factory worker ended in 1935. It occurred in a humble fishing village in Portugal, where she watched a procession of fishermen's wives blessing the ships. This saint's day procession, accompanied by mournful music, struck Weil as both ancient and expressive of quintessential human sadness. This ritual in the fishing village centered on women, and it evoked the continuity of Mediterranean culture with pre-Christian religion. Such processions do not reflect the imperial church or a distant father God, but local patron saints identified with the community and nature. Weil saw that many such saints and Holy Mothers are continuous with pagan deities, who wield power not as lawgivers and judges, but as mediators and comforters.[37] As she watched the procession, her exhaustion from factory work was reflected in the women's mournful voices. In recollection, Weil observes that at that moment she became convinced that "Christianity is pre-eminently the religion of slaves, that slaves cannot help belonging to it, and I among others."[38] Identification with the poor, she thought, was a bridge between Christian mysticism and Marxism.

From a feminist perspective, it is significant that Weil's insights were formulated through her experiences as a female factory worker and her witnessing of a women's ritual procession. Not only does she observe slavery or oppression, but she seeks to share it, and philosophically considers it the most profound insight into the human condition. This valorization of oppression is not found in Beauvoir, who idealizes equal autonomy for women and men, or Irigaray, who advocates women's mysticism as resistance to patriarchy. Their condemnation of masculine oppression imputes responsibility for social wrongs one-sidedly to men, failing to theorize broader reasons for hierarchical power exerted by both women and men. Related to this neglect of women's agency as potential oppressors is inattention to social class, a matter of growing concern among recent feminists connected with awareness of minority-group oppression. Her consciousness of power domination and social position are two feminist assets in Weil's approach.

The oppressive character of force and the ubiquity of enslavement lead towards the notion of mystical self-annihilation. Weil transmutes her first-hand insights about suffering and oppression into an ontology of negation. According to her account, creation itself requires an act of withdrawal and renunciation by God, in order to allow the existence of creatures distinct from God. Thus creation is a divine act of humility, generosity and love, and goodness is not enforced by God's power. God allows human selves autonomous power that is used selfishly to dominate. The self-emptying (*kenosis*) of God in Christ is the paradigm of divine power, which explains Weil's conjecture that Christ has been crucified since the beginning of the world.[39] Evil and suffering display divine withdrawal. There is a feminist sensibility evident in this understanding. Rather than paternal command, God displays maternal renunciation of power to allow relation between independent beings.[40] In comparison, Irigaray's female mysticism also makes divine power dependent on human recognition, whereas Beauvoir does not pursue mysticism for feminist ends. But Irigaray presumes that a deity who does not display coercive power is feminine, or like the elements. Perhaps any mystical posture that undermines patriarchal construction is acceptable to Irigaray. The apophatic approach taken by Weil has the advantage of embracing natural and personal metaphors for God, remaining androgynously open to gendered images, but committed to none as ultimate truth. Although God is experienced mystically, God's reality cannot be fully expressed by human concepts.

By grace, God's absence, which is necessary to permit created beings, is not total. In reciprocity to the divine renunciation of creation, a person can accomplish *decreation* which opens space for God. God awaits the opportunity afforded by human renunciation of the ego. Self-annihilation is voluntary. It may occur when a person feels affliction, which is physical, psychological or social suffering, often caused by manual work or illness.

It may also occur in love, and more rarely as an act of grace. Weil identifies the grace of annihilation in God[41] as quite distinct from destructive self-annihilation, such as that which is caused by debasing factory work. Decreation and annihilation are also positively described as love. God withdraws out of love to allow us to be. Then the self may withdraw for God's sake; in this way, human agents show love for God. With the assistance of humanity, God's love enters creation and is made real.

The ethical implications of self-annihilation are expanded in her essay "Forms of the implicit love of God." These forms are love of neighbor, love of beauty and natural order, and love of religious practices. Weil describes love as a consensual passive activity. The self which exerts controlling power is negated. Readiness for love is voluntary, but loving is not an assertive act of will.[42] It involves attention and waiting. Love of neighbor involves acceptance of affliction, but the mystic does not seek suffering masochistically. Irigaray complicates notions of self and the other, focusing on women who are pervasively framed by the male gaze and lacking a vocabulary apart from male dominance. The permeable self envisioned by Irigaray approaches self-negation in refusing identity as the other to the male and rejecting appropriative love, which is why she inserts "to" in the phrase "I love to you."[43] Compared to Beauvoir, both Weil and Irigaray de-center the separate self, refuse binary self-other relations, and struggle with the confines of language. Both admire mystical relationality for subverting the confines of gender identity, and overcoming the false dichotomy of activity and passivity in self-other interaction.

Conclusion: Weil's Feminist Potential

To do justice to the multiple connections between Weil and French feminist thought would require many more pages. Nevertheless, this chapter at least demonstrates that Weil is a vibrant interlocutor for feminist reflection. To position Weil in the development of feminist thought, I propose that we consider her as a "pre-post-feminist."[44] This elliptical label highlights her ambiguous position. Given her death in 1943, she precedes the French feminist movement galvanized by Beauvoir. Yet she can be considered feminist because of her biography and the relevance of her writings. Further, to view her as post-feminist highlights the way in which her thought challenges traditionalist feminist assumptions about women as subjects. The term "post-" also indicates departure from a status quo, whether in philosophy, theology, literature or art. For example, postmodern thinkers destabilize unified discourses of reason and systems of knowledge, and post-colonial authors uncover layers of internalized oppression. Certain feminist theologians have identified themselves as "post-Christian" because of their radical reimagining of theological doctrines and biblical texts, and some identify mysticism as contributing to their post-Christian vision where gaps of reason and understanding lie in tension with faith affirmations and theological claims.[45] Among such authors there is also post-feminist questioning of feminist assumptions about subjectivity, agency, and liberation. The claim to be "post-" is intended to highlight departures from a given system of thought, and among religious thinkers, the categories postmodern, post-colonial, post-Christian and post-feminist may often overlap. Weil could be described as pre-post-feminist since she offers new perspectives on modern philosophy, oppression, patriarchal theology, and white women's feminism.[46]

Overall, in comparing the three French writers, Weil stands closer to Irigaray, even though Weil and Beauvoir belong to the same generation. To find Weil ahead of her time is not surprising, since she is famous for her precocious intelligence. Weil anticipates criticisms of feminist authors, like Beauvoir and many others, who philosophize about women collectively without attention to material aspects of selfhood. Weil also rejects the subject-object dualism that Beauvoir portrays. Although Weil's approach reflects the importance of mysticism for empowerment as developed by Irigaray, she would object to how Irigaray links mysticism with sexual difference. Weil does not assume a unitary social position for women, or binary opposition between the sexes. She challenges Beauvoir's liberal notion of equality, as well as the sexual morphology of Irigaray. Moreover, she advocates neither the vertical transcendence of classical theism nor the horizontal transcendence of feminism, but a material transcendence.[47] Subjectivity is destabilized in Weil's thinking. Paradoxically, it is self-loss that offers release from female and male social roles, and integrates nature, the human, and the divine.

For feminist reflection, a major reason why Weil's approach to mystical selfhood is appealing is its sensible quality. She carefully examines material conditions of existence and the relationship of the embodied self with nature, as well as examining physical labor and the attention of love. God's immanence in creation is discovered through self renunciation correlated with ethical commitment. Weil's vision of mystical self-annihilation is implicitly feminist in its concrete approach to selfhood and its ethical implications. To view Weil as a pre-post-feminist is a thought-experiment intended to show her complex relevance to feminist religious reflection in the twenty-first century.

Notes

[1] Siân Reynolds, "Simone Weil and women workers in the 1930s: *condition ouvrière and condition féminine*," *Cahiers Simone Weil*, Vol. XIX, No. 1 (1996), 97–113.

[2] For major investigations of women's mysticism and feminism, see Carolyn Walker Bynum, *Fragmentation and Redemption: Essays on Gender and the Human Body in Medieval Religion* (New York: Urzone Publishers, 1991); Grace Jantzen, *Power, Gender and Christian Mysticism* (Cambridge: Cambridge University Press, 1995); and Amy Hollywood, *Sensible Ecstasy: Mysticism, Sexual Difference, and the Demands of History* (Chicago: University of Chicago Press, 2002).

[3] Simone Pétrement, *Simone Weil: A Life*, trans. Raymond Rosenthal (New York: Pantheon Books, 1976), 28.

[4] Simone de Beauvoir, *The Second Sex*, trans. H. M. Parshley (New York: Knopf, 1957).

[5] Jane Duran, "The two Simones," *Ratio* Vol. XIII, No. 3 (September 2000), 201–12.

[6] Simone de Beauvoir, *Memoirs of a Dutiful Daughter*, trans. James Kirkup (New York: Harper & Row, 1974), 252; and Pétrement, *Simone Weil: A Life*, 51.

[7] One prominent critique of white middle-class bias in feminism is found in bell hooks, *Feminist Theory: From Margin to Center* (Boston: South End Press, 1984), 34.

[8] Debates among Marxist feminists are represented in Lydia Sargent, ed., *Women and Revolution: A Discussion of the Unhappy Marriage of Marxism and Feminism* (Boston: South End Press, 1981).

[9] Beauvoir, *Second Sex*, xxix.

[10] Beauvoir's ontology derives from the existentialism developed in Jean Paul Sartre, *Being and Nothingness: An Essay in Phenomenological Ontology* (1943; New York: Citadel Press, 1966).

[11] Beauvoir, *Second Sex*, 670.

[12] Beauvoir, *Second Sex*, 678.

[13] Beauvoir, *Second Sex*, 680.

[14] Beauvoir, *Second Sex*, 671.

[15] For broad feminist criticism of Beauvoir, see Josephine Donovan, *Feminist Theory: The Intellectual Traditions* (New York: Continuum, 2004), 139–41.

[16] The prominence of mysticism in the writings of contemporary French feminists Luce Irigaray, Julia Kristeva, Catherine Clément and Hélène Cixous is displayed in Morny Joy, Kathleen O'Grady and Judith L. Poxon, eds, *French Feminists on Religion: A Reader* (London: Routledge, 2002).

[17] Luce Irigaray, *Speculum of the Other Woman*, trans. Gillian C. Gill (Cornell: Cornell University Press, 1985), 191.

[18] The term *jouissance*, meaning "enjoyment," "pleasure" or "bliss," is employed in the work of psychoanalyst Jacques Lacan, Julia Kristeva, Luce Irigaray and others, but typically it is not translated into English because of its multivalent meanings.

[19] Irigaray, *Speculum*, 195.

[20] Ibid., 197.

[21] Ibid., 191.

[22] For exposition of Irigaray's views on mysticism in relation to Beauvoir, see Amy Hollywood, *Sensible Ecstasy*, 193–203.

[23] Luce Irigaray, "Divine woman" (1984) in *Sexes and Genealogies*, trans. Gillian C. Gill (New York: Columbia University Press, 1993), 57–72.

[24] Ibid., 71.

[25] Ibid., 62.

[26] Luce Irigaray, *An Ethics of Sexual Difference*, trans. Carolyn Burke and Gillian C. Gill (Ithaca: Cornell University Press, 1993), 115.

[27] Martin Heidegger, "Building dwelling thinking," in *The Question Concerning Technology, and Other Essays*, trans. William Lovitt (New York: Garland Publishers, 1977), 319–40.

[28] Irigaray, *Ethics of Sexual Difference*, 129.

[29] Flora Keshgegian, *God Reflected: Metaphors for Life* (Minneapolis, MN: Fortress Press, 2008).

[30] For exploration of how Irigaray's proposal is not essentialist in rethinking God, see Ellen T. Armour, "Divining differences: Irigaray and religion," in Morny Joy, ed., *Religion in French Feminist Thought: Critical Perspectives* (London: Routledge, 2003), 29–39.

[31] Irigaray's use of the term "divinity" operates on a relational and ethical level, which leaves her open to changes of secularizing religious vocabulary. Penelope Deutscher, "'The only diabolical thing about women': Luce Irigaray on divinity," *Hypatia* Vol. 9, No. 4 (Fall 1994), 88–111.

[32] Luce Irigaray, *I Love To You: Sketch of a Possible Felicity in History*, trans. Alison Martin (New York: Routledge, 1996).

[33] Ibid., 104.

[34] Ibid., 116.

[35] In Greek, *apophasis* means without image, and Christian apophatic mysticism is associated with negative theology and Platonism. For philosophical analysis of Weil's mysticism of decreation, see Miklos Vetö, *The Religious Metaphysics of Simone Weil*, trans. Joan Dargan (Albany: State University of New York Press, 1994), 26–40.

[36] Editors' note: See Chapters 14 and 15 of this volume.

[37] Andrea Nye, *Philosophia: The Thought of Rosa Luxemburg, Simone Weil, and Hannah Arendt* (New York: Routledge, 1994), 96.

[38] WG, 67.

[39] WG, 145.

[40] FLN, 140.

[41] NB, 463.

[42] WG, 149.

[43] Irigaray, *I Love To You*, 60.

44 The term "pre-post-feminist" is applied to Weil by Mary Orr in an unpublished paper, "Genesis, gynesis and ontogenesis," delivered at the Feminist Theory Conference, Glasgow Scotland, 12–15 July 1991. Cited in Siân Reynolds, "Simone Weil and women workers," 113.

45 Pamela Sue Anderson, "The 'post-' age of belief: wither or whither Christianity?" in Lisa Isherwood and Kathleen McPhillips, eds, *Post-Christian Feminisms: A Critical Approach* (Aldershot, UK: Ashgate, 2008), 38.

46 See Pui-lan Kwok, *Postcolonial Imagination and Feminist Theology* (London: SCM Press, 2005), and Ellen Armour, *Deconstruction, Feminist Theology, and the Problem of Difference: Subverting the Race/Gender Divide* (Chicago: University of Chicago Press, 1999).

47 Anne Elvey, "Material elements: The matter of women, the matter of earth, the matter of God," in Isherwood and McPhillips, eds, *Post-Christian Feminisms*, 57–8.

Chapter 14

Truly Incarnated: Simone Weil's Revised Christianity

Inese Radzins

I think, and so do you, that our obligation for the next two or three years, an obligation so strict that we can scarcely fail in it without treason, is to show the public the possibility of a truly incarnated Christianity.[1]

In particular, the belief that a man can be saved outside the visible Church requires that all the elements of faith should be pondered afresh, under the pain of complete incoherence. For the entire edifice is built around the contrary affirmation, which scarcely anybody today would venture to support. No one has yet wanted to recognize the need for such a revision . . . If, therefore, salvation is possible outside the Church, individual or collective revelations are also possible outside Christianity. In that case, true faith constitutes a very different form of adhesion from that which consists in believing such-and-such an opinion. The whole notion of faith then needs to be thought out anew.[2]

Introduction

It has always been clear that Simone Weil had a contradictory relationship to Christianity, as both biting critic and serious admirer. This is evidenced in her suggestions that Christianity required her *not* to be baptized, or that it would have been better if the resurrection never occurred.[3] These heterodox ideas arise from Weil's liminal spacing in regard to Christianity. In her *Spiritual Autobiography* she positioned herself as not in the Church, but nevertheless as inspired by Christianity.[4] I suggest that this marginal place allows Weil to extricate Christianity— or at least the idea of Christian inspiration—from the Church. She does this by suggesting a "revision" of Christianity that calls for thinking it *otherwise* than through adherence to an "opinion."[5] A central aspect of this rethinking is her figuration of the idea of incarnation—the topic of this chapter.

Even today, 100 years after her birth, Weil's proposal for a more incarnated Christianity remains unique, and perhaps even unmatched. I suggest that the surprising element in her work—and something that has heretofore not been sufficiently explored—is the framing of incarnation in terms of materiality. To illustrate this I follow a provocative suggestion by Robert Chenavier. He writes: "It is less the combining of Christianity and Platonism—which in the final analysis is quite a traditional combination—that defines the originality of Simone Weil than the articulation of a Christian Platonism together with a consistent materialism."[6] In this chapter I develop Chenavier's insight regarding materialism, and argue that it offers the clue to deciphering Weil's idea of a *truly incarnated Christianity*. In other words, I am taking materiality as the site of Weil's revisioning of Christian incarnation.

What is material for Weil is the world, understood in two different senses. On the one hand, the world is considered as the material relationships, both natural and social, that produce human life. On the other, the world is regarded cosmologically, as the horizon of all that *is*. In order to understand Weil's materialism and how it reformulates traditional notions of Christian incarnation, I will take two steps. The first is to ground her understanding of materialism, along with the first meaning of the world, in terms of her relationship to Marx. Weil's thought is permeated throughout with Marxist ideas and yet is never limited to either Marx or Marxism in any of its early twentieth-century forms—whether materialist, socialist, or communist.[7] What drew her to Marx, I suggest, was her concern with oppression or suffering, whether that be in the form of ancient Greek slavery, the dynamics of war, modern factory work, the reality of poverty, or the effects of French colonialism. What defines Weil's materialism is an emphasis on social forces and their potential to alienate. In this section I will argue that Weil merges Marxist and Christian insights to develop a strong critique of institutional structures, like capital and the Church.

The second step I will take is to frame Weil's idea of incarnation in terms of the second meaning of world, cosmology. She herself does this by connecting Marx's notion of labor to a cosmological sensibility. If our relationship to the world is severed by the alienation that occurs through social force, the only possibility of repair comes from "outside" the material connections that determine this world. This implies a very different praxis, and one that fundamentally reorients the idea of incarnation to the universe. The world, matter itself, turns out to be spiritual. No spirit lies behind, above, or even below, the world. Rather, spirit is this material cosmos in its entirety. It is only this cosmos and a particular orientation to it that can counter the alienation produced by social forces.

What emerges from these two steps is an uncanny synthesis of Marxist materiality and Greek cosmology that takes the world as the site of Christian truth. This synthesis is rooted in a strong orientation to the world, and differs from traditional models of Christianity in three crucial respects. First, in orienting itself to the world, it will be more universal and less institutional. The emphasis is on the cosmos, rather than the Church. Second, in grounding her thinking in the world, Weil will emphasize cosmology over Christology. Finally, as regards the individual, this idea of incarnation will be focused on developing a spirituality of work rather than emphasizing the idea of salvation. Throughout, I suggest that Weil's position both diverges from the traditional and offers a recovery of certain elements of Christianity long forgotten or marginalized.

Weil's Materialism: Marx's Labor and His Social Force

I position Weil's idea of materiality in terms of her appropriation of two Marxist categories: labor and social force. Beginning with labor allows us to see that Weil's anthropology concerns doing, or working, rather than being. We are created as workers, laborers. An engagement with the world grounds her idea of materiality. It is this engagement that is the root of human incarnation: we are created to engage the world in work. I suggest that Weil appropriates Marx's idea of labor as "life activity, productive life."[8] Human beings are characterized by what they do, how they work. I do not mean to imply that her emphasis on labor comes exclusively from Marx. As Chenavier clearly shows, her "philosophy of work" is multifaceted and depends upon many other thinkers.[9] What is important for both Weil and Marx is understanding labor as "the central activity of human life and a source of humanity's dignity."[10] Laboring involves (re)producing life. It is an engagement with the world and with natural matter in supplying our means of subsistence. Human beings live by *producing*—eating, building, gathering. I suggest that for both Weil and Marx production is best understood as a broad category that defines our fundamental humanity. It is not to be narrowly conceived as some-*thing* we do, or by the product we make. Rather, it is how we always and already find ourselves; it is our life activity.

What distinguishes human beings from other creatures and from one another is the particular *way* we work, our capacity to produce, to create. On the one hand, human beings are distinguished from other creatures because we are conscious of our production; we think about how, what and why we produce. For example, we create cuisine; we do not simply eat. Likewise, we design and decorate. On the other hand, we are distinguished from one another by our work. No two persons produce in exactly the same manner. This offers the idea of a radical singularity to which we will return in the second section.[11] My labor is mine alone and is not—as capital would have it—comparable to that of others. For Weil this productivity, because it defines our engagement in the world, is our most profound and spiritual capacity. To be human is to labor. "This schema is the form of all our actions in the sense that it is a condition of all our actions to be labor, that is to say, to be totally lacking in immediacy."[12] Weil's understanding of labor encompasses any and all human action: crying, playing, reading, building, writing, making. I suggest that this broad conception of labor grounds her understanding of incarnation. Later, we will see how this idea of labor depends upon a crucial Weilienne category, decreation.

Whereas productivity defines an individual's relationship with the material world, force characterizes one's relationships with others. This relates to Weil's second appropriation of a Marxist idea, social force. Materiality depends upon "the double burden imposed on man by nature and society."[13] On the one hand, human beings are subject to the forces of nature—the rotations of the planet, the seasons, the movement of waves, and weather. These forces have an uncontrollable element and can be equally beautiful and devastating. Weil called this natural determination necessity, or gravity. On the other hand, human beings are also subject to social forces:

> Marx's truly great idea is that in human society as well as in nature nothing takes place otherwise than through material transformations. "Men make their own history, but within certain fixed conditions." To desire is nothing; we have got to know the material conditions which determine our possibilities of action; and in the social sphere these conditions are defined by the way in which man obeys material

necessities in supplying his own needs, in other words, by the method of production.[14]

Unlike natural forces however, the fixed conditions of social life are much harder to identify. This is the case because they concern the manifold dynamics of social existence: politics, religion, workplace structures, family units, economies, and so on.

In order to understand these material/social forces, Weil observed that Marx offered a radical revisioning of history. In Western Europe prior to Marx, history was understood to be guided by unseen forces: be they the gods of the ancient Greeks, the idea of Providence or divine will for Christians, Hegel's movement of Spirit in history, or the Enlightenment emphasis on progress. These mysterious forces were seen as guiding history towards a specific end. Marx suggested that these attributions created the idea, or illusion, that society and its history was beyond the control of individuals or groups. The problem with this conception of history is that it minimizes human responsibility. Both Weil and Marx note that when history is guided by unknown forces, suffering can become a necessary *step* toward a better future. Likewise, oppression— such as colonialism, racism, sexism or fascism—can be normalized in the service of either progress or history.

Following Marx, Weil sought to demystify this understanding of history by locating the cause of oppression in social forces:

Marx was the first and, unless I am mistaken, the only one—for his researches were not followed up—to have the twin idea of taking society as the fundamental human fact and of studying therein, as the physicist does in matter, the relationships of force. Here we have an idea of genius, in the full sense of the word. It is not a doctrine; it is an instrument of study, research, exploration and possibly construction for every doctrine that is not to risk crumbling to dust on contact with a truth.[15]

The importance of identifying society as a powerful material force was that it allowed one to place the onus for suffering in human hands— whether as a result of capital, democracy, totalitarianism, Church, state, or clan.

For Weil, society involved a powerful contradiction between individual and collective existence. It is a human need to live with and among others. In this sense, society positively roots individuals—in a family, culture, or religion. Simultaneously, however, society also suppresses individuality: to become part of a group implies some form of constraint on the part of the individual. This is true of family units, local citizenship, church membership, workplaces, and national identity. Individuals are subject to the constraints that mark any given social group. The problem with society is that it distorts the life of the individual—slavery, factory work, colonial oppression and poverty are only a few of the worst examples. Marx and Weil—and perhaps Weil because of Marx—contend that these social forces produce various constraints, and inevitably suffering. Although they frame their concerns differently, both asked why the dynamic of social existence necessarily produced suffering. Marx's terms were "alienation" and "estrangement," whereas Weil chose "oppression," "suffering," or "affliction."[16]

Marx's explanation of social forces occurs through the development of the specific force of capital. He suggested that the movement of capital is increasingly alienating to the individual worker. What capital does is deprive the worker of the means of production, their capacity to determine their own productivity. Blum and Seidler explain thus: "[t]he source of oppression lies in the deprivation of the use of intelligence in the operation of work."[17] In other words, alienation occurs when individuals are severed from a relation to the means of production. When someone or something else—capital, militarization, colonialism, increasing bureaucracy—controls the means of an individual's production, alienation occurs. Marx noted that this happens on four specific levels: alienation from the product of labor, from oneself, from one's species-being, and from others.[18] What occurs is a dangerous transposition: labor is disassociated from the individual. Work is no longer an end in itself, no longer how I live and actually exist. Rather, work becomes the means to my end; I work in order to receive a paycheck. Modern existence is characterized by a dangerous separation of life and work, encapsulated in the phrase *working for the weekend.*[19]

I suggest that what distinguished Weil's idea of incarnation was the conviction that materiality concerns not only natural forces, but also social ones. In order to expand upon this, I will turn to a discussion of the relationship between Marx and Christianity in Weil's work. In constructing her idea of materiality, Weil puts Marx in dialogue with Christianity. In this she presaged the work of later German political theologians and Latin American liberation thinkers.[20] Weil produces a fruitful conversation that can attend to the limits of both perspectives. On the one hand, she criticizes Christianity on Marxist grounds insofar as it developed as a social institution that did not hesitate to use force to oppress various others. On the other hand, she argues that the insights of Christianity parallel those of Marx and even, perhaps, surpass them (that is, they are more Marxist than Marx himself). This dialogue between Marx and Christianity has numerous implications. I will focus on just three that have relevance for her idea of incarnation.

The first implication concerns the Church as a social structure which, she confessed, "frightens" her.[21] The problem with the Church is the same as that of capital—it produces alienation. For Weil any social group (for example Church, state, business or civic group) is interested in its own wellbeing and the consolidation of its power. This occurs because groups are focused on building membership, strengthening ranks and raising revenue. In Weil's logic, the greater the institutionalization, the greater the levels of oppression. This was for her clear in the case of the Church, which after the fourth century became the religion of the empire, and an example of social power *par excellence*. Through the centuries, the Church participated in and instigated the destruction of numerous *others*. The drive toward institutionalization, with its requirement of conquering, converting, or destroying *others*, came as the Church consolidated its power and allied with political regimes. Weil is not alone in identifying the problematic nature of the Church as a social structure. More recently, liberation philosopher Enrique Dussel has suggested that Marx was absolutely correct in calling for a rejection of religion, because the religion of his day concerned only Christendom and its social power.[22]

The second implication, and the one that offers a counter to the institutionalization of the Church, is Weil's observation that Christianity is "pre-eminently the religion of slaves."[23] She contends that Christianity understands slavery as the submission to social forces. In her meditation on the Lord's Prayer she makes a radical suggestion: "Our personality is entirely dependent on external circumstances which have unlimited power to crush it. But we would rather die than admit this."[24] These external circumstances are the social forces alluded to previously. What is critical for Weil is that we understand our place in the world as radically determined not by ourselves, but by the social forces that produce and surround us. Contemporary psychoanalysis makes a similar point.[25] Weil's Jesus is unique because he was aware of these social dynamics, whether religious, political, or economic. This is clear in the Gospel stories of Jesus's relationship to religious and secular authorities, his actions in overthrowing the vendors in the temple, his particular attention to those who are marginalized, and his singular life (as we will see below). For now, I suggest that Weil's Christianity, like her Marxism, helped her identify the very real power of social forces in determining human existence. The third implication is a crucial divergence from Marx. Although Weil uses Marx's ideas, she also criticizes his method for being too beholden to modern ideas of progress and history. Weil suggested that Marx's thinking was still too limited by a notion of historical progress, or the idea that humanity and history are moving towards a better future. Marx would place this progress in human hands by suggesting that a revolution could overcome the alienation which capital produced. Weil was less optimistic—or perhaps more realistic—when she questioned both the idea of progress and of revolution. I suggest that this critique arises from her version of Christianity, with its emphasis on eternality rather than temporality.

Weil is skeptical of any revolution precisely because it can only offer *more of the same* in terms of social force. Revolution is another form of social power, and thus is no less oppressive than the existing powers.[26] In addition, she is skeptical of the idea of progress. For Weil, the alienation produced by social forces is a by-product of social existence and not something that can be overcome. It is an "absurdity lying at the very heart of social life."[27] As such, it is ever-present. Thus capital becomes one manifestation of this force. An intriguing aspect of Weil's work in this regard is her anachronistic use of Marx's methodology to understand history.

> Marx was right to begin by positing the reality of a social matter, of a social necessity . . . This idea was original in relation to his time; but, absolutely speaking it is not original . . . Plato felt above all very strongly that social matter is an infinitely greater obstacle to overcome between the soul and the good than the flesh properly so called. That is also the Christian conception . . . social matter is the cultural and proliferating medium *par excellence* for lies and false beliefs.[28]

This position allowed Weil to offer numerous examples of social forces: Plato's "Great Beast," the anti-Christ of the Book of Revelation, the violence of the *Iliad*, the Crusades, French colonialism, European militarism, and Christian missionary activity. They produce different forms of oppression, but all nevertheless manifest the power of any social force. Perhaps the most compelling example is her reading of the *Iliad*, which demonstrates how all individuals, both victors and vanquished, are defined by their particular material conditions and in relation to the main character, force.[29]

Weil's dialogue between Marx and Christianity produces a unique understanding of materiality that is not limited to nature, body, or matter. Rather, materiality includes both our natural and social interactions. What is crucial is that Weil's Christianity does not deny materiality, but rather reconstructs it. Instead of rejecting matter, or nature, as much of traditional Christianity might, her thinking challenges the power of the social relationships that determine our materiality in alienating ways.[30] Thus her understanding of sin is social, rather than individual. It is not a moral category, but rather a structural one. Thus the human condition involves navigating these forces and enduring the alienation, suffering and oppression they produce. Her materialism takes suffering as a part of the dynamic of all human relationships—present in the ancient Greeks no less than in modern society. If this is the case, the task can never be to eliminate these social forces, whether by revolution or through a Christian understanding of "salvation history." Rather, the task becomes their minimization.[31]

Whereas the previous section addressed what Weil called "necessity," or "gravity," I now turn to another force, Good, or "grace."

If we examine human society and souls closely and with real attention, we see that wherever the virtue of supernatural light is absent, everything is obedient to mechanical laws as blind and as exact as the laws of gravitation.[32]

These *laws of gravitation* are, I suggest, the social forces identified above. The difficulty is that when confronted with these laws, human beings adamantly insist upon their freedom. For Weil, via Marx, this freedom is an illusion because our situation is always determined by these social laws. The only possibility for countering this social force is what she terms *supernatural.*

However, her supernatural is not (as tradition often has it) a point outside nature. Rather, it is *super* in two distinct ways. First, because it remains outside the dynamics of social force, it is not determined by the social structures that define our material existence. The second meaning of this *super* is as the highest, or most appropriate, form of the natural. The key for Weil's incarnation lies in understanding the supernatural as something that arises in and through matter and our working, rather than as something that stands above and beyond nature. In order to understand this supernatural, or Good, it is necessary to turn to Weil's cosmology.

Materialism as Cosmology: Making the Universe One's Country

Having identified Weil's materiality as being defined by social and natural forces and the alienation of work, I turn now to a discussion of the only possible counter to these forces—a cosmological orientation. For Weil, the only point outside this world of social forces is the universe, or cosmos. The determination of this world by nature and society lies in opposition to the universe, which is by definition unlimited. Her notion of materiality is complete when the world is considered not only in its material, but also in its cosmological, components. I suggest that Chenavier's proposal for a "consistent materialism" involves considering both necessity (natural and social forces) and Good (cosmology). The limit of worldly necessity is met by the infinity of cosmos. Weil's Christianity is thus rooted in a particular interpretation of the cosmos, or universe, as that which frames and defines materiality.

This materiality depends upon a cosmology that displaces the traditional subject of Christianity, Jesus Christ. In other words, incarnation was for Weil more cosmologic than Christological. Although certain strands of Christianity—especially the Eastern ones—emphasize cosmology, Western theology has prioritized Jesus Christ. At the heart of the dominant Christian message in the West is the historical figure of Jesus, who is considered *the* unique and complete incarnation of God in the world. In this understanding, God stands outside the universe and enters the world principally in the figure of Jesus. Instead, Weil prefers an emphasis on the Johannine account, the Word that is with God and is God from the beginning of time.[33] Before the historic incarnation, Jesus was already the Word, the Truth of the world. She explains: "Christ likes us to prefer truth to him because, before being Christ, he is truth."[34] *This preference for truth* is an extension of John's emphasis on the Word's primacy, and crucial to the Gospel's message.[35] Christ is then a particular and crucial revelation of Truth, not an exclusive one. In other words, if Truth is universal, it cannot be limited to the figure of Christ.

Displacing Christology in favor of a cosmological Christianity allowed Weil to locate truth in the cosmos, or universally, rather than in any particular event, religion or person. Incarnation is for Weil this Word/Truth

of the eternal universe. She is clear that this Truth is not the earth, or the
human experience of the world, but rather the cosmos as the whole
totality of what is. The universe is the ground, or horizon, for all that is.
By way of explanation, I suggest that Weil's idea of truth can be understood in terms of contemporary phenomenology's idea of *horizon*.[36] As
such, it offers the condition for the possibility of all things and yet
remains fundamentally unknowable. Because it is the condition, that in
which we always and already find ourselves, it can never become a positive object of knowledge. This is precisely why the cosmos cannot be
known: it is not a thing like other things in the world to be known
(whether natural or social). It is like a canvas that holds a work of art,
necessary but unseen. Like the chlorophyll that sustains life, it is active
but not visible to the eye.[37] Like the creative process of inspiration that
allows the artist to create a beautiful work of art, it remains mysterious.
As horizon, the universe is both determinative of—and irreducible to—
human categories of knowledge.

This emphasis on cosmology relativizes institutional Christianity as the
unique locus of God's incarnation. If cosmos is the site of incarnation,
worldly wisdom rather than any one institution or religion is central.
Weil explains: "The children of God should not have any other country
here below but the universe itself . . ."[38] She proposed that a *preference for
truth* required "making the universe one's country," or living universally.
Christian Truth *is* the universe itself. Truth is not an abstract form, or
God standing behind or above the world. Rather, Truth is the cosmos in
its wholeness. This implies that "in everything that exists there is most of
the time more truth than falsehood."[39] If social force is a *negative* aspect
of her materialism, cosmology is the *positive*. The universe, and all that is,
is True and Good and divine.

Weil offered various ways of referencing this world that is to be our
country below including Good, Truth, God, Mystery, Incarnation, Love,
and Inspiration. All of these words express the world's incomprehensibil-
ity and its indispensability for human beings. The world is what forms
human beings and allows them to be. As is often noted, this cosmological
emphasis is related to Weil's reading of the Greeks and to a particular
appropriation of Greek truth.[40] Rémi Brague argues that a cosmological
orientation was prevalent in the West up until the Middle Ages. He
observed that this orientation located truth in the universe, or cosmos,
rather than in human knowledge. Truth was worldly, including the cosmos itself and all that it revealed.[41] For the Greeks this meant being
determined by, and understanding themselves within, a universal schema,

in the rotation of the planets and among the stars. This is in sharp contrast to a modern sensibility, which locates knowledge in the individual. With the Enlightenment came the view that human beings could explain the universe. Weil rejects this modern emphasis on the knowing subject and seeks to reorient humanity toward the unknowable world. Her idea of Christian incarnation demands being at home in the world, not looking to another world or searching for heaven.

In order to better understand Weil's cosmology, I have identified three crucial aspects that relate to her materiality. The first idea is that the universe is an ongoing activity of "worlding."[42] On this point, Weil's thoughts could resonate with certain contemporary process philosophers or theologians. The universe is not some-*thing* that God creates *ex-nihilo*, or outside of Godself. Rather, the universe is the generative, moving, acting, revolving, eternal activity of God. Weil's idea of creation, not surprisingly, differed from the traditional Christian notion of creation *ex nihilo*. The cosmos is not the something that God makes out of nothing. The universe, as *horizon*, can never reveal itself as some*thing* to be seen. Precisely because the universe is what defines, contains, inspires and determines all creation, it can never become an objective anything. Weil's world, like her God, is in the words of Plato "beyond being." It is not to be conceived as something but rather as a creative inspirational activity, spiriting, energizing and upholding all that is.

Although "worlding" is an eternal activity as I have suggested, it is so in a negative way. For Weil's world to be, God had to renounce Godself. Blanchot connects this Weilienne idea of renunciation to the Kabalistic, and specifically Lurianic, notion of *tsimtsum*.[43] In this schema, God creates by contracting: by renouncing a part of Godself so that something else can be. If God is all that is, for the world to be, God must withdraw Godself. Weil refers to this as divine decreation. The world is for Weil the renunciatory and decreative activity of worlding. For Weil, this renunciation means sacrifice. The universe was the Johannine "lamb slain from the foundation of the World."[44] In other words, worlding is the activity of the mother who must make room for the growing child in her womb. Another image Weil provided was that of the artist, who must continually negate themselves in order to create. However, the personal metaphors remain limited because God, as previously noted, is not a being but rather the activity of worlding. In fact, Weil goes so far as to argue that God's presence is only available as absenting activity.[45] This means that the world is not to be thought of as an image of God, but rather as ongoing and decreative activity.[46]

The second characteristic of Weil's cosmology is its eternality. It defies temporality, historicity or chronology. A cosmological Christianity underscores that God, Universe, Good, is eternal. God is "in the beginning" only as an *arche*, understood as an eternal point of reference rather than a temporal origin. That is, cosmos is not subject to the temporality that human beings construct and employ. Although the early Christians had a sense of this eternity, Weil suggests that the Church displaced this eternity in favor of chronology.[47] This is primarily the case when the work of Christ takes on historical significance in the form of the idea of salvation history.

There is no reason whatever to suppose that after so atrocious a crime as the murder of a perfect being humanity must needs have become better; and, in fact, taken in the mass, it does not appear to have done so. The Redemption is situated on another place—an eternal plane . . . Christianity was responsible for bringing this notion of progress, previously unknown, into the world; and this notion, become the bane of the modern world, has de-Christianized it. We must abandon the notion. We must get rid of our superstition of chronology in order to find Eternity.[48]

Emphasizing chronology, in Weil's judgment, allowed the development of the Church as an institution. What was ignored in this process was a relationship to the universe, or eternality.

The third and final characteristic of Weil's cosmology is its impersonality. The universe, understood as what is Good itself or as God, Godself, is impersonal. For Weil, a truth of Christianity is God's acting on behalf of everyone through the world and thus not acting for or against anyone in particular.

The words "Be ye perfect, even as your Father which is in heaven is perfect", coming immediately after the words "Your Father which is in heaven, who maketh his sun to rise on the evil and on the good, and sendeth rain on the just and on the unjust" imply a whole doctrine which, as far as I know, is not developed anywhere. For Christ cites as the supreme characteristic of God's justice precisely what is always brought forward (example of Job) with the object of accusing Him of injustice namely that He favors the good and the wicked indifferently. There must have been in Christ's teaching the notion of a certain virtue attaching to indifference, similar to that which may be found in Greek stoicism and Hindu thought.[49]

This impersonality creates a theological dilemma: does Weil equate God and world.[50] Is her God the cosmos itself? The answer implies, I believe, a Weilienne contradiction. On the one hand, the universe and God are identified. It is the *horizon* of all that is. On the other hand, Weil suggests that God can be personally encountered in a myriad of ways: the smile of a beloved, the act of sharing bread, and the movement of the waves in the water.[51] I would suggest that Weil's idea of the impersonality of God requires what Mayra Rivera calls a different form of divine touch.[52] For Weil, God is not a person and yet may be experienced personally in and through the world. The two are not for her incompatible.

Conclusion: The Implications of a Truly Incarnated Christianity

Weil's idea of a truly incarnated Christianity begins to emerge from her conception of materiality. This incarnation roots human beings in a three-fold manner: in work, social relations, and our larger horizon— cosmos. To be rooted implies a positive connection to our world through what Marx called production and Weil identified as a *spirituality of work*. We are incarnated as laboring, creating individuals. Human beings are most human and thus most spiritual when they can work with the least possible degree of restraint, in other words, when they can determine their means of production. However, human beings are also social creatures, which means that they root themselves in other forces such as nations, churches, class structures, or money. The problem with these social forces is that they all, in varying degrees, alienate the individual from their spiritual capacity to labor. In order to lessen this alienation, Weil proposes a cosmological sensibility. The only means of minimizing the dynamic of social force is found "outside" necessity and in cosmology, the Good. In other words, social force can only be minimized by a cosmo- logical orientation. I suggest that this idea of incarnation requires a radi- cal positioning of the individual that involves three aspects.

The first is contemplation. Instead of imitating society and its tendency towards power—as the Church has so often done—a cosmological Christianity suggests a particular relation to the world. If Truth is cosmo- logical, human beings should be determined by contemplation. A con- templative stance resists what Weil understood to be a problem of modern existence—objectifying the universe and understanding it as a collection of things to be manipulated and used. This resistant form of contemplation is not unique to Christianity. Rather, it is a universal characteristic, or possibility, of all human persons.

The contemplation practiced in India, Greece, China, etc., is just as supernatural as that of the Christian mystics. More particularly, there exists a very close affinity between Plato and, for example, St John of the Cross. Also, between the Hindu Upanishads and St John of the Cross. Taoism too is very close to Christian mysticism. The Orphic and Pythagorean mysteries were authentic mystical traditions.[53]

Weil noted that the same contemplative stance that orients one towards cosmos is what orients one towards work. In other places she calls this "attention." Contemplation turns our gaze towards the world as horizon and thus relativizes all the *things* in the world. As such, it may minimize the impact of social forces.

The second aspect of Weil's incarnation is imitation. Human beings not only contemplate the universe, they must also copy it. This is difficult because the universe, as previously noted, is characterized by its negating activity. What this involves for individuals is decreation. If the world arises and is upheld by renunciation, human beings themselves must undergo such an activity. I am suggesting that Weil's idea of decreation takes on a very specific meaning here: renouncing the ideas of truth created by social forces. It is not so much a moral category as a structural one: for example, giving up the attitude of accumulation so prevalent in capitalism. This negative attitude, Weil suggests, allows the *space* and *goods* for others to be. Jesus, in the Gospels, displays this stance.

The import of Christ lies in his acceptance of a renunciatory stance. Jesus orients himself cosmologically, towards the Father, and in the process resists the social forces of his time, only to be murdered in the process. For Weil, the cross reveals the inability of social forces to accept a cosmological sensibility. Jesus is crucified because he questions societal norms. I suggest that this is what she means by the supernatural "use" of suffering.[54] She is not suggesting that suffering be something to be desired. Rather, she understands suffering as an outcome of a specific—and singular— relationship to social force. And herein lies Weil's desire to emphasize the crucifixion rather than the resurrection. This is a calculated decision on her part. In her judgment the resurrection leads to a certain form of Christian triumphalism, the illusion that history or heaven will offer something better. Whereas crucifixion reveals Jesus's relationship to suffering, resurrection displaces suffering and suggests that it can be overcome. For Weil, the veracity of Christianity lies in its comprehension of the very material reality of suffering. The message of Jesus is crucial: the cross is central to understanding the work of Truth in the world.

The third and final point to make about Weil's incarnation is its emphasis on what I call "singularity." The Truth of Christianity reveals for Weil the negative effects of social forces that alienate us from world, one another, and ourselves. If the problem of existence lies in our social structures, the response can only be something singular. It is crucial to note that Weil rarely—except in the case of the Cathars and perhaps the Pythagoreans—suggested groups as a model for meaningful work. By their very nature, groups are unable to take a contemplative stance. In other words, society cannot offer a remedy to itself. This is the unique *work* of the individual. I suggest that there is a correspondence between Weil's idea of the singularity of labor and that of a relation to cosmology. Meaningful work and a cosmological sensibility are, perhaps, two sides of the same coin. Just as we contemplate matter in work, so also we contemplate the world as our horizon. In fact, for Weil, it is through our individual labor—under the minimal amount of social force—that we contemplate the universe. Likewise, contemplating the universe allows for meaningful labor. Incarnation refers to this attentiveness to our laboring in the world. For Weil, this attention translates into a cosmic attention.

However, as noted above in the example of Jesus, this singularity of action is incredibly difficult. The illustrations Weil provided of singular individuals ready to labor are well known: Plato's *just man*, Prometheus, Joan of Arc, Patroclus, and perhaps even Marx. What characterizes these individuals is the ability to read their situations and respond differently than social forces would dictate. That is, they can say *no* to social force, to capital, empire, government, and even Church. The reason they can do so is that they understand creation, or activity, in terms of decreation. Weil affirms that "creation means self-loss."[55] Other examples could include Socrates, Eckhart, Porete, Martin Luther King, Jr, Gandhi, Romero, and the many *disappeared* of Latin America. What is revelatory of these figures is that their actions are considered questionable, dangerous, or heretical by the powers-that-be. Most suffer: Eckhart was tried, and Socrates, Joan of Arc, Porete, King, Romero and the *disappeared* were murdered. The importance of these singular figures, like Jesus, is that they attend to and act upon their cosmological sensibility. It is a position other than the social, and one that counters the existing status quo.

In conclusion, I suggest that Weil's idea of a fully incarnated Christianity is rooted in her concern with a spirituality of work. The reality of social force is a powerful counter to individual labor. By alienating and oppressing, social forces divorce individuals from their means of production, and thus from the world or cosmos. Under these conditions, a truly incarnated Christianity requires developing a cosmological sensibility that minimizes social forces while maximizing an individual's ability to labor and thus to live spiritually. This, for Weil, is not easy to achieve because it demands a difficult posture: both contemplation and renunciation. Central to Weil's conception of incarnation is the emphasis on decreation as a way of understanding both cosmos and the individual. It is only this posture that allows the development of a spirituality of work in which the divine is understood as what is encountered in laboring: in the shovel hitting the dirt, in the breaking of bread, in the contemplation of a geometric proof, and even in the act of smiling at a beloved.

Notes

1. WG^I, 32/AD, 82. (Emphasis added.)
2. LP, 46. (Emphasis added.)
3. WG^I, 31, 46 and LP, 55.
4. See Weil's "Spiritual autobiography" in WG^I especially WG^I, 22, 32, 46/AD, 83.
5. Weil is distinguishing *believing* in Christianity from contemplating, or recognizing, its truth.
6. E. Jane Doering and Eric O. Springsted, *The Christian Platonism of Simone Weil* (Notre Dame, IN: University of Notre Dame Press, 2004), 74. See also Robert Chenavier, *Simone Weil: philosophe du travail* (Paris: Les Études Cref, 2001).
7. On this topic see Lawrence Blum and Victor Seidler, *A Truer Liberty: Simone Weil and Marxism* (London: Routledge, 1989).
8. Karl Marx, *Early Writings* (London: Penguin, 1992), 328. This is found in Marx's "Economic and philosophical manuscripts," which were only published in 1932. It is unclear to me whether Weil had read these. In this work Marx elaborates: "Man lives from nature, i.e. nature is his body, and he must maintain a continuing dialogue with it if he is not to die. To say that man's physical and mental life is linked to nature simply means that nature is linked to itself, for man is a part of nature . . . for man reproduces himself not only intellectually, in his consciousness, but actively and actually, and he can therefore contemplate himself in a world he has created . . . (328–9).
9. See also Chenavier, *Simone Weil.*
10. Blum and Seidler, *A Truer Liberty,* 48.
11. On the idea of the singularity of work in Marx, see Michel Henry, *Marx: A Philosophy of Human Reality* (Bloomington, IN: Indiana University Press, 1983).

[12] OC I, 154. As translated by Aedín Ní Loingsigh in Chenavier, "Simone Weil: Contemplating Platonism through a consistent materialism," in Doering and Springsted, eds, *The Christian Platonism of Simone Weil*, 65. See also NR, 302, and OL, 37. For a longer discussion, see Chenavier, *Simone Weil*, 441–517.

[13] OL, 56.

[14] OL, 45. This quote resonates with Marx's famous dictum in the "Eighteenth Brumaire of Louis Bonaparte": "Men make their own history, but they do not make it just as they please; they do not make it under circumstances chosen by themselves, but under circumstances directly encountered, given and transmitted from the past" (Karl Marx, *Selected Writings* [Indianapolis, IN: Hackett, 1994], 188).

[15] OL, 171.

[16] It is important to remember that the word *affliction* (*malheur*) was used in a very specific way by Weil. See "The love of God and affliction," WG[I], 67–82. Throughout this work, I am referring to what she calls more generally suffering, or oppression.

[17] Seidler and Blum, *A Truer Liberty*, 39.

[18] Marx, *Early Writings*, 58–68.

[19] See OL, 37.

[20] See OL, 170 and the works of Ernst Bloch, Johannes Baptist Metz, Enrique Dussel, and Gustavo Gutiérrez. Editors' note: See also Chapter 15.

[21] WG[I], 11.

[22] Enrique Dussel, *Beyond Philosophy: Ethics, History, Marxism and Liberation Theology* (Oxford: Rowman and Littlefield, 2003), 27.

[23] WG[I], 26.

[24] WG[I], 149.

[25] On this convergence of Marxist and psychoanalytic thought, see Julia Kristeva's "Prolegomena" to *Revolution in Poetic Language* (New York: Columbia, 1984). Editors' note: See also Chapter 12.

[26] OL, 78.

[27] OL, 71.

[28] OL, 179.

[29] Cf. IC.

[30] In a fascinating commentary, Weil suggests that the New Testament Greek word η οικουμενη (often translated as *world* in English), or *la terre habitée* in Weil's French, signifies a relationship to the Roman Empire. This would imply that specific New Testament passages were referencing not the world, as a generic cosmos, but rather the world as a specific social force, i.e. Rome. See OC VI.II, 327 and 478.

[31] Just as Marx criticized religion for focusing on an illusory future, or heaven, Weil criticized Marx for focusing on an illusion—revolution. For Weil, both heaven and revolution are illusory: "The problem is, therefore, quite clear; it is a question of knowing whether it is possible to conceive of an organization of production which, though powerless to remove the necessities imposed by nature and the social constraint arising therefrom, would enable these at any rate to be exercised without grinding down souls and bodies under oppression" (OL, 56).

[32] WG¹, 75. See also OL, 88.

[33] See the Gospel of John, Chapter One, *New Oxford Annotated Bible* (New York: Oxford University Press, 1977), 1286.

[34] WG¹, 27.

[35] For example, see Mark 10.18 and Luke 18.19, *New Oxford Annotated Bible*, where Jesus asks a question: "And Jesus said to him, 'Why do you call me good? No one is good but God alone. . .'"

[36] See Michel Henry, *I Am the Truth* (Stanford: Stanford University Press, 2003) and Edmund Husserl, *Ideas Pertaining to a Pure Phenomenology and to a Phenomenological Philosophy: First Book* (Dordrecht: Kluwer, 1982). Editors' note: See also Anthony J. Steinbock, *Phenomenology and Mysticism: The Verticality of Religious Experience* (Bloomington, IN: Indiana University Press, 2007).

[37] PSO, 13–20.

[38] WG¹, 49.

[39] WG¹, 76.

[40] There are numerous articles and books on Weil's relationship to the Greeks, and especially to Plato. See: Doering and Springsted, eds, *The Christian Platonism of Simone Weil*; Miklos Vetö, *The Religious Metaphysics of Simone Weil* (Albany: State University of New York, 1994); and Michel Narcy, "Le donaine grec" (OC VI.I), 919–33. Cf. IC.

[41] Rémi Brague, *The Wisdom of the World* (Chicago: University of Chicago Press, 2003).

[42] In this emphasis on worlding, Weil's work seems to resonate with that of Heidegger. Both criticize modern conceptions of the world rooted in subjectivity. See Maria Villela-Petit, "Simone Weil, Martin Heidegger et la Grece," in *Cahiers Simone Weil* XXVI, No. 2 (Juin 2003), and Martin Heidegger, *The Question Concerning Technology and Other Essays* (New York: Harper, 1977).

[43] Maurice Blanchot, *The Infinite Conversation* (Minneapolis, MN: University of Minnesota Press, 1993), 118.

[44] IC, 93.

[45] See the section "Love of the Order of the World" in WG¹, 99–117.

[46] Editors' note: See Ann Pirruccello, "Interpreting Simone Weil: Presence and absence in attention," *Philosophy East and West* Vol. 45 (1995).

[47] LP, 48.

[48] LP, 48. Editors' note: See also Jacques Cabaud's "Preface" to this volume.

[49] LP, 69.

[50] This question often arises with Spinoza. Because Weil's journals contain many references to Spinoza it would be interesting to explore her relationship to Spinoza's thoughts on *natura naturans* and *natura naturata*. See Alain Goldschlager, *Simone Weil et Spinoza: essai d'interpretation* (Sherbrooke: Naaman, 1982).

[51] See WG¹, 27, 84 and 90.

[52] Mayra River, *Touch of Transcendence: A Postcolonial Theology of God* (Louisville: Westminster John Knox, 2007).

[53] LP, 47/LR, 53.

[54] GG, 96.

[55] WG¹, 92.

Chapter 15

Affliction and the Option for the Poor: Simone Weil and Latin American Liberation Theology

Maria Clara Lucchetti Bingemer
(Translated by Bryan Lueck)

In many respects Simone Weil's life and thought foreshadow liberation theology. Ten years before the worker-priests descended into the underworld of the modern factory to proclaim the gospel of justice, and thirty years before liberation theology proclaimed that the most profound encounter with God could happen only through the face of the poor, Weil attended to the oppressed, worked alongside them in the factories, educated them, toiled in the fields with them, and spoke out against injustice which oppressed them. She did all of these things on the basis of a philosophy that sees justice as existing in both the political and religious spheres, resulting in unlikely bridges and radical demands.

The intersection between political engagement and mystical experience constitutes Weil's primary originality, and is an important part of her legacy to the generations that follow her.[1] I would like to reflect comparatively on the convergences between the life and thought of Simone Weil and the proposals of Latin American liberation theology, which were put forward in the 1970s and which changed the face of the Church and of Latin American society.[2]

In the twenty-first century, when disenchantment with politics has alienated human beings, transforming them from thinking beings into consuming subjects, it seems to me that Weil's legacy can help to revive the inevitable and fecund tension between faith and life, mysticism and practice, which has always accompanied Judeo-Christian civilization in its itinerary of feeling and realization.

Engagement with the Poor as Identity and a Way of Life

Proximity and friendship with the poor, as well as the "spirit of poverty," were integral parts of Weil's life since earliest childhood.[3] To get a sense for the significance of proximity and friendship with the poor in Weil's life, one need only read the biography written by her friend Simone Pétrement.[4] The importance of the spirit of poverty, on the other hand, is expressed clearly in Weil's own "Spiritual autobiography," written to the Dominican priest Joseph Marie Perrin before she left for the United States during World War Two.[5] Weil's studies and professional life would merely give concrete form to these experiences.

After completing her *aggrégation* in philosophy, Weil was appointed to a teaching position at a *lycée* for girls in Le Puy. Before taking up her duties as a professor, though, she took a vacation in the coastal village of Reville. There she befriended the local fishermen and their families, working alongside them. She would go out with the fishermen at night, taking care of the nets and winding up the fishing lines. When the weather was bad and the fishermen could not go out, Weil gave them lessons. And the fishermen remembered her well: "She wanted to live like us."[6] She shared work and meals with them. And she gave them what she had to give: her knowledge and her intellectual training. She wanted to be like them, and so she drew near to their lives at the most profound levels.

At Le Puy, teaching would be only one of Weil's many responsibilities. Having already participated in the national congress of the General Confederation of Labor, Weil immediately sought out contacts with the trade union movement, in which she participated actively. She joined the National Teachers' Union and went on to organize meetings between militants of all political persuasions, fighting for unity within the trade union movement.[7]

Weil was working at a truly feverish pace. In addition to her regular courses at the *lycée*, she offered free courses to the miners. Depriving herself of sleep and meals, she contributed to Alain's journal *L'Effort* and wrote articles for the union bulletins.[8] Her union activity earned her trips to the police station, reprimands from educational authorities, and threats of transfer. The alliances that she made during this period were increasingly with the left, and even with the radical left. Her sympathies with anarchism were clear, and her criticisms of capitalism explicit. Nonetheless she maintained her lucidity and her critical independence with regard to ideologies.

In March of 1934, Weil began to withdraw from partisan political activity. In a letter to her friend Simone Pétrement, she wrote: "I have decided to withdraw entirely from any kind of political activity, except for theoretical work. This does not absolutely exclude possible participation in a great spontaneous movement of the masses (in the ranks, as a soldier), but I don't want any responsibility, no matter how slight, or even indirect, because I am certain that all the blood that will be shed will be shed in vain, and that we are beaten in advance . . ."[9] We can sense in this letter the sad lucidity of someone discouraged from the belief that party politics and violence could solve the problems that were afflicting Europe and the world. Without abandoning her engagement with the downtrodden, and still continuing to participate in strikes and mass movements, she found developing more and more strongly within her the great project that would distinguish her forever: to know, through her work in the factory, the world of poverty and oppression from the inside.

During her final months at Roanne, where she had been assigned to teach in the fall of 1933, Weil worked on what would become one of her most famous texts, "Reflections on the causes of liberty and social oppression," which she considered her "magnum opus," her "testament."[10] It contained in brief form all of her thinking on the relations between the individual human being and the society of her time. Around this same time, she made her decision to leave for the factory. The project was too important to her to wait any longer and to risk never carrying it out. Weil was seeking through this project a way to reconcile the kind of organization needed by an industrial society with the conditions of work and life necessary for a free proletariat.[11] She would not seek the answer to this question as other intellectuals did, by shutting herself up in the library and immersing herself in books. She would seek it rather in the infernal heat of the factory, in proximity to the suffering of the workers. Her "testament," which contains her best thinking on politics and oppression, was finished in December of 1934. She had gone into the factory on the fourth day of that same month. She went to verify in her own flesh what she had been thinking about since her classes with Alain at the Sorbonne.

Incarnation in the Life of the Poor

Weil's almost complete rupture with the political organizations of the left did not imply an alienation from the reality of poverty and injustice that marked the context in which she lived.[12] She remained convinced that one could combat injustice only by getting close to it and living it from within. This is how she understood her project of going to work in the factory, which came to shape her life in increasingly concrete ways.[13]

It is impressive to see Weil's intuition transformed into a decision, into a practice taken up and lived by her during the 1930s. It was a practice that would closely resemble that of the worker-priests and of other European laypersons in the 1940s. These Christians who went into the factories to live with the poor and to proclaim the Gospel would be among the greatest inspirations for later Latin American liberation theology which, supported by the bishops of the Latin American continent, gained force in the 1970s.[14] Weil made the departure from her professorship to the factory alone, drawing strength solely from the call that she felt inside her and from her desire to benefit workers through a better understanding of their living conditions.

Weil rented a small room on the top floor of a building on the rue Lacourbe in order to be closer to her workplace and to live solely on her own wages, without help from her family. No one in the factory was to know that she was a professor.[15] She experienced in her own flesh not only the most obvious burdens of poverty (exhaustion, hunger, despair, fear of orders, and punishments), but she also arrived at profound and poignant insights into the progressive dehumanization that the enslaving labor of modern society inflicts on individuals. She determined that the society of her time was built on a kind of labor that forced human beings not to think. In a letter to a former student, for instance, Weil wrote that

if you think, you work more slowly; and there are norms of speed, laid down by pitiless bureaucrats, that must be observed—both to avoid getting fired and in order to earn enough (payment being by piecework). I am still unable to achieve the required speeds, for many reasons: my unfamiliarity with the work, my inborn awkwardness, which is considerable, a certain natural slowness of movement, headaches, and a peculiar inveterate habit of thinking, which I can't shake off.[16]

These conditions stultified the workers, rendering them incapable of discerning their real situation and of rebelling against it.

Weil's true motivation for going into the factory was to determine how to achieve the liberation of the workers. She wanted to be alongside them in their workplace in order to determine from within the causes of their oppression, and to help them to attain a more human life.

The cruel consequences of this choice made themselves felt on Weil's fragile body. In her diary she recounts crying ceaselessly during work, and succumbing to fits of sobbing upon returning home. With the passing of weeks, she was reduced to a state in which even thinking became impossible. She describes this deplorable state in which she found herself as follows:

> Exhaustion ends by making me forget the real reasons for my working in the factory, renders almost invincible the strongest temptation which this life brings with it: that of no longer thinking, the only and sole means of not suffering from it. It is only on Saturday afternoon and Sunday that I am visited by some memories, shreds of ideas . . . The terror that seizes me when I realize my dependence on external circumstances: it would be enough if one day I were forced to work without a weekly rest . . . and I would immediately become a beast of burden.[17]

This incarnation in the life of the poor produced a profound transformation in the young intellectual. From the depths of her pain and weariness emerged Weil's most lucid reflections on labor, and on the foolish pretension of modern ideologies that claimed from the height of their theories to liberate the workers, who lived like slaves in the factories: "When I think that the great Bolshevik leaders proposed to *create* a free working class and that doubtless none of them . . . had ever set foot inside a factory . . . politics appears to me a sinister farce."[18] She once told a student movingly that "[a]bove all, I feel I have escaped from a world of abstractions to find myself among real men—some good and some bad, but with real goodness or badness. Goodness especially, when it exists in a factory, is something real; because the least act of kindness . . . calls for victory over fatigue and the obsession with pay. . ."[19]

Weil reflected upon and evaluated her experiences in the factories once they had come to an end. And her reflections reveal just how painful they were for her. She wrote in a letter to Albertine Thévenon:

> What working in the factory meant for me personally was . . . that all the external reasons . . . upon which were based my sense of personal dignity, my self-respect, were radically destroyed within two or three weeks by the daily experience of brutal constraint. And don't imagine that this provoked in me any rebellious action. No, on the contrary; it produced the last thing I expected from me—docility. The resigned

docility of a beast of burden. It seemed to me that I was born to wait for, and receive, and carry out orders—that I had never done and never would do anything else . . . When I was kept away from work by illness, I became fully aware of the degradation into which I was falling, and I swore to myself that I would go on enduring the life until the day when I was able to pull myself together in spite of it. And I kept my word. Slowly and painfully, in and through slavery, I reconquered the sense of my human dignity—a sense that this time relied upon nothing outside myself.[20]

What Weil had experienced developed into a theory of working life in the factories of her time and place. In a text from the end of 1937, Weil describes the situation of factory workers as follows:

If the workers are exhausted by fatigue and want, this is because they do not count for anything and the growth of the factory counts for everything. They do not count for anything because the role that the majority of them play in production is that of mere cogs, and they are degraded into this role of cogs because intellectual labour has become separated from manual labour, and because the development of machinery has taken away the privilege of skill from man so as to transfer it to inert matter.[21]

The young professor of philosophy left her youth and her happiness behind in the factory. But despite this she was still able to say she was "glad to have lived through it."[22] This was the same conclusion that the worker-priests reached in the 1940s and 1950s. Such also was the feeling of the Latin American Church in 1968 when it proclaimed in Medellín, Colombia, that the struggle for justice and commitment to the liberation of the poor were inseparable from the proclamation of the Gospel.[23] Such was the perspective of the theologian Gustavo Gutiérrez in laying the groundwork for a new way of doing theology, based on the reality of oppression and poverty.

In his *Theology of Liberation*, the Peruvian theologian affirms that "it is not a question of idealizing poverty, but rather of taking it on as it is— an evil—to protest against it and to struggle to abolish it." He adds that "Christian poverty has meaning only as a commitment of solidarity with the poor, with those who suffer misery and injustice. The commitment is to witness to the evil which has resulted from sin and is a breach of communion."[24] The poor about whom Gutiérrez speaks—like those who preoccupied Weil—are not sentimentalized and idealized figures, but are rather a concrete class, marginalized by society: the poor are "the oppressed. . . the member[s] of the proletariat struggling for the most basic rights; the exploited and plundered social class, the country struggling for its liberation." And he adds that "in our times . . . to be in solidarity with the 'poor,' understood in this way, means to run personal risks—even to put one's life in danger. And so there are emerging new ways of living poverty which are different from the classic 'renunciation of the goods of this world.'"[25] Simone Weil, just like Gustavo Gutiérrez and, after him, other liberation theologians, understood that the option for the poor would not be possible without a concrete and physical proximity to the life of the poor, or without sharing their suffering, their privations, and their longing for liberation.

The Encounter with Christianity as Encounter with the Poor

Weil's encounter with Christianity would influence her life and thought in fundamental ways. On the basis of this encounter she effected a new synthesis of her previous ideas and reflections, one which bore a distinctly Christian stamp. Proximity to the poor and the effort to liberate them would be an important part of this, as evidenced by the account she gave to Father Perrin of her first encounter with Catholicism and of the indelible mark it made on her. The encounter took place in Póvoa de Varzim, a fishing village in Portugal. Weil had just left the factory feeling enfeebled and branded forever with the red-hot iron of slavery. This direct contact with affliction had killed her youth.[26] The procession of fishermen in Portugal was the light that deflagrated her whole internal life:

> In this state of mind, then, and in a wretched condition physically, I entered the little Portuguese village, which, alas, was very wretched too, on the very day of the festival of its patron saint. I was alone. It was the evening and there was a full moon over the sea. The wives of the fishermen were, in procession, making a tour of all the ships, carrying candles and singing what must certainly be very ancient hymns of a heart-rending sadness. Nothing can give any idea of it. I have never heard anything so poignant unless it were the song of the boatmen on the Volga. There the conviction was suddenly borne in upon me that Christianity is pre-eminently the religion of slaves, that slaves cannot help belonging to it, and I among others.[27]

It remains a curious fact that Weil, in describing her encounter with the procession, so typical of popular Portuguese Catholicism, would morally invert Nietzsche's thesis about the slave revolt. For Nietzsche, the great critic of Christianity, this revolt took place because the slaves were powerless to destroy either slavery or the Roman Empire that supported it. The new Christian religion, according to Nietzsche, became an expression of the impotent hatred of the slaves, who had to content themselves with an imaginary revenge.[28]

Weil described her experience before the procession in Póvoa do Varzim in Nietzsche's own terms—Christianity as the religion of slaves—but drew a completely opposite conclusion. While Nietzsche had viewed the connaturality of the poor with Christianity as the source of the decadence of Western aristocracy and society, Weil, who had been branded by slavery in her experience in the factory, saw in it her place of belonging. For her, Christianity is on the side of the last of this world, of those who are despised and regarded as insignificant; this is where Weil felt she should be as well.

Weil's route towards an immediate and explicit mystical experience of union with Christ passed through the urgent need to kneel down at Assisi. It passed through the stabbing pain of headaches, transfigured by the beauty of the Gregorian chant at Solesmes, introducing her to thoughts of the Passion of Christ. And it culminated in Christ's taking possession of her during a recitation of the poem "Love" by George Herbert.[29] After this, Weil's life and thought would undergo a profound transformation. All that she thought and wrote would henceforth bear a definitively Christian stamp. This represented a new stage in her personal and intellectual journey; her previous experience would not be lost, but it would be taken up again in a new light. It is here, it seems, that Weil's thought approaches most closely the writings of the liberation theologians, while nonetheless maintaining some notable differences.

The movement that shaped Weil's life from the beginning reached its apex in her experience of immersion in the Paschal Mystery. This immersion, being a real experience of God in the Passion of Christ, was for Weil always just as much an immersion in the passion of the poor and afflicted of the world, first in the factory workers, then in Christ in person, the "beloved face" of Weil's spiritual experience.[30] This fascinating spiritual discovery would not immobilize Weil in passive and alienated contemplation, but would rather deepen her compassion for the last of the earth, whom she did not dissociate from Christ, finally and lovingly encountered.

The gift of her calling and of union with Christ, and her experience of the ardent desire of his Cross, did not separate Weil from her experience of the centrality of "affliction" (*malheur*), to which her compassion had attracted her from earliest childhood.[31] It was this affliction that Weil experienced in its most extreme consequences in the factory, where she was subjected to routine so monotonous, and "production" so exacting, that she felt herself being reduced to a brute mechanism.[32] Therefore, she would continue to turn her "attention"—a central category in her thought—to the poor and unfortunate of every kind, that is, to the afflicted with whom God identifies Himself and through whom He manifests Himself. Weil's writings after 1938, the year in which she most likely had her mystical experience, testify abundantly to this.

The "Afflicted": Weilienne Name for the "Poor"

For Weil, human suffering contains within itself a category that is "something apart, specific and irreducible": affliction.[33] It is important to establish that for Weil, affliction is something greater than, and different from, physical, moral or any other kind of suffering. It is, moreover, something that must not be treated as a merely individual situation. Weil herself affirms that "there is not real affliction unless the event that has seized and uprooted a life attacks it, directly or indirectly, in all its parts, social, psychological, and physical. The social factor is essential. There is not really affliction unless there is social degradation or the fear of it in some form or another."[34]

Weil considered this affliction "the great enigma of human life."[35] This is because it is "surprising that God should have given affliction the power to seize the very souls of the innocent and to take possession of them as their sovereign lord."[36] Because affliction is something so radical and so structural, rendering those who have never experienced it incapable of comprehending the experience of the afflicted, and rendering the afflicted incapable of helping anyone at all, Weil considered compassion for the afflicted an impossibility in human terms, and only possible through God's grace. "When it is really found we have a more astounding miracle than walking on water, healing the sick, or even raising the dead."[37]

Weil claims that affliction is so terrible because it renders God absent and hidden from human perception, submerging the soul in the horror of not having anything to love. In this darkness into which the soul finds itself plunged, it may cease to love. That is the mortal danger. "The soul has to go on loving in the emptiness, or at least to go on wanting to love, though it may only be with an infinitesimal part of itself. Then, one day, God will come to show himself to this soul and to reveal the beauty of the world to it, as in the case of Job. But if the soul stops loving it falls, even in this life, into something almost equivalent to hell."[38]

Turning one's attention to the afflicted, and helping them to emerge from the lethal state into which affliction has put them, becomes possible only through the descent of God, which makes Christ live within them. To give, and to give oneself to the afflicted is, according to Weil, a mystical experience, since the one who gives feels no distance whatever between the person before her and themselves, but rather transfers to the other the whole of their being. From this moment on the impulse to feed the other becomes as instinctive, as immediate, as our impulse to nourish ourselves when hungry.[39] It does not become so through a reflection that would link the act to our love for God; we feed the other simply because he or she needs it. "Christ will thank the people who give in the way they eat."[40]

Weil understood this impulse to give the afflicted what they need, an impulse possible only through God, as something with Eucharistic connotations. For it is "the benefactor himself, as a bearer of Christ, who causes Christ to enter the famished sufferer with the bread he gives him. The other can consent to receive this presence or not, exactly like the person who goes to communion. If the gift is rightly given and rightly received, the passing of a morsel of bread from one man to another is something like a real communion."[41]

For those who are genuinely compassionate, though, it is not a matter of giving material things, even things of such vital necessity as food. "They do for the afflicted something very different from feeding, clothing, or taking care of them. By projecting their own being into those they help they give them for a moment—what affliction has deprived them of—an existence of their own."[42] Once the one who gives to the unfortunate can see Christ himself in that person, the Christian burden of giving becomes bilateral. "Affliction is essentially a destruction of personality, a lapse into anonymity. Just as Christ put off his divinity for love, so the afflicted are stripped of their humanity by misfortune."[43]

But also, in carrying out the act of giving, one is being formed to Christ himself:

To project one's being into an afflicted person is to assume for a moment his affliction, it is to choose voluntarily something whose very essence consists in being imposed by constraint upon the unwilling.

And that is an impossibility. Only Christ has done it. Only Christ and those men whose whole soul he possesses can do it. What these men give to the afflicted whom they succour, when they project their own being into them, is not really their own being, because they no longer possess one; it is Christ himself.[44]

But Weil goes on to identify charity and justice, and to defend both as attitudes owed to the afflicted. This, I believe, is where her thought is intertwined most closely with that of liberation theology. Weil writes that

> Christ does not call his benefactors loving or charitable. He calls them just. The Gospel makes no distinction between love of our neighbor and justice. In the eyes of the Greeks also a respect for Zeus the suppliant was the first duty of justice. We have invented the distinction between justice and charity. It is easy to understand why. Our notion of justice dispenses him who possesses from the obligation of giving. If he gives all the same, he thinks he has a right to be pleased with himself. He thinks he has done a good work.[45]

Weil thus understands love of one's neighbor, the heart of the Bible's message and of the Gospel, purely and simply as justice. "Only the absolute identification of justice and love makes the coexistence possible of compassion and gratitude on the one hand, and on the other, of respect for the dignity of affliction in the afflicted—a respect felt by the sufferer himself and the others. It has to be recognized that no kindness can go further than justice without constituting a fault under a false appearance of kindness."[46]

Only the practice of justice, according to Weil, can bring about equality between human beings, between the strong and the weak, the powerful and the afflicted. For the stronger party, the supernatural virtue of justice consists in conducting him/herself exactly as if there were equality. For the weaker party, justice consists in not believing that there really is an equality of strength, and in recognizing that the other's generosity is the only reason for this treatment. It is what is called gratitude.[47] Weil recognizes in a creature who acts justly a reproduction of the original attitude of the Creator, and declares that this virtue is the Christian virtue *par excellence*.[48] This virtue, according to Weil, is identical with real, active faith in the true God. "The true God is the God we think of as almighty, but as not exercising his power everywhere . . ."[49]

After her encounter with Christianity, Weil never dissociated her profound love of the crucified Christ, of God the Father of Jesus Christ, from her consciousness of the urgency of justice, or from her engagement with the poor and afflicted. These sentiments, making her so alive to the suffering of others, would never abandon her. On the contrary, they became ever more present and acute. They would constitute forever her great passion and her severest torture. As Father Perrin noted in his preface to *Waiting for God*, "Compassion is torture for anyone who truly loves."[50] This torment accompanied Weil until the end of her life. Exiled in London, prevented from entering occupied France and giving her life there—which had been her most profound desire—she came to experience the temptation to hopelessness that was produced in her by her contact with the misfortune of others. And there she recalled the one thing that consoled her: "I reassure myself a little by remembering that Christ wept on foreseeing the horrors of the destruction of Jerusalem. I hope that he will forgive my compassion."[51]

For Weil, the love of God and of Christ were inseparable from the love of the other who was suffering and afflicted. "To treat our neighbor who is in affliction with love is something like baptizing him," for to do so is to return to him the dignity and the humanity that affliction has taken from him.[52] Making a most beautiful comparison with the parable of the Good Samaritan, Weil says that the one who is devoid of everything has no identity. He is a piece of bloody, inert flesh at the side of the road.[53] Several people pass by without even seeing him. Only one stops and attends to him. The acts that follow are nothing but the automatic effects of this moment of attention. Weil insists that this attention is creative, but at the same time kenotic, full of renunciation. The one who practices this gesture of attention consents to diminish, or to not increase, his power—to act only so that the other might exist, independently of himself. He transports himself into the other and participates in the fallen state in which the other dwells.[54]

Creative attention to the afflicted is thus something like genius, bringing into existence what did not previously exist. The other who falls injured by the side of the road does not really exist in their humanity. Creative attention, the carefulness of the one who attends to and cares for the other, brings that other into existence as a person, a human being. There we find faith which, just like love, makes visible those who were previously unseen. The poor, the afflicted, are invisible. Faith inspired by love sees the invisible.[55] It sees the invisible because God Himself is present in the one who acts for and in the afflicted other. Attention is an event of love that only exists and only takes place in and through God.

For Weil, love of one's neighbor is something that happens in the sphere of gratitude, and not in the sphere of commerce, where everything has a price and corresponds to a right. Such love is something that does not even proceed from the domain of charity, *as understood colloquially*. Love of one's neighbor pertains rather to justice, which is the only practice that can raise humanity to the level of equality. Finally, for Weil this love has a creative power. Once it is directed to someone deprived of their most fundamental dignity, and thus of their humanity, restoring them and returning to them their human condition, it has the power to bring into existence what did not previously exist. God Himself descends into the heart of affliction in order to reveal Himself in the persons who suffer from it, and in those who suffer with them.[56] It is God Himself, therefore, who enables human beings to get outside the sphere of self-sufficiency and to experience faith, which operates by charity in the attention paid to the afflicted, returning their subjectivity to them and making them the subjects of their own histories.

Liberation theology proposed something analogous in Latin America. It is not a matter of reinforcing the millenarian practice, already assumed on a greater or lesser scale by Christians, of giving what was left over, of holding back excesses in order to give to those who lack everything. It is a matter rather of reinforcing the fact that effective attention to the poor is a question of justice. It means being charitable by renouncing any and all "privileges," so that suffering is shared. And it means doing so freely, not in order to render the poor debtors, thankful to the one who has done them this favor from above, but rather helping them to become conscious of their situation and to assume their places as subjects in history.

Attention to the Poor as Constitutive of Faith: Simone Weil and Liberation Theology

If there is a point on which all the currents and tendencies of liberation theology agree, it is that the option for the poor is theocentric. For liberation theology, in other words, the reason to opt for the poor is God Himself, not an ideology, a theory, or a result of an analysis of reality.[57] While affirming categorically and in accordance with biblical revelation that God loves all His creatures equally, making no exceptions for human beings, liberation theology contends that God nonetheless reveals Himself especially radically in the field of justice. God sides with justice, taking up completely the cause of those who have been wronged. Those who believe in this God, in the God of revelation, the God of the Bible, the God of Jesus Christ, have no path to follow other than that of the option for the poor.[58]

In the context of liberation theology, the term "poor" must not be taken in its colloquial sense as referring to the economically or materially poor. Nor should it be taken to refer to "the poor in spirit." The concept of "the poor" refers rather to the oppressed, to the victims of an organization of the world that is unjust, and that therefore fails to correspond to the justice desired by God. The option for the poor, then, should not be understood as something different from the option for the victims of racism, or of gender discrimination, or of cultural marginalization.[59] The most renowned liberation theologians have emphasized the tremendous interpellation that the existence of poverty, conceived in this sense, represents for humanity, situating this problem at the very center of theological thought. They have endeavored to discover the causes of poverty and the means to combat it. They have promoted the creation of base communities which, through readings of the Bible, would help the poor to see their situation more clearly and to make the decisions necessary to transform it. Liberation theologians have fought not so much against atheism, but against idolatry as the principal enemy of faith. The idolatry against which the liberation theologians have fought is the kind that deifies consumerism, wealth, power, and in sum everything on which modern capitalist society is based.

The theology of Leonardo Boff, for example, proposes a radical rupture with the logic of the capitalist system, one that aims to liberate the poor and the oppressed.[60] Jon Sobrino, in his theology, identifies the poor with the "victim," proclaiming the necessity of a political holiness that would assume the risks of an incarnation in the life of the poor in order to fight for their liberation.[61] Following closely the life and memory of Oscar Romero, the archbishop of San Salvador who was assassinated while celebrating the Eucharist in 1980, Sobrino argues that "political holiness is historically necessary today for the poor to receive the good news and for history to move toward the coming of God's kingdom."[62] It is necessary as well in order for the Church to return to the Gospel and to show the world a more credible face, which it can do only by means of a radical and effective love of the poor.[63]

From the beginning, liberation theology has understood itself as the bearer of a qualified word which, added to those of others in history, could contribute to the liberation of the poor and the oppressed of every kind.

But it has always maintained very clearly that there would be no real liberation unless the poor raised their voices freely and expressed themselves directly and creatively, in society and history.

Like Weil, the liberation theologians believe that the look which liberates the poor from their poverty, the afflicted from their affliction, is the one that is creative through its emptiness and renunciation, that does not give material things with which to satisfy immediate needs. It is rather the look that gives them the possibility of regaining their human dignity, of assuming fully their mission of transforming the history and destiny of their people.

Conclusion: The Hidden God Revealed in the Face of the Poor

Simone Weil and the liberation theologians both struggled with the same dilemma: their consciousness of the love and kindness of God seemed to be in tension with their consciousness of the violence and the hiddenness of this same God.[64] For Weil, God was revealed through close acquaintance with the poor and their suffering. The same was true for the liberation theologians. What perhaps differentiates the one from the other—Weilienne philosophy from liberation theology—is their different conceptions of praxis. While liberation theology understands praxis as a collective and transforming movement of history, in which a whole people is both subject and protagonist, Weil conceives the practice of justice as something more individualized, something shaped by attention to the other who lies injured and mistreated at the side of the road.

In both of these reflections, however, it is clear that God is revealed not through a fulgurant glory that would dazzle human eyes, but rather through a kenotic hiddenness in the face of the poor and oppressed who cry out for liberation and whose poverty interpellates us epiphanically. One's own salvation is at stake in responding to this interpellation. And the path of this response leads necessarily to kenosis and to the Cross.

From the 1970s through the 1990s, liberation theology called on the Church of Latin America, and of the entire world, to leave behind its place of privilege and its alliances with elites and to go out resolutely to the margins of society, to be at the side of the poor and to realize there its evangelizing mission. Much earlier, in the 1930s and 1940s, the young Jewish philosopher Simone Weil lived this in her own flesh. Obeying an irresistible internal impulse, she descended into the underworld of the factory, allowing herself to be marked forever by the red-hot iron of slavery. And she encountered truth in the experience of union with the crucified Christ, who formed her to himself, teaching her the path of attention to the afflicted as a condition for the practice of justice. Liberation theology certainly owes many of its insights to Weil. To know her life and works better would help this theology to rediscover the freshness and radicality of its sources, at a time when the great social questions continue to interpellate those who believe in the God who reveals Himself as justice for the poor.

Notes

¹ Cf. Josep Otón, "A la luz de lo sagrado: experiencia religiosa y compromiso politico," presented at the conference "Simone Weil. La conciencia del dolor y la belleza. Una revision crítica en el centenario de su nacimento" in Valencia, Spain, October 24–28, 2008.
² It would take too long to list all the works written on liberation theology, so I will refer here only to its founding text: Gustavo Gutiérrez, *A Theology of Liberation: History, Politics, and Salvation*, Revised Edition with a new introduction, trans. and ed. Sister Caridad Inda and John Eagleson (Maryknoll, NY: Orbis Books, 1988).
³ Cf. ibid., especially Chapter 13, "Poverty: Solidarity and Protest."
⁴ Simone Pétrement, *Simone Weil: A Life*, trans. Raymond Rosenthal (New York: Pantheon Books, 1976).
⁵ WG, 61–83.
⁶ LDP, vi.
⁷ Pétrement, *Simone Weil*, 79.
⁸ Ibid., 89. Alain was the pen name of Émile Chartier (1868–1951), who was an influential teacher and philosopher. Weil studied with him at Lycée Henri-IV. See Pétrement, *Simone Weil*, Chapter 2.
⁹ Pétrement, *Simone Weil*, 198.
¹⁰ OL, 36–117.
¹¹ Pétrement, *Simone Weil*, 204.
¹² Cf. Pétrement, *Simone Weil*, 217–8.
¹³ Cf. Pétrement, *Simone Weil*, 218.
¹⁴ Cardinal Emmanuel Suhard of Paris had founded the "Mission de France," allowing some priests to work in the factories in order to move nearer to the lives of the workers. Among these priests were the well-known Dominican Jacques Loew, who worked as a stevedore at the port of Marseille, and the priest Michel Favreau, who was killed in an accident at work. The laywoman Madeleine Delbrel, author of *We, the Ordinary People of the Streets*, immersed herself in the world of workers at Ivry. And 1950 saw the publication of Henri Godin and Yves Daniel's *France, pays de mission?* The worker-priests were accused of being communists and denounced for subversive activities.

Liberation theologians would experience a similar conflict with the Vatican in the 1980s.

[15] Pétrement, *Simone Weil*, 225.

[16] Ibid., 226.

[17] Ibid., 230.

[18] Ibid., 232, quoted from *CO*, 20.

[19] Ibid., 235–6.

[20] Ibid., 245, quoted from CO, 27.

[21] OL, 149.

[22] Pétrement, *Simone Weil*, 246, quoted from CO, 21.

[23] Cf. Consejo Episcopal Latinoamericano (CELAM), *A Igreja na atual transformação da América Latina à luz do Concílio: conclusões de Medellín* (Petrópolis: Vozes, 1973).

[24] Gutiérrez, *Theology of Liberation*, 172.

[25] Ibid., 173.

[26] WG, 66.

[27] WG, 67.

[28] Cf. Friedrich Nietzsche, *The Genealogy of Morals* and *The Antichrist*.

[29] See WG, 65–8.

[30] WG, 69.

[31] Cf. WG, 83. In her "Spiritual autobiography," Weil writes that "every time I think of the crucifixion of Christ I commit the sin of envy."

[32] WG, 67.

[33] WG, 117.

[34] WG, 119.

[35] WG, 119.

[36] WG, 119–20.

[37] WG, 120.

[38] WG, 121.

[39] Cf. what Gustavo Gutiérrez has written about this in *We Drink from Our Own Wells: The Spiritual Journey of a People* (Maryknoll, NY: Orbis Books, 2003).

[40] GTG, 94. This is a clear allusion to Matthew 25.36–45.

[41] WG, 139.

[42] GTG, 94.

[43] GTG, 94.

[44] GTG, 94–5. Cf. Galatians, 2.19–20.

[45] WG, 139.

[46] WG, 140.

[47] WG, 143.

[48] WG, 144.

[49] WG, 144.

[50] J. M. Perrin and G. Thibon, *Simone Weil as We Knew Her*, trans. Emma Craufurd (London: Routledge & Kegan Paul, 1953), 20.

[51] WG, 91.

[52] WG, 146.

[53] WG, 146. Cf. Luke, 10.25–37.

[54] WG, 147.

[55] WG, 149.

[56] *"Deus mesmo desce ao centro da desventura para a partir daí reveler-se nas pessoas que a padecem e nas pessoas que dela se com-padecem."* In hyphenating the verb "com-padecer se," the author emphasizes its literal sense of "suffering-with." The more straightforward translation of the verb would be "to pity."

[57] Cf. Gustavo Gutiérrez, "El Dios de la Vida," *Christus* 47 (1982), 53–4.

[58] Cf. Ronaldo Muñoz, *The God of Christians* (Maryknoll, NY: Orbis Books, 1994), Chapter 2.

[59] Cf. José María Vigil, "A Opção pelos Pobres é opção pela justiça. Para um reenquadramento teológico-sistemático da opção pelos pobres," *Perspectiva Teológica* XXXVI/99 (maio/agosto 2004), 241–52.

[60] Boff defends this thesis in many different books. Among these are Leonardo Boff, *Jesus Christ Liberator: A Critical Christology for Our Times* (Maryknoll, NY: Orbis Books, 1978); Leonardo Boff, *Trinity and Society* (Maryknoll, NY: Orbis Books, 1988); Leonardo Boff, *E a Igreja se fez povo. Eclesiogénese, a Igreja que nasce da fé do povo* (Petrópolis: Vozes, 1986).

[61] Cf. Sobrino's best-known works: Jon Sobrino, *Christology at the Crossroads: A Latin American Approach* (Maryknoll, NY: Orbis Books, 1978); Jon Sobrino, *Christ the Liberator: A View from the Victims*, trans. Paul Burns (Maryknoll, NY: Orbis Books, 2001); Jon Sobrino, *Jesus in Latin America* (Maryknoll, NY: Orbis Books, 1987); Jon Sobrino, *True Church and the Poor* (Maryknoll, NY: Orbis Books, 1984).

[62] Jon Sobrino, *Spirituality of Liberation: Toward Political Holiness*, trans. Robert R. Barr (Maryknoll, NY: Orbis Books, 1988), 86.

[63] Ibid.

[64] Cf. Alexander Nava, *The Mystical and Prophetic Thought of Simone Weil and Gustavo Gutiérrez: Reflections on the Mystery and Hiddenness of God* (Albany: State University of New York Press, 2001), 158–9.

Bibliography

Ali, Anwar J. and Suada al-Salhy. "Need dire and aid scant, Iraq war widows suffer." *New York Times*, 24 February 2009: 1, 6.

Alishan, Leonardo. "Tired thoughts." Burning Bush Publications, 2003. http://www.bbbooks.com/winner2003.html (accessed on 10 March 2009).

Alvarez, Lizette. "Sucides of soldiers reach high of nearly 3 decades." *New York Times*, 29 January 2009. http://www.nytimes.com/2009/01/30/us/30suicide.html (accessed on 8 March 2009).

Anderson, Pamela Sue. "The 'Post-' age of belief: Wither or whither Christianity?," in *Post-Christian Feminisms: A Critical Approach*, ed. Lisa Isherwood and Kathleen McPhillips. Aldershot, UK: Ashgate, 2008.

Andic, Martin. "Commentary on Matthews," *Proceedings of the Boston Area Colloquium in Ancient Philosophy* 13 (1997): 56–68.

Appiah, Anthony. "Identity, Authenticity, Survival," in *Multiculturalism*, ed. Amy Gutman. Princeton, NJ: Princeton University Press, 1994.

Arendt, Hannah. *The Human Condition*. Chicago: University of Chicago Press, 1998.

———. *Responsibility and Judgment*, ed. Jerome Kohn. New York: Schocken Books, 2003.

Aristotle, *Nicomachean Ethics*, trans. W. D. Ross and J. O. Urmson, in *The Complete Works of Aristotle*, ed. Jonathan Barnes. Princeton: Princeton University Press, 1995.

Armour, Ellen T. *Deconstruction, Feminist Theology, and the Problem of Difference: Subverting the Race/Gender Divide*. Chicago: University of Chicago Press, 1999.

———. "Divining differences: Irigaray and religion," in *Religion in French Feminist Thought: Critical Perspectives*, ed. Morny Joy. London: Routledge, 2003.

Augustine. *Confessions*, trans. F. J. Sheed. Indianapolis, IN: Hackett Publishing Company, 1993.

Baldwin, James. *Nobody Knows My Name: More Notes of a Native Son*. New York: Vintage International, 1993.

Beauvoir, Simone de. *The Second Sex*, trans. H. M. Parshley. New York: Knopf, 1957.

———. *Memoirs of a Dutiful Daughter*, trans. James Kirkup. New York: Harper & Row, 1974.

Benedict XVI. "First message of His Holiness Pope Benedict XVI at the end of the Eucharistic Concelebration with the members of the College of Cardinals in the Sistine Chapel," No. 4 (20 April 2005). http://www.vatican.va/holy_father/benedict_xvi/messages/pont-messages/2005/documents/hf_ben-xvi_mes_20050420_missa-pro-ecclesia_en.html (accessed on 17 January 2009).

————. *Saved in Hope*. San Francisco: Ignatius Press, 2008.

Bernauer, James W. "Michel Foucault's Ecstatic Thinking," in James Bernauer and David Rasmussen, eds, *The Final Foucault*. Cambridge, MA: MIT Press, 1987.

Bingemer, Maria Clara Lucchetti. "Simone Weil et Albert Camus: Sainteté sans Dieu et mystique sans Église," *Cahiers Simone Weil* XXVIII, No. 4 (2005).

Birou, Alain. "L'Articulation entre le surnaturel et le social chez Simone Weil," *Cahiers Simone Weil* Vol. VIII, No. 1 (1985).

Blanchot, Maurice. *The Infinite Conversation*, trans. Susan Hanson. Minneapolis, MN: University of Minnesota Press, 1993.

Blum, Lawrence and Victor Seidler, *A Truer Liberty: Simone Weil and Marxism*. London: Routledge, 1989.

Boff, Leonardo. *Jesus Christ Liberator: A Critical Christology for Our Times*. Maryknoll, NY: Orbis Books, 1978.

————. *E a Igreja se fez povo. Eclesiogênese, a Igreja que nasce da fé do povo*. Petrópolis: Vozes, 1986.

————. *Trinity and Society*. Maryknoll, NY: Orbis Books, 1988.

Bordo, Susan. *Unbearable Weight: Feminism, Western Culture, and the Body*. Berkeley: University of California Press, 1995.

Brague, Rémi. *The Wisdom of the World*. Chicago: University of Chicago Press, 2003.

Bullivant, Stephen. "From 'Main Tendue' to Vatican II: The Catholic engagement with atheism 1936–1965," *New Blackfriars* Vol. 90, No. 1026 (March, 2009).

Butler, Judith. *Giving an Account of Oneself*. New York: Fordham University Press, 2005.

Bynum, Carolyn Walker. *Fragmentation and Redemption: Essays on Gender and the Human Body in Medieval Religion*. New York: Urzone Publishers, 1991.

Calder, James. "Labour and thought in the philosophy of Simone Weil: Preface to a philosophy of education," Ph.D. thesis, Dalhousie University, 1985.

Carrette, Jeremy R. "Prologue to a confession of the flesh," in Michel Foucault, *Religion and Culture*, ed. Jeremy R. Carrette. New York: Routledge, 1999.

Carson, Anne. *Eros: The Bittersweet*. USA: Dalkey Archive Press, 2000.

Center for Public Integrity. Charles Lewis and Mark Reading-Smith, *False Pretenses*. 23 January 2008. http://projects.publicintegrity.org/WarCard/ (accessed on 8 March 2009).

Chenavier, Robert. *Simone Weil: philosophe du travail*. Paris: Les Études Cref, 2001.

Clark, Ronald W. *The Scientific Breakthrough*. New York: G. P. Putnam's Sons, 1974.

Clarke, Arthur C. *Profiles of the Future*. New York: Harper & Row, 1973.

Cohen, Richard A. "Introduction: Humanism and Anti-humanism—Levinas, Cassirer, and Heidegger," in Emmanuel Levinas, *Humanism of the Other*, trans. Nidra Poller. Chicago: University of Illinois Press, 2006.

Coles, Robert. *Simone Weil: A Modern Pilgrimage*. Woodstock, VT: SkyLight Paths Publishing, 2001.

Conrad, Joseph. *Victory*. Oxford: Oxford University Press, 1986.

Consejo Episcopal Latinoamericano (CELAM). *A Igreja na atual transformação da América Latina à luz do Concílio: conclusões de Medellín*. Petrópolis:Vozes, 1973.

Cosgrove, Joseph K. "Simone Weil's spiritual critique of modern science: An historical critical assessment." *Zygon* Vol. 43, No. 2 (June 2008).

Dabashi, Hamid. *Islamic Liberation Theology: Resisting the Empire.* New York: Routledge, 2008.

Le Dantec, Félix. *Athéisme.* Paris: Flammarion, 1907.

Davies, Brian. "Phillips on belief in God," *Philosophical Investigations* Vol. 30, No. 1 (July 2007): 219–44.

Deutscher, Penelope. "'The only diabolical thing about women': Luce Irigaray on divinity," *Hypatia* Vol. 9, No. 4 (Fall 1994): 88–111.

Dickinson, Emily. *Selected Poems,* ed. Christopher Moore. New York: Gramercy Books, 1993.

Dietz, Mary. *Between the Human and the Divine: The Political Thought of Simone Weil.* Totowa, NJ: Rowman and Littlefield, 1988.

Doering, Jane and Eric O. Springsted, eds, *The Christian Platonism of Simone Weil.* Notre Dame, IN: University of Notre Dame Press, 2004.

Donovan, Josephine. *Feminist Theory: The Intellectual Traditions.* New York: Continuum, 2004.

Dreyfus, Hubert and Paul Rabinow, *Michel Foucault: Beyond Structuralism and Hermeneutics.* Chicago, IL: University of Chicago Press, 1982.

Duran, Jane. "The two Simones," *Ratio* Vol. XIII, No. 3 (September 2000): 201–12.

Dussel, Enrique. *Beyond Philosophy: Ethics, History, Marxism and Liberation Theology.* Oxford: Rowman and Littlefield, 2003.

Eisenhower, Dwight D. "Farewell address to the nation." Delivered 17 January 1961. http://www.vlib.us/amdocs/texts/ddefarew.html (accessed on 10 March 2009).

Eliot, T. S. "Preface," in Simone Weil, *The Need for Roots: Prelude to a Declaration of Duties towards Mankind,* trans. Arthur Wills. New York: Routledge, 2002.

Ellert, F. C. "Introduction," in Simone Weil, *Oppression and Liberty,* trans. Arthur Wills and John Petrie. Amherst, MA: The University of Massachusetts Press, 1973.

Ellul, Jacques. *Propaganda: The Formation of Men's Attitudes,* trans. Konrad Kellen and Jean Lerner. New York: Vintage Books, 1973.

———. *The Technological Bluff.* Grand Rapids, MI: Wm. B. Eerdmans Publishing Co., 1990.

Elvey, Anne. "Material elements: The matter of women, the matter of earth, the matter of God," in *Post-Christian Feminisms: A Critical Approach,* ed. Lisa Isherwood and Kathleen McPhillips. Aldershot, UK: Ashgate, 2008.

Finch, Henry Leroy. *Simone Weil and the Intellect of Grace,* ed. Martin Andic. New York: Continuum, 1999.

Flew, Antony and Alasdair MacIntyre, eds. *New Essays in Philosophical Theology.* London: Macmillan, 1955.

Foster, Michael. *Mystery and Philosophy.* Westport, CT: Greenwood Press, 1980.

Foucault, Michel. "About the beginnings of the hermeneutics of the self," reprinted in Michel Foucault, *Religion and Culture,* ed. Jeremy R. Carrette. New York: Routledge, 1999.

———. *Discipline and Punish: The Birth of the Prison,* trans. Alan Sheridan. New York: Pantheon, 1977.

————. *The History of Sexuality: An Introduction, Vol. I*, trans. Robert Hurley. New York: Vintage, 1990.

————. *The History of Sexuality, Vol. II: The Use of Pleasure*, trans. Robert Hurley. New York: Vintage Books, 1990.

————. *"Society Must Be Defended": Lectures at the College de France, 1975–1976*, trans. David Macey. New York: Picador, 1997.

————. "The will to knowledge," in Michel Foucault, *Ethics: Subjectivity and Truth*, trans. Paul Rabinow. New York: New Press, 1997.

Franklin, Ursula. *The Real World of Technology*. Toronto: House of Anansi Press, 1999.

Freire, Paulo. *Pedagogy of the Oppressed*, trans. Myra Bergman Ramos. New York: Continuum, 1997.

Gabellieri, Emmanuel. *Être et don: Simone Weil et la philosophie*. Leuven: Peeters, 2003.

Goldschlager, Alain. *Simone Weil et Spinoza: essai d'interprétation*. Sherbrooke: Naaman, 1982.

Gould, Stephen Jay. *Rocks of Ages*. New York: Library of Contemporary Thought, 1999.

Grant, George. "The paradox of democratic education," in *The George Grant Reader*, ed. William Christian and Sheila Grant. Toronto: University of Toronto Press, 1998.

————. *Technology and Empire*. Toronto: House of Anansi Press, 1969.

————. *Technology and Justice*. Toronto: House of Anansi Press, 1986.

Guitton, Jean. "Quelques observations sur la pensée de Simone Weil concernant l'Eucharistie." *Cahier Simone Weil* Vol. V, No. 1 (1982).

Gutiérrez, Gustavo. "El Dios de la Vida," *Christus* 47 (1982).

————. *A Theology of Liberation: History, Politics, and Salvation*, revised edition with a new introduction, trans. and ed. Sister Caridad Inda and John Eagleson. Maryknoll, NY: Orbis Books, 1988.

————. *We Drink from Our Own Wells: The Spiritual Journey of a People*. Maryknoll, NY: Orbis Books, 2003.

Halley, H. H. *Halley's Bible Handbook*. Grand Rapids: Zondervan Publishing House, 1965.

Hedges, Chris. *War Is a Force that Gives Us Meaning*. New York: Anchor Books, 2002.

Heidegger, Martin. *The Question Concerning Technology, and Other Essays*, trans. William Lovitt. New York: Garland Publishers, 1977.

————. *Being and Time*, trans. John Macquarrie and Edward Robinson. New York: Harper Collins, 1962.

Henry, Michel. *I Am the Truth*, trans. Susan Emanuel. Stanford: Stanford University Press, 2003.

————. *Marx: A Philosophy of Human Reality*. Bloomington: Indiana University Press, 1983.

Hobbins, Daniel, ed. and trans., *The Trial of Joan of Arc*. Cambridge, MA: Harvard University Press, 2005.

Hollywood, Amy. *Sensible Ecstasy: Mysticism, Sexual Difference, and the Demands of History*. Chicago: University of Chicago Press, 2002.

hooks, bell. *Feminist Theory: From Margin to Center*. Boston: South End Press, 1984.

Hume, David. *An Enquiry Concerning Human Understanding.* Indianapolis, IN: Hackett Publishing Co., 1977.

Husserl, Edmund. *Ideas Pertaining to a Pure Phenomenology and to a Phenomenological Philosophy: First Book.* Dordrecht: Kluwer, 1982.

Idinopolus, Thomas. "Necessity and nihilism in Simone Weil's vision of God," in *Mysticism, Nihilism, Feminism: New Critical Essays on the Theology of Simone Weil,* ed. Thomas Idinopolus and Josephine Knopp. Johnson City, TN: Institute of Social Science and Arts, 1984.

International Commission of Jurists. Report of the Eminent Jurists Panel on Terrorism, Counter-terrorism and Human Rights. *Assessing Damage, Urging Action.* Geneva, Switzerland, 2009.

Iraq Body Count. http://www.iraqbodycount.org/ (accessed on 8 March 2009).

Irigaray, Luce. "Divine woman," trans. Gillian C. Gill, in *Sexes and Genealogies.* New York: Columbia University Press, 1993.

———. *An Ethics of Sexual Difference,* trans. Carolyn Burke and Gillian C. Gill. Ithaca: Cornell University Press, 1993.

———. *I Love To You: Sketch of a Possible Felicity in History,* trans. Alison Martin. New York: Routledge, 1996.

———. *Speculum of the Other Woman,* trans. Gillian C. Gill. Cornell: Cornell University Press, 1985.

Irwin, Alexander. *Saints of the Impossible: Bataille, Weil, and the Politics of the Sacred.* Minneapolis, MN: University of Minnesota Press, 2002.

Jacoby, Susan. *The Age of American Unreason.* New York: Pantheon Books, 2008.

Janicaud, Dominque, et al. *Phenomenology and "The Theological Turn": The French Debate.* New York: Fordham University Press, 2001.

Jantzen, Grace. *Power, Gender and Christian Mysticism.* Cambridge: Cambridge University Press, 1995.

John Paul II. *Ecclesia de Eucharistia* (17 April 2003). http://www.vatican.va/holy_father/special_features/encyclicals/documents/hf_jp-ii_enc_20030417_ecclesia_eucharistia_en.html (accessed on 17 January 2009).

Joy, Morny, Kathleen O'Grady and Judith L. Poxon, eds, *French Feminists on Religion: A Reader.* London: Routledge, 2002.

Jungk, Robert. *Brighter Than A Thousand Suns.* New York: Harcourt Brace, 1958.

Kammen, Daniel M., Alexander I. Shlyakhter and Richard Wilson. "What is the risk of the impossible," *Technology: Journal of the Franklin Institute,* Vol. 33, 1 A (1994): 97–116.

Kearney, Richard. *Modern Movements in European Philosophy.* Manchester and New York: Manchester University Press, 1986.

———. *Strangers, Gods and Monsters: Interpreting Otherness.* New York: Routledge, 2003.

Keener, Craig S. *The IVP Bible Background Commentary: New Testament.* Downer's Grove: InterVarsity Press, 1993.

Keshgegian, Flora. *God Reflected: Metaphors for Life.* Minneapolis, MN: Fortress Press, 2008.

Kierkegaard, Søren. *The Book on Adler,* ed. and trans. Howard V. Hong and Edna H. Hong. Princeton: Princeton University Press, 1998.

———. *Upbuilding Discourses in Various Spirits*, ed. and trans. Howard V. Hong and Edna H. Hong. Princeton: Princeton University Press, 1993.

———. *Works of Love*, ed. and trans. Howard V. Hong and Edna H. Hong. Princeton: Princeton University Press, 1995.

King, Jr., Martin Luther. "Letter from Birmingham City jail," in *A Testament of Hope: The Essential Writings and Speeches of Martin Luther King, Jr*, ed. James M. Washington. New York: HarperOne, 1990.

Kristeva, Julia. "Prolegomena," in *Revolution in Poetic Language*, trans. Margaret Waller. New York: Columbia, 1984.

Kwok, Pui-lan. *Postcolonial Imagination and Feminist Theology*. London: SCM Press, 2005.

LeBlanc, John Randolph. *Ethics and Creativity in the Political Thought of Simone Weil and Albert Camus*. Lewiston, NY: Edwin Mellen Press, 2004.

Lewis, C. S. *A Grief Observed*. San Francisco: Harper, 2001.

Loades, Ann. "Eucharistic sacrifice: Simone Weil's use of a liturgical metaphor," *Religion and Literature* 17, No. 2: 43–54.

Maran, Rita. *Torture: The Role of Ideology in the French-Algerian War*. New York: Praeger, 1989.

Marcel, Gabriel. *Mystery of Being* Vol. I. South Bend: Gateway, 1950.

Marion, Jean-Luc. *Being Given: Toward a Phenomenology of Givenness*, trans. Jeffrey Kosky. Stanford: Stanford University Press, 2002.

Marx, Karl. *Early Writings*. London: Penguin, 1992.

———. *Selected Writings*. Indianapolis: Hackett, 1994.

Matthews, Gareth B. "The career of perplexity in Plato," *Proceedings of the Boston Area Colloquium in Ancient Philosophy* 13 (1997): 35–55.

McInytre, Alasdair. "Miller's Foucault, Foucault's Foucault," *Salmagudi*, No. 97 (Winter 1993).

McKibben, Bill. *Deep Economy: The Wealth of Communities and the Durable Future*. Oxford: Henry Holt, 2007.

Meaney, Marie Cabaud. *Simone Weil's Apologetic Use of Literature: Her Christological Interpretations of Ancient Greek Texts*. Oxford: Oxford University Press, 2007.

Miller, James. *The Passion of Michel Foucault*. London: Harper Collins, 1993.

Morgan, Vance. *Weaving the World*. Notre Dame, IN: University of Notre Dame Press, 2005.

Muñoz, Ronaldo. *The God of Christians*. Maryknoll, NY: Orbis Books, 1994.

Nagel, Thomas. *The View From Nowhere*. Oxford: Oxford University Press, 1986.

National Center for Health Statistics. *Prevalence of Overweight and Obesity Among Adults: United States, 1999–2002*. http://www.cdc.gov/nchs/products/pubs/pubd/hestats/obese/obse99.htm (accessed on 20 March 2009).

Nava, Alexander. *The Mystical and Prophetic Thought of Simone Weil and Gustavo Gutiérrez: Reflections on the Mystery and Hiddenness of God*. Albany: State University of New York Press, 2001.

New Oxford Annotated Bible. New York: Oxford University Press, 1977.

Niebuhr, H. Richard. *The Kingdom of God in America*. Hanover, NH: Wesleyan University Press, 1988.

Nielsen, Kai. *An Introduction to the Philosophy of Religion*. London: Macmillan, 1982.

———. *Philosophy and Atheism*. New York: Prometheus, 1985.

―――. "Can anything be beyond human understanding?," in *Philosophy and the Grammar of Religious Belief*, ed. Tim Tessin and Mario von der Ruhr. London: Macmillan, 1995.

Nielsen, Kai and D. Z. Phillips. *Wittgensteinian Fideism?* London: SCM Press, 2005.

Nye, Andrea. *Philosophia: The Thought of Rosa Luxemburg, Simone Weil, and Hannah Arendt.* New York: Routledge, 1994.

O'Connelli, D. P. *Richelieu.* London: Weidenfeld and Nicolson, 1968.

Orwell, George. "Politics and the English language," in *A Collection of Essays.* San Diego: Harvest Books, 1981.

Padfield, Peter. *Himmler. Reichsführer – SS.* London: Macmillan, 1990.

Pascal, Blaise. *Pensées and Other Writings*, trans. Honor Levi. Oxford: Oxford University Press, 1995.

Patel, Raj. *Stuffed and Starved: The Hidden Battle for the World Food System.* Brooklyn, NY: Melville House Publishing, 2007.

Perrin, J. M., ed. *Réponses aux questions de Simone Weil.* Paris: Aubier/Éditions Montaigne, 1964.

Perrin, J. M., and G. Thibon. *Simone Weil as We Knew Her*, trans. Emma Craufurd. London: Routledge & Kegan Paul, 1953.

Pétrement, Simone. *La Vie de Simone Weil.* 2 Volumes. Paris: Fayard, 1973.

―――. *Simone Weil: A Life*, trans. Raymond Rosenthal. New York: Pantheon Books, 1976.

Phillips, D. Z. *Death and Immortality.* London: Macmillan, 1972.

―――. "Dislocating the soul," in *Can Religion Be Explained Away?*, ed. D. Z. Phillips. London: Macmillan, 1996.

Pirruccello, Ann. "Interpreting Simone Weil: Presence and absence in attention," *Philosophy East and West* Vol. 45 (1995).

Plato. *Crito*, trans. David Gallop, in *Defense of Socrates, Euthyphro, and Crito.* Oxford: Oxford University Press, 1997.

―――. *Republic*, trans. F. M. Cornford, in *The Republic of Plato.* Oxford: Oxford University Press, 1945.

―――. *Republic*, trans. G. M. A. Grube. Indianapolis, IN: Hackett Publishing Co., 1992.

―――. *Symposium*, trans. Alexander Nehamas and Paul Woodruff. Indianapolis, IN: Hackett Publishing Co., 1989.

Rahner, Karl. *Concern for the Church* Vol. 20, *Theological Investigations*, trans. Edward Quinn. New York: Crossroad, 1981.

Ratzinger, Joseph Cardinal. "The presence of the Lord in the Sacrament," in *God Is Near Us: The Eucharist, The Heart of Life*, ed. Stephan Otto Horn and Vinzenz Pfnür, trans. Henry Taylor. San Francisco: Ignatius, 2003.

Reynolds, Siân. "Simone Weil and women workers in the 1930s: *Condition Ouvrière* and *Condition Féminine*," *Cahiers Simone Weil*, Vol. XIX, No. 1 (1996).

Rice, David. "Misreading Simone Weil: Psychobiography, pathos, and politics." Paper presented at the annual meeting of the American Political Science Association [APSA] annual meeting, 29 Aug 2008.

River, Mayra. *Touch of Transcendence: A Postcolonial Theology of God.* Louisville: Westminster John Knox, 2007.

Rose, Gillian. *Judaism and Modernity: Philosophical Essays.* Oxford: Blackwell, 1993.

Rozelle-Stone, A. Rebecca. "Voiding distraction: Simone Weil and the religio-ethics of attention." Ph.D. dissertation, Southern Illinois University Carbondale, 2009.

Ruhr, Mario von der. "Theology, philosophy, and heresy: D. Z. Phillips and the grammar of religious belief," in *D. Z. Phillips' Contemplative Philosophy of Religion*, ed. Andy Sanders. London: Ashgate, 2007.

Said, Edward. *Orientalism*. New York: Vintage Books, 1979.

———. "Islam as news," in *The Edward Said Reader*, ed. Moustafa Bayoumi and Andrew Rubin. New York: Vintage Books, 2000.

Sappho. *Sappho: The Poems*, trans. Sasha Newborn. Santa Barbara, CA: Bandanna Books, 2000.

Sargent, Lydia, ed. *Women and Revolution: A Discussion of the Unhappy Marriage of Marxism and Feminism*. Boston: South End Press, 1981.

Sartre, Jean Paul. *Being and Nothingness: An Essay in Phenomenological Ontology*. New York: Citadel Press, 1966.

Schmidt, Lawrence E. and Scott Marratto. *The End of Ethics in a Technological Society*. Montreal: McGill Queen's University Press, 2008.

Schumacher, E. F. *Small is Beautiful: A Study of Economics as if People Mattered*. London: Sphere Books, 1974.

Schweizer, Harold. *On Waiting*. New York: Routledge, 2008.

Sharp, Travis. Center for Arms Control and Non-proliferation (2009). As cited by Anup Shah, *World Military Spending*, http://www.globalissues.org/article/75/world-military-spending (accessed on 16 March 2009).

Sobrino, Jon. *Christ the Liberator: A View from the Victims*, trans. Paul Burns. Maryknoll, NY: Orbis Books, 2001.

———. *Christology at the Crossroads: A Latin American Approach*. Maryknoll, NY: Orbis Books, 1978.

———. *Jesus in Latin America*. Maryknoll, NY: Orbis Books, 1987.

———. *Spirituality of Liberation: Toward Political Holiness*, trans. Robert R. Barr. Maryknoll, NY: Orbis Books, 1988.

———. *True Church and the Poor*. Maryknoll, NY: Orbis Books, 1984.

Sontag, Susan. "Simone Weil," in *Against Interpretation*. New York: Farrar, Straus & Giroux, 1961.

Springsted, Eric O. *Christus Mediator: Platonic Mediation in the Thought of Simone Weil*. Chico: Scholars Press, 1983.

———. "Contradiction, mystery and the use of words in Simone Weil," in *The Beauty that Saves*, ed. J. Dunaway and E. O. Springsted. Macon: Mercer University Press, 1996.

———. "Théorie weilienne et théorie platonicienne de la necessité," *Cahiers Simone Weil* Vol. IV, No. 3 (1981).

Steinbock, Anthony J. "Interpersonal attention through exemplarity," *Journal of Consciousness Studies* Vol. 8, Nos. 5–7 (2001).

———. *Phenomenology and Mysticism: The Verticality of Religious Experience*. Bloomington, IN: Indiana University Press, 2007.

Szasz, Ferenc Morton. *The Day The Sun Rose Twice*. Albuquerque: University of New Mexico Press, 1984.

Taylor, Charles. "The politics of recognition," in *Multiculturalism*, ed. Amy Gutman. Princeton, NJ: Princeton University Press, 1994.

————. *A Secular Age*. Cambridge: Harvard University Press, 2007.

Torgerson, Jon M. "Socrates: outwardly a monster, all beauty within," *Metaphilosophy* 22:3 (1991), 239–50.

Ullman, Harlan K. and James P. Wade. *Shock And Awe: Achieving Rapid Dominance*. Washington, DC: National Defense University, 1996.

Vetö, Miklos. *La Métaphysique religieuse de Simone Weil*. Paris: Vrin, 1971.

————. *The Religious Metaphysics of Simone Weil*, trans. Joan Dargan. Albany: State University of New York Press, 1994.

Vigil, José María. "A Opção pelos Pobres é opção pela justiça. Para um reenquadramento teológico-sistemático da opção pelos pobres," *Perspectiva Teológica* XXXVI/99 (maio/agosto 2004).

Villela-Petit, Maria. "Simone Weil, Martin Heidegger et la Grece," *Cahiers Simone Weil* XXVI, No. 2 (Juin 2003).

Watts, Alan. *The Way of Zen*. New York: Vintage Books, 1989.

West, Cornel. *Democracy Matters: Winning the Fight Against Imperialism*. New York: Penguin Books, 2004.

Wilde, Oscar. "The decay of lying," in *Complete Works*. London: Collins, 1983.

Winner, Langdon. *The Whale and the Reactor: A Search for Limits in an Age of High Technology*. Chicago: University of Chicago Press, 1986.

Wittgenstein, Ludwig. *Tractatus Logico-Philosophicus*, trans. D. F. Pears and B. F. McGuinness. London: Routledge & Kegan Paul, 1961.

Woelfel, James. *Albert Camus on the Sacred and the Secular*. Lanham, MD: University Press of America, 1987.

Wolfteich, Claire. "Attention or destruction: Simone Weil and the paradox of the Eucharist," *The Journal of Religion* 81, No. 3 (July 2001): 359–76.

Index

Bush, George W. 156n. 44, 157n. 55,
172
Butler, Judith 194–6, 199, 201
Bynum, Caroline Walker 27, 28,
218n. 2

Cahiers (Weil) 43, 44
Calder, James 124
Camus, Albert 66, 71, 74n. 66, 176
captivity
human 183–4
soul's 184
caricatures 142–3
Carson, Anne 26, 147
charity 250
Chenavier, Robert 222, 223, 230
Christian asceticism 178, 179
Christian incarnation
cosmologic 230–1
materiality and 222–3
true 234–7
Christianity 82, 214
Greek culture and 39, 185
Himmler and 62–4, 74n. 54
idolatrous 57–64
Marx in dialogue with 226–9
missionary expeditions 60–1
Nietzschean challenge to 8
orthodox 64–9
slavery and 227
suffering and 235–6
Weil's relationship to 221–2, 246–8
see also religion
Christian Platonism 66, 177, 205, 222
Christian poverty 245–6
Christ, Jesus 60, 215
afflicted and 249–50
contradictory teachings of 85–6
cosmological orientation of 235–6
God and 95
as incarnation of God 230
miracles of 114–15, 117
resurrection 70–1
Saint Peter's betrayal of 63–4
Church
approach to faith 98
divinity of Jesus and 95

eternality and 233
idolatrous self-adulation 59–60
liberation of poor 245, 254
as social structure 227
Cixous, Hélène 209
clarity 91–3
Clarke, Arthur C. 123
classical science 127
limitations of 127–8, 129
see also modern science; science
Clément, Catherine 209
Cold War 165
Coles, Robert
critique of Weil's life 20
colonialism/colonization 60, 228
France 171
Communism 40, 44–5
Compton, Arthur 130–1
Confessions (St. Augustine) 43
Congar, Yves 56
Conrad, Joseph 68
conscience
of privileged 198
replaced by public opinion 111,
129
suppression of 141
"consistent materialism" 222, 230
consumer capitalism 19
consummation
consumption and 21–2, 25
etymology and modern
definition 21
consumption 20–1, 33
consummation and 21–2, 25
etymology and modern
definition 21
contemplation 92, 234–5
contradiction 96–7
values and 100–1
Cosgrove, Joseph K. 138n. 56
Copernican revolution 7
cosmological sensibility 234, 236, 237
Marx's notion of labor and 222–3
cosmology 222–3
materialism as 230–4
Couturier, Paul, Father 71
Crauford, Emma 80

Nietzsche, Friedrich 7, 8, 10, 15n. 6,
    39, 55, 178, 247
Noddings, Nel 80
non-believers 82
  neighbor love and 86–7
  relevance of education 82–3
non-interference 31–2
Nye, Andrea 33

obedience
  to divine will 65–6
obesity 19, 24, 36n. 35
Operation Iraqi Freedom 169, 172,
    174n. 21, 174n. 23
Oppenheimer, Robert 130, 132
oppression 4, 30, 228
  causes of 5–6
  history and 225
  masculine 215
  overcoming women's 211
  in social forces 225
Orphic mystery 235
Orthodox Christianity 64–9
Orwell, George 143, 144–5, 150

pacifism
  Weil's rejection of 159–60
Padfield, Peter 63
parable of the wise and foolish
    virgins 76–7, 82–3, 85–6
Pascal, Blaise 42, 43
Paschal Mystery 247
The Passion of Michel Foucault
  (Miller) 179
Patel, Raj 18
Patroclus 236
Pedagogy of the Oppressed (Freire) 30
Perrin, Joseph-Marie, Father 21, 59,
    71, 81, 241, 246, 251
personality 197
  social manifestation of 199
personal Providence 116–17
person-society relationship 13–14
La Peste (Camus) 66, 74n. 66
Peter, St., 114–15
  betrayal of Christ 63–4
Pétrement, Simone 241, 242

phenomenology 3, 231
Phillips, D. Z. 54–5, 66, 72n. 13
philosophical life 102–3
Planck, Max 128
Plato xx, 5, 55, 56, 77, 78, 80, 92, 93,
    96, 141, 145, 155n. 39, 181, 184,
    210, 228, 232, 235, 236
  allegory of the cave 40–2, 84
  criticism of sophists 150–1
  poetry 97, 104n. 23, 139, 150, 152–3,
    157n. 66
poor
  see poverty
'Popular Front' 56
Porete, Marguerite 236
"La Porte" (Weil) 45–6
Posternak, Jean 132
Postman, Neil 80
poverty
  Christianity and 245–8
  identification with 241–2
  liberation theology and 252–4
  Weil's identification with 214,
    242–5, 254–5
  see also affliction
power
  Foucaultian 182–3, 185–6, 187–9
  of society 5
  subjects and 188
  "The power of words" (Weil) 143
Principle of Non-Overlapping
    Magisteria (NOMA) 108–9
privileges 197–8
probability 128–9
  necessity and 130–3
problems 91–2
  distinction between mystery 92
productivity 224
Prometheus 236
propagandistic language xxiv,
    156n. 50, 156n. 53, 157n. 55
Providence
  see divine Providence
pure necessity 119
Pythagorean mystery 235

quantum theory 128, 131–2

Index 275